Let's Blow Up the Elite College Admissions Black Box

It's Roiling Young Lives, Rigged for the Rich, and Wrong for America

Terry Connelly

LET'S BLOW UP THE ELITE COLLEGE ADMISSIONS BLACK BOX

LET'S BLOW UP THE ELITE COLLEGE ADMISSIONS BLACK BOX

TERMINOLOGY AND PERSONAL ACKNOWLEDGMENTS

The terms *elite colleges and exclusive colleges* are used interchangeably in this book to refer to those nonprofit higher education institutions in the United States, whether they are officially colleges or universities, that have an undergraduate acceptance rate of 35 percent or less and hold an endowment of at least $500 million. References to *power colleges*, *ultra-elite colleges*, *most elite colleges* and *systemically important colleges* refer to about two dozen elite colleges that regularly admit 20 percent or less of their applicants and have endowments of $1 billion or more. In text citations, where the author has two or more referenced articles during the same year, the full date of the cited article is shown.

The author most gratefully acknowledges the advice, support, and encouragement of his wife, Jennifer McFarlane; his brother and sisters, Dan, Carolyn, and Virginia Connelly; and all his children and their spouses (Lianna, Kaelyn, Jenny and Charles, Blair and Jen, Mark and Char) during the course of this project, as well as the following individuals: Todd Collins, Chris Compton, Janet Foster, Denise Herrmann, Robby Jones, John Luhtala, Evan Lurie, Beth Most, Jamie O'Keeffe, and Catherine Wolff.

LET'S BLOW UP THE ELITE COLLEGE ADMISSIONS BLACK BOX

CONTENTS

LET'S BLOW UP THE ELITE COLLEGE ADMISSIONS BLACK BOX

INTRODUCTION

Why One More Book on College Admissions Is Necessary — And Timely

Silicon Valley gets up early. Unofficial calculations of stock option values begin to reset when the stock market opens at 6:30 a.m. local time. Fresh venture capital is on the breakfast menus at Buck's and Coupa Cafe. Before dawn, scores of bright-vested crossing guards fan out to protect Palo Alto's kids from biking commuters and self-driving cars. But our town went one step further: trained security personnel stood guard day and night at all commuter rail grade crossings — to stop our high school students from committing *suicide by train*. (Kapp 2015) They did so for the entire seven years my own daughters attended high school here, until replaced by surveillance cameras in 2018.

The cameras, however, did nothing to address the causes of suicide clusters among students approaching their college years. When the COVID-19 pandemic of early 2020 kept all children home with only virtual classes to stream, those cameras had no children to track on their way to high school, while the pressure of our kids to make their way to college only got worse. Technology rich Palo Alto parents readily sheltered in place and switched their work time online, escaping much of the mass layoffs that swept the nation At the onset of the April 2020 initial coronavirus peak in America,

1

Brookings reported that 70 percent of the top income quintile was working from home, compared to not more than 50 percent of all other workers. (Guyot and Sawhill 2020) Although upper class children were better equipped to manage online and work the web to maximize their college admissions chances, COVID-19 only heightened the intense pressure to ace admissions tests and navigate the admissions maze, which even before the pandemic was driving some of their parents to bribery schemes to secure the "right" college placements.

For low income and many racial minority Silicon Valley families for whom finding and financing college was already a stretch or even impossible, the pressure on their high school age children became even worse with COVID-19. The pandemic quickly revealed that America's increasing wealth gap was also reflected in a *broadband* gap directly impeding disadvantaged children's ability to be present in classes, complete homework, take admissions test offered only online, or excel in sports, arts or other activities that were shut down by COVID-19 risks. (Hoover April 24 and 29, 2020) Plus that, the pandemic hit to colleges' bottom lines could make admissions departments even more likely to favor wealthy applicants.

The respiratory virus further aroused local and national concerns about mental and emotional health because of social isolation, including the distress of school age children in particular. Seniors at Palo Alto's high schools expressed their sadness and frustrations at missing out on graduation ceremonies and particularly the one chance to celebrate and share their excitement in person with relatives and long-time friends before they leave the community. (Kadvany May 2020) A high school junior in New York published an essay ("There Is No Vaccine for Teenage Despair") mourning the suicide of her 13- year old friend, who was "feeling the stress of quarantine" and wondering if she as "so sad at that moment that she couldn't imagine ever being happy." The author wondered what she herself might be capable of doing "trapped in my own room with my own thoughts." (Rosen 2020)

Intense anxiety emerged especially among high school and college juniors and seniors caught up in the college admissions and post-graduation employment cycles, while being denied the traditional closure ceremonies celebrating their accomplishments that would otherwise mitigate the special 2020 stress of needing to move on but with no sure place to go. Even the *Wall Street Journal* devoted a special weekend section (Chua et al. 2020) acknowledging and addressing the additional emotional and psychological burdens thrust upon those students now coming of age in what will be known as the *pandemic generation*. We obviously do not want any them feeling hopeless at what should be one of the most hopeful times in their lives.

Roiling Young Lives

The question of why two clusters totaling a dozen teenagers in one of the most advantaged towns in America lost hope in their own lives (and 12 percent of their peer group report having thoughts along the same lines) has produced multiple reactions, few definitive answers, and one emerging psychological diagnostic term: academic dysmorphia. Akin to body dysmorphia disorder, this serious anxiety condition is due to an imaginary or severely exaggerated intellectual deficiency that must be obsessively hidden or disguised — perhaps especially in a community that revels in its "genius bar" minds and educational excellence. Our children live in an age of multiple competitive dysmorphias, mediated through the latest social media technologies. Some plastic surgeons report an alarming rate of interest of patients who ask to be made to look more like their photo-shopped Snapchat pictures. (Chiu 2019)

Among responses to the suicide clusters (besides adding grade crossing guards), a community committee was formed to revise public high school academic schedules to place students' emotional well being on equal footing with their academic achievement. As a university dean with substantial experience with schedules, I volunteered. But I had much to learn about high school, especially how students in Palo Alto and similar high-achievement localities are coping (or not) with the pressure to perform at an A-level sufficient to secure the perceived social necessity of admission to an elite college, and the resulting hyper-intense peer competition.

I am a parent of three children educated in New York City prep schools in the '80s and '90s, and lately two more who attended Palo Alto public schools. I know today's new stresses are both unrelenting and unprecedented. The college admissions process now is radically different than it was in our New York days. The competition among colleges to prove and improve their own relative status in terms of their selectivity ranking has become more sophisticated and intense. The widespread adoption of the digitized "common app" encourages students (who generally have only a limited awareness of the standards for admission that any particular college will apply when push comes to shove) to submit twice or triple the number of applications typical a few decades ago.

Elite college admissions departments know that most of those applications will not meet their unpublished minimum standards but aggressively seek them out anyway to pad the denominator of their all-important selectivity ratios. Their established business and financial models leave little to manage those ratios by shrinking their enrollment — the numerator of that all-important ratio. Even Harvard uses this application-padding technique, knowing that, as its own witness put it in a recent trial regarding allegations of admissions discrimination, three-quarters of applications to the university will be "'out of the money'" with no chance to get in. (Hoover October 31, 2018) If Harvard has to stuff its applications channel to preserve its prestigious ranking, what can we expect from the other elite colleges, and all the others that want to be elite?

Combined with data on standardized test scores and other factors tracked by the infamous *US News* annual college rankings, low admissions ratios have come to define the level of a college's selectivity. That one number purports to signify *success* on the admissions scoreboard for both the colleges and the students who gain entry to them, identifying the chosen few schools that select the chosen few applicants. Relatively few (about 5 percent) of America's 2,000-plus nonprofit colleges and universities are comfortable winners of the admissions game. About the same percentage applies to college applicants as well when it comes to admission to elite institutions where they are well qualified for enrollment. Admissions is a game that more and more requires great wealth to win: wealth that most deserving applicants' families do not possess, and that many excellent but tuition-dependent colleges can only dream will enrich their enrollment profiles.

Getting in to an exclusive college is in one sense the academic equivalent of "making the playoffs" in major league sports. It is the best way to preserve or create membership in America's moneyed class. It is increasingly the case, however, that *pre-existing* family money will be the most significant number on the scoreboard that determines whether a student will make America's socio-economic playoffs.

Todays' winner-take-most national economy displays a rigidifying wealth disparity between the haves and the have-nots — as well as between the haves and the have-mores. The pressure is so great to be among the "chosen few" college applicants that even very wealthy parents have chosen to pursue blatantly corrupt pathways to elite colleges for their children. Meanwhile, colleges with otherwise stellar academic and societal reputations have resorted to cheating on their own data submissions to *US News*.

Most parents and their applicant children have no idea that published admissions rates have themselves been manipulated by colleges so much that they are often simultaneously factually lower than commonly stated because of undisclosed special admissions lanes reserved for the wealthiest and most well-connected applicants and also artificially higher than they appear due to the "denominator padding" achieved through deceptive marketing techniques that invite hopeless applications.

As a parent, experienced business executive, and retired business school dean, I find the current elite college admissions market a national disgrace. Elite colleges leverage self-perpetuating endowments to fund sophisticated marketing techniques that exploit the anxieties of children and their parents in order to achieve a self-inflating and essentially meaningless aura of ranked selectivity. As one commentator wrote in the *Chronicle of Higher Education:* "[C]olleges are given a lot: not just money and trust of families, but tax-exempt status, federally financed student aid and millions in research dollars. Can they make the case that they give enough back?" (McMurtrie 2019) I think not.

Elite colleges could (but probably won't) start with a hard look at what their admissions processes have become: a peer-pressure cooker. Today's high school experience is not that of our fathers or mothers, or our own before we became parents. For a rising generation Z that has been brought up in an era of school shootings — and the highest suicide rate our nation has ever recorded beginning in the middle school years — the pressure to perform like an Apple app in the all-important admissions game is all too real. One tenth-grade girl in Palo Alto said with innocent irony that she chose to run hurdles in track after school because "that's the only time at school when I don't feel pressured to perform!" Another told our high school schedule committee: "School is my whole life, twenty-four seven."

I worked in the twenty-four seven legal and investment banking worlds; I once billed a twenty-five-hour lawyer's day (full credit to the late, lamented Concorde). Must we now push our children into that world in order to quench an admissions anxiety artfully stoked and exploited by colleges themselves to validate and enhance their own ranking status? Do ninth graders really need to start crafting resumes and pulling all-nighters?

There comes a time in a lengthy career (including mine) when the last version of one's resume morphs into the first draft of an obituary. I am lately too accustomed to reading those of friends and colleagues I've met along the way. But I never expected to be — and can no longer abide — reading yet another obituary of a contemporary of my daughters drawn to suicide amid the intense pressure of today's high school years, much of which stems from the admissions black box invented by our nation's most elite colleges. Attempting to decode that black box for a price has become a billion-dollar, inside-knowledge industry, accessible only to those who can afford to pay the going rates for a variety of consulting help in addition to the official price of admission.

Rigged for the Rich

College degrees and increasingly graduate studies are the prime differentiators in terms of income and employment in the US economy, which lately features more personal downside than upside. It is not surprising, then, that parents' anxiety (and derivatively their children's) intensely focuses on admission to an *elite* college, lest their offspring graduate but live in a down-market zip code (or maybe worse, just move back home). In this book, the term "elite colleges" in its broadest sense refers to about 120 private nonprofit and state-funded colleges and universities that dominate college rankings, admit 35 percent or less of their undergraduate applicants and hold endowments of at least $500 million. There is also a smaller coterie of about 25 super-elite colleges that includes the Ivy League schools, plus MIT, Stanford and the University of Chicago as well as universities such as Duke and Northwestern, together with smaller liberal arts schools primarily in the Northeast (the "Little Ivies") plus the Claremont Colleges consortium in California. Together these "elites of the elite" — with endowments averaging into the billions and acceptance rates in single digits or the teens. Like the "top 25" college teams that take the lead in the competition for the best football and basketball athletes, these academic power schools set the tone and the terms for how the college admissions game is played.

Colleges in the broader group of elites tend to aspire to the enrollment results, revenues and endowments of the "top 25" and therefore align their admission strategies and practices with those power colleges. They persist in this approach even when the cost of doing so puts them under ever-increasing pressure to meet their annual full-tuition-paying enrollment goals and thereby maintain their academic quality. They fear the ultimate jeopardy of being relegated to "non-elite" status. The pressure to keep up also can lead even elite schools to sacrifice other goals, especially in terms of expanding the racial and economic diversity of their student bodies. (Douthat 2019) And colleges lacking elite status increasingly face the most threatening financial jeopardy and enrollment pressures of a far more existential character, driven by the need to keep up with the power elites' approach to the admissions process.

The admissions strategies and practices of the top-25 most elite colleges and universities will largely constitute the focus of this book. They account for roughly the top quintile of all elite colleges, and this book will show that it is no accident their enrollment profiles decisively favor the top quintile (or better) of American wealth.

As a factual matter, scores of schools other than the elite colleges could fill the bill in terms of pathways to successful careers and lives. As a group, however, elite colleges do little to dispel the myth of their indispensability. Instead, they nurture that image, thrive on their aura of exclusivity, and exploit the admissions angst it creates. In turn, that anxiety makes admission itself a pearl of great price, but at what cost in terms of teenage stress, family lives, and societal values? Broadly speaking, there has been a too passive tolerance even of the growing number of high school suicides, and of the web of clinical anxiety and depression in which they occur, as unfortunate but unavoidable "collateral damage" of a process that amounts to a teenage rite of passage, which they and their parents should strive to game rather than tame. As a private school counseling director, Brennan Barnard, described it in the "Answer Sheet" section of the *Washington Post*: "The message to students is fundamentally Darwinian: Only the fittest survive, rising to the top in a game to endure an application process that focuses on external rather than internal depth...The more applicants a school can deny and the more accepted students who enroll, the higher ranked a college is." (Barnard 2016)

To that end, elite colleges have designed and imposed on their less-endowed peers a highly competitive, secretive, and unpredictable admissions environment, the better to enhance their own relative rankings and related revenue flows. Our nation's most distinguished and well-capitalized institutions of higher learning seem determined to emulate their original roles as agents and guardians of a self-perpetuating upper-class establishment: not the former WASP aristocracy but a new privileged class that might be labeled as the *EGGS:* Entitled Graduates of Gold-plated Schools. Higher education reforms in the second half of the twentieth century that sought to make broad access to higher education an engine of social and economic mobility have mutated into a manifestly self-interested elite college business model to build their income streams and endowment resources through cultivating a rich clientele and leveraging their shared tax-avoiding privileges.

Precisely when did the role of family wealth and "lineage" (as a Harvard official put it) in gaining admission to elite colleges become so pervasive that a graph of America's increasing income disparity and a contemporaneous graph of elite admissions disparity between economic subgroups become virtually interchangeable? When did admission to elite colleges "won" by teenagers become an entry on their parents' social resumes? At what point did family-wide anxiety associated with trying to decode the admissions black box become so prevalent that it threatened to earn designation as its own category of psychological disorder? And when did admissions departments become wholly owned subsidiaries of their colleges' advancement offices and athletic departments (or the other way around when it comes to the rosters of certain "aristocratic" college sports teams)?

We cannot pinpoint an exact date for any of these developments. We now know, however, the exact date when the corrupting mix of wealth, social status, and the elite college admissions process broke through to public consciousness enough to provoke real demand for accountability and reform: March 12, 2019. That is the date the United States Attorney for the District of Massachusetts announced federal indictments of dozens of parents, admissions consultants, college coaches, and standardized test administrators in a scheme to secure admission to several elite colleges through falsified standardized test scores and sham athletic records for children from very wealthy families across the country, involving bribes ranging from $200,0000 to $6 million totaling $25 million in aggregate. (Medina, Benner, and Taylor 2019)

Some of the accused allegedly also paid off psychiatrists and other doctors to certify falsely that their children suffered from learning disabilities that warranted special test-taking accommodations that facilitated substituting professionally corrected answers for their own. One of the indicted admissions consultants even felt compelled to remind a parent to tell his daughter to "be stupid" in her interview with the examining doctor, extending the corrupting scheme to include both members of the medical profession and the indicted parents' children. (Mangan March 13, 2019) Even after the indictments, it was revealed that some parents have stooped to giving up their parental custodial rights and assigning them to relatives of limited financial means so that their children will qualify for financial aid — taking away resources intended to help children from families that truly cannot afford to pay today's college costs. (Gluckman July 30, 2019)

The profound public policy importance of these revelations has not been the indictments themselves or the amount of money involved, but rather the centrality of money in the whole elite college admissions process that it exposed. This reality was brought home by the depth, scope, and tenor of media coverage the indictments immediately attracted. It was not merely a leading headline in the *Chronicle of Higher Education*, the leading journal of academic affairs. Nor was it just front-page coverage (and the equivalent on their websites) in the main national circulation newspapers like the *New York Times,* the *Wall Street Journal* and *USA Today,* or on the twenty-four seven cable outlets and nightly broadcast network shows. My hometown *Palo Alto Weekly* and its online editions also ran with the story for days, especially since the central perpetrator of the bribery scheme (Rick Singer, who decided to sing when he got caught) had found Silicon Valley a fertile hunting ground among status-anxious parents who insist that their admissions-anxious children are "all above average" (apologies to Lake Wobegon), and that they have the money to prove it.

More significantly on the financial front, the indictments became a lead story on the most prominent business and financial cable news networks from *CNBC* to *Fox Business* to *Bloomberg.* The business news corollary of "If it bleeds, it leads" is "If it smells, it sells." The very first edition of *Bloomberg Businessweek* magazine after the admissions indictments carried the cover headline "College Is a Racket." The indictment story uncapped the stench of the elite college admissions process — the "secret" that everybody knew — especially the applicants themselves. More than a few high school and college students quoted in the immediate aftermath of the indictments essentially responded, "Why are you surprised? It's always been about the money."

The political professionals in Washington, DC also began to take serious notice of admissions corruption. Their morning bible, the online news aggregator Axios, bore the headline "A few of the legal ways admissions are rigged for the wealthy." (Allen 2019) These include preferences for early decision applicants, donors' children and the related and enabling income tax deductions, certain kinds of athletes, full-tuition paying wealthy foreigners, legacy applicants, as well as beneficiaries of professional-level test tutoring. Let's call the source of these preferences collectively the admissions game's own class of PEDs — Performance-Enhancing *Dollars*.

The *Palo Alto Weekly*, obviously cognizant of our community's history of student suicides, concluded its editorial on the indictment by focusing on the stress the admissions process loads onto our children: "The arms race aiming at gaining advantage over others in college admissions is fueling student stress and unhappiness, increased risk of depression and suicide and now exposes parents and their children to prosecution and humiliation…[P]arents need to recognize it is their kids, not them, who must find their passions and pursue their own dreams for a happy and fulfilling life." Unfortunately, even those the *Weekly* called "the most highly qualified high school students" are forced to compete for admissions and must do so under a system "where the wealthy and influential already have so many advantages." (Editorial, *Palo Alto Weekly*. 2019)

Jason England, former admissions official at an elite college, lamented in a commentary in the *Chronicle of Higher Education* that "[t]he US Department of Justice filings confirm what we already know, or should have known: Elite-college admissions exists chiefly to replicate class privilege."

> I saw how the system is rife with inequities and loopholes; how unscrupulous wealthy people are willing to pay admissions fixers to exploit those loopholes; and how grifters adjacent to the process cash in on whatever influence they have…To harp on this cluster of odious dimwits and greedy fixers obscures the insidious day-to-day practices in which the entire community of elite prep schools, independent college advisors, and admissions officers are complicit. (England 2019)

Within hours of the federal indictment, Robert Frank, a regular contributor on *CNBC*, commented that the bribery approach, expensive as it was, must have "looked a lot cheaper" than the traditional way of buying a college admission with a multi-million-dollar donation. The prosecutors in the case distinguished the donation route from the indicted conduct because the former would be "perfectly legal." This book, however, will reconsider that assumption, and whether it should be true going forward. In that connection, the most revealing description of the bribery scheme was the marketing pitch of Rick Singer captured on tape. He referred to the donation route as the "back door" donation route to admission that he compared unfavorably with his significantly cheaper "side door" of bribing test proctors and athletic coaches. (Chaffin 2019)

We will delve into details of the bribery scheme as necessary in chapters 4 and 5, which deal directly with standardized admissions tests and the back-door donation route to admission. At this point, it is sufficient to note that virtually nobody involved in the elite admissions game has to date had the temerity to blame just "a few rotten apples" — they intuitively know the public won't buy that defense. Their reticence creates an opportunity to pry open their admissions black box and chart a path to lasting systemic change.

Several excellent books by distinguished and experienced educators and commentators over the past three decades have exposed at least indirectly the perverse and corrupting elements of elite college admissions practices, as well as the related distortions amid the infamous college rankings. Reporters and columnists at the *Washington Post*, the *Chronicle of Higher Education, The Atlantic*, the *New York Times*, the *Wall Street Journal,* and even *Town & Country* have done the same as has, more recently, the Jack Kent Cooke Foundation, especially under the leadership of the late Harold Levy. I have relied on and gratefully acknowledge these books, publications and articles (listed on the references list at the end of this book) as bedrock research on the admissions practices of elite colleges. Those practices have resulted in what one author (Frank Bruni) called an admissions "mania" and others have decried for their adverse effects on many young lives, as well as the biases toward the rich and well-connected embedded in the process that are designed primarily to advance the colleges' financial interests even if the result is admittedly unfair to most applicants.

We will learn how the one-college-only early decision option requiring a promise to accept any offer (and nowadays increasingly accounting for a majority of admissions on some elite campuses) is cleverly and cynically marketed as a way to alleviate the stress on high school students and their parents. But this apparently sympathetic pitch masks a trifecta of big wins for the colleges: more full sticker-price tuition payers, higher admissions yields and selectivity rankings, and more future tax-deductible donations from grateful families that can afford to choose the early decision route because they do not mind foregoing any tuition bargaining leverage in the process. James Fallows, in his seminal September 2001 article on the evils of early decision in the *Atlantic*, called the process a "racket." (Fallows 2001) Unfortunately, it has spread further and deeper into the elite college universe since then. We will also see that, ironically, any prospective employer who traffics in similarly-styled "exploding" or "bullet" job offers to college students would likely be banned from on-campus recruiting by the career services offices of the very same campuses that engage in the equivalently coercive practice of early decision admissions

Likewise, even the test-optional application break for applicants can be corrupted in schools' reported admission stats to show higher SAT/ACT score averages and ranges (and thus earn a higher selectivity rank), while leaving applicants who cannot afford professional test tutoring to a Hobson's choice if they also lack the resources to produce enough "demonstrated interest" and shiny-object "enrichment experiences" to balance against the absence of standardized test scores. *Optional* should not really mean *if you dare* in actual practice, but it could: many high school seniors have found this out the hard way when they skip the so-called optional extra essay prompt in their applications!

We will also recognize the subtle and not-so-subtle ways that elite college admissions practices wind up providing special consideration to those applicants coming from wealthy and well-connected families: legacy admissions, which together with early decision admissions frequently account for well over 50 percent of elite college enrollment; children of major donors, celebrities and politicians; faculty children; and international students; and out-of-state applicants to public colleges who can pay full tuition. Even merit aid has been corrupted to attract athletes in "aristocratic" (that is, primarily white) sports and other highly sought-after wealthy applicants. Ironically, the parents who spent their money bribing the women's crew coach at USC to accept fake athletic credentials may not have realized that the women's crew roster (with the cooperation of the USC admissions department) had

15

grown to include as many as 150 walk-ons — their daughters might even have been admitted just by volunteering to try out!

More indirect but equally effective tilts toward the rich include "feeder" relationships with wealthy private prep schools and certain public schools in very wealthy communities; decisional bonus points for demonstrated interest shown by pre-application visits to campus and attendance at expensive summer learning camps; increasing standardized test score benchmarks that invite and ultimately compel costly tutoring; and weighting GPAs for advanced placement courses not broadly available in disadvantaged school districts. Elite colleges have accumulated the financial wherewithal to be increasingly need blind when it comes to admitting a few socioeconomically disadvantaged applicants each year — but they are rarely wealth blind when it comes to which applicants get to the front of the line. As we shall see, their marketing efforts and special admissions lanes to attract students from the latter income category far outpace their efforts to identify, recruit and support those from the lower reaches of the family income range.

Wrong for America

The previously published research materials I have referred to and credited throughout this book have collectively exposed many of the socially shameful aspects and effects of the elite college admissions. But shaming alone hasn't worked to change the system, and some (but not all) of the most critical analysis stops just short of suggesting change, focusing instead on providing very high-value advice on how best to play the admissions game as it lays (and, all too often, lies). As a result, while children growing up with the advantages of wealthy families and communities indeed suffer stress from the pressure of high expectations regarding their ability to win the elite admissions game, the broader risk to our children accrues to those in the lower four quintiles of income status (including those considered middle class) who are being further disadvantaged in terms of access not only to the most elite colleges and top-ranked universities, but also to the vast majority of far more tuition-dependent colleges. As a result, higher education no longer functions as a fundamental enabler of socioeconomic mobility in America but rather is proving to be one of the biggest obstacles to such personal and societal progress.

Middle-class and more economically disadvantaged families are not the only victims of the big squeeze of the elite college admissions marketing machine — so is a large and critically important segment of higher education overall that can't match the elites' market power. For the fall 2019 entering class, a study by the *Chronicle of Higher Education* found that 60 percent of nearly 300 private and public colleges surveyed had failed to meet their enrollment goals, and two-thirds had failed to meet their net revenue objectives as well. (Carlson 2020) Many colleges lack sufficient funding to underwrite elite-level mass marketing and can't compete otherwise without a combination of severe tuition discounting that shrinks their faculty and student support staffs, hurts their reputations and extends their average degree completion times to six years or more.

The emerging pattern is a self-reinforcing vicious circle that puts enormous and destructive pressure on both college applicants and many colleges themselves:

- The elite colleges compete aggressively among themselves for the most highly selective reputations, which will attract the most exclusive clientele, aided by very expensive marketing programs and budgets.
- Meanwhile, lesser-endowed, tuition-dependent colleges, which often actually do an equal or better job of preparing lower-income students to succeed after graduation, struggle to compete for applicants with higher and higher tuition "sticker prices" to offset the cost of competition

that must, however, be heavily discounted to attract enough of the best students.

- This, in turn, starves those lesser-endowed institutions' academic resources and over time turns off interest among the very best qualified candidates for admission.

- At the same time, these tuition-dependent schools face credit downgrades and higher borrowing costs while taking in the vast majority of qualified low-income, historically disadvantaged students, who often need more academic and social support through to graduation than these schools can afford to provide.

- Middle-income students who don't qualify for grants, however, will be saddled with a lifetime of loan payments that will leave them trapped in their economic and social status (at best), even if they are among the lucky 55 to 60 percent who actually graduate within six years.

This phenomenon is unquestionably bad for an American economy where income disparity is becoming locked in, and economic growth is already constrained because over six million jobs are reported unfilled almost every month, largely due to the lack of US workers educated enough to fill them.

When all the elements of the elite college admissions system that will be detailed in this book are taken together, it will become extremely difficult to conclude that the exploitation of anxiety and favoritism toward wealthy applicants inherent in elite college admissions is merely an unintended byproduct of an otherwise benign and "holistic" admissions selection process. There has been intelligent design at work here.

In fairness, thousands of dedicated college admissions professionals, as well as school counselors and private admissions consultants, work diligently to bring a measure of humanity to what, in practice, amounts to an inhumane and socially destructive college application system. Many parents, students, high school administrators, and college officials would assume that that most college applicants survive the process, gain admission to a college that is a fit for their potential and ability to pay, and proceed to graduate in a reasonable time and pursue the related economic benefits of their degrees. American higher education is reputedly the envy of the world. So why consider changing the fabric of the college admissions process for the sake of a minority of outliers? Why write, publish, read, or act on this book?

If the ultimate fit for each student in terms of college admissions results is so good, however, why do 40 percent of American college students never graduate, even after six years? Why did only 44 percent of our 2.9 million high school graduates in 2017, according to a federal report, go directly on to a four-year college despite our country's crying need for more graduates to work in the future economy? (National Center for Education Statistics 2019) Why does the composition of the student bodies of our nation's most respected and admired institutions increasingly reflect and reinforce our nation's expanding income and social disparities?

If our the-envy-of-the-world colleges are still effective in advancing economic and social mobility, why is the range and depth of income disparity in the United States one of the worst among developed economies? Why do so many state-funded colleges pursue the twin strategies of allocating increasing percentages of their admissions to full-paying foreign students and simultaneously offering their lower in-state tuition rates to many out-of-state applicants? And why do so many private colleges also feel forced to match lower public in-state tuition levels or risk teetering on the brink of insolvency? These schools are struggling to keep up in the student recruiting game dominated by the rich marketing budgets of elite colleges obsessed with winning a *US News* ranking that attracts the wealthiest families who want their children to own the most exclusive academic brand.

Catherine Bond Hill, former president of Vassar College and a leader in promoting need-blind admissions, in a *Wall Street Journal* commentary shortly after the Massachusetts admissions bribery indictments were announced, asked rhetorically why it's such a bad thing that many low- and moderate-income families will find their students priced out of elite colleges: after all, those families are also priced out of other markets for high-end cars, restaurants, homes.

> The difference is that taxpayers subsidize higher education in a variety of ways under the premise that benefits society as a whole. These subsidies are significantly higher selective institutions, which reap the benefits of preferential tax treatment on endowment earnings and charitable giving. As a result, wealthy students receive more of these subsidies than their lower-income peers today, a situation few would argue is ideal. (Hill 2019)

In other words, elite college admissions processes are not only offering affirmative action for the rich; they are literally providing federal welfare for the rich. This book will show how American taxpayers (and voters) can do something about that.

Elite Colleges Won't Willingly Change the Current Admissions System (It's Too Good for Them): But Litigation Disclosures, and Bribery Scandals and Even the COVID-19 Pandemic Have Triggered Public Interest in Reform

Thanks to the triggering event of the admissions bribery indictments, we now have the chance to do much more than simply advise high school students and their families about how to best play the admissions game. We can seize the moment to consider a way forward that decisively rejects and reforms elite college admissions processes that force not only our children but all higher educational institutions to play by their costly rules.

We can harness the powerful leverage of the government's taxing and regulatory power, as well as the leverage of federal tuition loans and grants already employed to enforce anti-discrimination and sexual misconduct investigatory processes under the federal Higher Education Act's Title IX. As a former securities lawyer, investment-banking executive, strategy consultant, and business school dean, I know a broken and one-sided marketing scheme when I see one. I also have learned how such a system can be reformed with clear standards of transparency, accountability, and fairness with respect to those entities that control the information that their stakeholders need to make rational decisions.

Intentional obfuscation and even outright duplicity have been the devils hidden in the details of the black box admissions practices at elite colleges. Meanwhile, mandatory transparency and fundamental fair dealing have been the heart and soul of the federal statutory responses to other rigged economic systems: the post-Crash Securities Acts of the 1930s, the Sarbanes-Oxley Act after the Enron fraud, the Dodd-Frank Act after the housing and banking crisis and Great Recession, and the establishment of the Consumer Finance Protection Bureau in the wake of that same financial crisis. Four-year elite college costs now exceed the combined average household's mortgage, credit card, and auto loan debt. Yet federal regulatory power remains largely unused in the face of admissions processes that could not survive the kind of rules already governing much smaller lifetime family investments.

The typical college brochure could not get past the SEC; the prospectus for initial public stock offerings, for example, contains multiple pages calling attention to risk factors, a kind of material disclosure nowhere evident on college admissions websites or in their recruiting brochures. The practice of ramping up college selectivity rankings by pushing out application invitations to many thousands of high school students who are highly unlikely to meet the schools' secret baseline admissions standards bears a striking resemblance to the infamous subprime mortgage marketing scams. Sure, the colleges often waive their prevailing sub-$100 admission fees to facilitate building their admissions pool. The real price of padded admissions, however, is paid in the dishonesty and lack of transparency in the admission process as a whole, especially in terms of the selectivity game.

The *US News* rankings are no more reliable as guides to higher education quality than the opinions of bond rating agencies were when it came to subprime mortgage securities. The college admissions process, reformed to achieve transparency, equity, and fairness, would be far better off without those rankings. Indeed, the reforms proposed in this book would likely consign them to oblivion. No valid argument remains against requiring colleges to publish the private baseline algorithms and point systems they use to score applications: the big data gurus of Silicon Valley will discern and disclose them sooner or later anyway.

Mandatory disclosures such as the average number and percentage of admissions reserved for legacies, major donor and faculty children, and other factors that distort reported college selectivity could undermine the corrupting competition for pride of place in the *US News* rankings, which are at the heart of the mischief in elite college admissions and force other, more tuition-dependent schools to play the same marketing game as their elite competitors or risk having their bond ratings downgraded or, in the worst case, jeopardizing their very existence.

Recent litigation concerning whether Harvard University, in its four-factor holistic admissions process, has deliberately discriminated against Asian-American applicants revealed many previously undisclosed aspects of Harvard admissions decisions, including the fact that 29 percent of entering students selected by Harvard were either legacies, children of donors, or athletes — and mostly Caucasian. The discovery process in the lawsuit has given us a first good look inside the heretofore secret "black box" that is the elite college admissions process, and it isn't pretty! Like the bribery indictments, this finding (resulting from the mandated court discovery process), combined with the predictable and similar statistical outcomes of the early decision process, suggests that the real discrimination at Harvard and other elite colleges is decisively in favor of those with high incomes and important social and political connections.

Asked by opposing counsel in the Asian discrimination lawsuit whether Harvard's entering class should have a makeup that "looks a lot more like America," the dean of the undergraduate College answered "'I don't'" — perhaps focusing on the racial profile of our nation's college-age population. But he also went on to assert the "'We are not trying to mirror the socioeconomic or income distribution of the United States.'" (Gluckman November 2, 2018) Yet Harvard undergraduate enrollment, year after year, is unquestionably replicating our country's pattern of income and wealth distribution. As the data in chapter 2 will show, the upper most income groups get the lion's share of admissions to the most powerful elite colleges — their business models are working as designed! The United States Attorney in Massachusetts, in announcing the admissions bribery indictments, said that there "'can be no separate college admissions system for the wealthy.'" (Barrett, Devlin, and Zapotoski 2019) But that is precisely what is going on among our most elite colleges.

We could be waiting until the ice age in hell for elite schools to voluntarily and systematically reveal full and meaningful data on the number of admissions reserved in advance for legacies (who are five times more likely to be admitted at Harvard than applicants without such connections) and other wealthy and well-connected applicants or to own up to the actual applicant screening and rejection criteria hidden within these exclusionary practices. Meanwhile, these same schools have also stepped up their reliance on certain admissions criteria that also favor wealthy applicants such as demonstrated interest, shown by expensive pre-application visits to campus, while concentrating their recruiting outreach to focus on wealthy-zip-code school districts and prestigious private prep schools.

After the bribery indictments, admissions leaders have been quick to promise internal reviews to discover if their practices somehow are biased in favor of the wealthy or contribute to growing income inequality. History suggests, however, that internal reviews are at best nearsighted. If admissions leaders truly want to find out how their black box tilts the playing field decisively to the wealthy and exacerbates admissions anxiety to a crisis point and find ways to rebalance the admissions scales, the data is available in this book and elsewhere for them to see. They can reread their schools' legal charters, which require them to serve the general public good. They can listen to the public disgust with how elite admissions process now works in favor of the wealthy and powerful. Some observers have proposed remedies like admissions lotteries skills-based rather than diploma-based professional hiring that should be giving admissions officers sleepless nights.

One knowledgeable commentator on the state of the elite colleges admissions market offered a most radical example of how to make the preferences for wealthy applicants at least more transparent. Shortly after the admissions indictments, the *Texas Tribune* posted the following suggestion from Wallace Hall, a former member of the Board of Regents of the University of Texas-Austin: "If a university wants to sell seats, auction them and be upfront about it. For example, tell the public, 'We're going to sell 200 seats because we need money for the university.' Maintaining the black box approach where nobody gets to know how we let people in is ridiculous. It's also almost always corrupt. The focus should be on transparent and objective admissions." (Root and Najmabadi 2019)

Auctioning admissions to elite colleges might please the 11 percent of Americans polled after the indictments by *The Hill* (which covers the U.S. Congress) who say they would be willing to pay a bribe to get their kids accepted, but nobody else. (Manchester 2019) Literally awarding a large portion of admissions to the highest bidders, however, would at least eliminate two major corrupting aspects of the current system. An admissions auction system would seriously undermine the *US News* ranking — the relative dollar level of successful bids for each college would constitute an efficient market rankings system that theoretically incorporates all relevant information. And the bids themselves, unlike donations, certainly would not be tax-deductible, because the presence of a clear quid pro quo exchange of benefits between the college and the applicants' family would be indisputable.

At this moment in time, however, we have the opportunity to do better than just making the role of money in admissions nakedly transparent, while it remains in place with grotesquely inequitable outcomes. But change will not come easily. While the revelations of outright bribery of coaches and other officials to secure admissions has led to some immediate reforms in athletic recruiting, record-keeping and supervision, the severe short-term and long impacts of the COVID-19 pandemic on college finances could lead admission officials to tip their decision scales even more decisively toward donors' children, legacies and wealthy early decision applicants. Well before the bribery crisis and the pandemic hit, Sheryll Cashin, a Georgetown law professor and expert on affirmative action, quoted in a September 17, 2017 *New York Times* article ("When Affirmative Action Isn't Enough"), observed that the elite colleges are propagating a "system of segregation," and that their student populations will not fairly reflect America's overall demographics until the schools *"blow up the system."* (Emphasis supplied). That is precisely what this book proposes to do.

As was the case with America's most elite financial institutions in the years before their collapse in the 2007 through 2009 period, reliance on self-regulation and self-reform are not realistic options in terms of the elite college admissions system. Their leaders, like a pre-crisis former CEO of Citigroup, apparently feel the need to "keep on dancing" as long as the admissions money machine music keeps playing — no matter what they are saying publicly in response to the bribery indictments.

As we shall examine more deeply in chapter 6, scores of admissions officers from elite schools subscribed to a 2015 report from the Harvard School of Education that proposed major shifts in admissions practices. Among other recommendations, the report advised applicants not to be concerned (regardless of what college recruiters may say) about marginal differences between their own results and those of others on standardized tests and GPAs. The report also discouraged applicants from loading up on advanced placement courses and pursuing too many extracurricular activities. College brochures and recruiters (who later in the admissions cycle double as gatekeepers), however, have continued to push the opposite messages. Surely it should not be left to *applicants* to change their behavior (against their self-interest) to help elite colleges mitigate the destructive effects of their own self-interested and secretive admissions criteria and marketing practices.

This book will connect the dots within the multifaceted admissions maze to reveal the true picture of dark and interconnected elements of elite college admissions practices, despite the commercial-in-confidence secrecy officially guarding them. These "black box" practices have a virtually perfect and mutually reinforcing strategic fit focused on enhancing college wealth. The elements of the system work together toward that goal: deliberate focus on prep school recruiting and recommendations; extra weight on the scales for demonstrated interest that costs money; early decision opportunities known to be mainly workable for relatively wealthy applicants, including legacies and athletes; and special consideration for donors' children. Wealth-related admissions will beget grateful future donors and recycle the process into the next generations.

This book will also provide the focused exposure, indignation, and imagination necessary to rethink and replace the prevailing admissions system at its core, starting with our most elite colleges and universities. Twenty-first-century America features systemically important elite admissions departments that have set the prevailing tone for what has become the college admissions "mania" (in Frank Bruni's apt choice of words). We need a special set of rules to govern their conduct lest they continue to put our entire higher education system at risk.

New admissions norms, imposed through federal power to regulate schools that receive financial benefits from the government, must put an end to the exclusionary practices specifically designed and implemented to favor the wealthiest families and even exploit student anxiety to pad elite colleges' selectivity rankings. In particular, special rules will be required to realign the balance of marketplace power between applicants and elite colleges to attack directly the effects of their admissions practices that are embedding social immobility in the United States. More generally applicable regulations are also needed to expand radically the degree of transparency and disclosure associated with the admissions criteria and results of all public and private colleges and universities.

We need no longer tolerate college admissions as a mania we willingly put our children through while hoping for fairness from a system dominated by a wealthy few on both sides of the market. Secrecy is at the heart of the corruption of admissions: character is what you are in the dark. It is precisely the black box aspects of elite admissions that must be blown up, but in a perfectly legal, even elegant, manner. What's more legal than a good new law?

"College admissions as usual" is not worth the risk of losing one more student's life to suicide. Nor is it worth the damage it will continue to inflict on our nation's higher education system, economic progress, and reputation as a more just and equitable society. We may be on the cusp of finding the national *will* to admit that the elite college admissions system has the look of a racket as well as the feel of a mania. If we are alert to the moment, there is definitely a *way* to make real change.

Part I

The State of Play in the Admissions Game: Applicant Anxiety Reaches a Crisis Level While Elite Colleges Make the Rules to Suit Their Business Models

CHAPTER 1

Recovering from Teen Suicides: A Work in Progress Confronts the Nationwide College Admissions Mania

Pressure in Paradise

A conspicuously advantaged community was forced to look within and beyond itself after a rash of high school suicides by train. Palo Alto, California, is a weather-blessed town of nearly 70,000 in the center of Silicon Valley, the location of Stanford University and an original base for technology, social media, and data analytics giants from the early days of Hewlett-Packard to the new world of Facebook and Palantir. The income disparity gap in and around Palo Alto is as dramatic as anywhere in the nation. Santa Clara and neighboring San Mateo counties are home to 76,000 millionaires and billionaires; over 12,500 families have liquid assets (excluding home values) over $5 million. The *median* home price in Palo Alto at decade's end was $3.21 million. Two of Palo Alto's public high schools consistently rank in the top five in California and also among the best in the nation in terms of academic excellence. But

Palo Alto schools have a poor track record in terms of closing the so-called achievement gap among children in historically disadvantaged economic and social neighborhoods, which also exist in and around Palo Alto and populate the town's public schools. By the time students from low-income families in the Palo Alto school district reach middle school, they are not performing well enough to be on track through high school for a college degree: of the approximately 270 low-income middle school children in the town's public school, only 40 percent are performing at grade level, compared to 88 percent of their middle-income and high-income peers. Of those in the two public high schools, barely over 10 percent are college math ready, according to the California Early Assessment program.

Public and private efforts to address Palo Alto's achievement gap for socially and economically disadvantaged children have perhaps been overwhelmed by concerns among Palo Alto's high-achieving families about what could be termed an "overachievement gap" that disadvantages their own high-performing children. Despite their outstanding academic records, test scores, and extracurricular achievements, they fear children may be falling behind those classmates who are turning in world-class level performance in Olympic sports as well as science competitions, robotics tourneys, and other technology driven competition — or who are already making money by designing the latest social media or gaming app to already be in the highest income tax bracket while they fill out their college applications!

The Pew Research Center defines the economic middle class as those who earn between two-thirds of median household income for a given area and double the median within a given area. Palo Alto's median household income was reported in 2018 as $137,042 (more than double the estimates for the United States as a whole. By Pew's measure then, middle-class households in Palo Alto encompassed incomes from $92,362 to $274,086. This range dwarfs the levels in other college towns like Charlottesville, Virginia ($33,818 to $101,454), or Ann Arbor, Michigan ($38,464 to $115,394). The national middle-class income range was measured at $38,441 to $115, 224, which certainly means that Palo Alto is in the economic high-performance category. A newspaper survey in 2018 found that some families earning as much as $349,000 per year in Palo Alto considered themselves *lower* middle class compared to their neighbors. (May 2018) In Palo Alto, 95 percent of residents have college degrees, and 70 percent have graduate degrees, far above the national averages in each case. (Kelliher 2018)

Yet, for all its academic, creative, and financial success, Palo Alto has suffered in the recent decade from multiple clusters of suicides among the students in its high-performing high schools, and students at those schools have also exhibited alarming rates of anxiety and depression. Even the otherwise-robust Silicon Valley health care system was forced to acknowledge that it was overwhelmed and under-resourced to deal with the outbreak of teenage distress: not nearly enough local professionals or facilities or programs to care for scores of kids at any one time.

The Palo Alto community has begun to work through painful self-examination and reflection to come to grips with the factors driving the unprecedented surge in anxiety, depression, and self-harm among their school-age children. Parents with abundant means have begun asking themselves whether they might be not so much *raising* their children as *curating* them to embellish their own social resumes, and to eventually display wins in the competition for admission to the most elite colleges that would assure their futures as part of the economic and social upper classes. Some students have rediscovered enough peer empathy to move a student graduation speaker in Palo Alto to refer to a new standard form of greeting on campus: "How are you? I mean, really?" (Dremann 2016)

Some educators have begun to consider whether the chase for the elite admissions trophy is materially responsible for changing the high school experience to what one local student referred to as a "twenty-four seven" high-performance culture. High school students themselves have been moved to consider whether they risk becoming ultracompetitive automatons driven by anxiety about their fates as determined by the college admissions "black box." That term was borrowed for this book's title: it was used to describe the elite college admissions process by James Fallows in his seminal September 2001 article in *Atlantic* entitled "The Early Decision Racket."

In a general letter to Palo Alto High School's community, the editors of the student newspaper observed that "[A]s seniors, we have emerged from the dark cloud of the college admissions process and have witnessed firsthand the way that it erodes one's sense of value and place...The carrot of college corrupts...The majority of our student body's current system of values prioritizes a competitive cycle of chasing unfulfilling goals, fueling a rat race that can continue throughout one's entire life." (Ethan, Leyton, Kaylie, Ujwal, and Waverly April 2019) The *Washington Post* even noticed that the student newspapers at both of Palo Alto public high schools in 2019 ceased publishing editions mapping the colleges that each of their named graduates will be attending, because they concluded that practice was contributing to heightened stress and anxiety during the application process. The *Post* referenced one school newspaper's conclusion that "the map contributes to the toxic, comparison driven culture....Our community fosters a college-centric mindset which erodes one's sense of value and can lead to students with less traditional plans feeling judged, embarrassed or underrepresented.'" (Strauss June 11, 2019)

Like the local student editors, some adult Silicon Valley residents are even asking themselves why their own ultra-intense business culture and professional class is so willing to accept (and even honor) F's in terms of innovation failures among Silicon Valley entrepreneurs — Stanford's design thinking initiative celebrates the mantra "Fail Quickly" (learn and move on) — but stubbornly considers even a B+ earned by their own children while giving their best efforts to be totally unacceptable. What is driving so much parental, school, peer, and social pressure in a direction that always demands A-level or (weighted) better performance in high school? Call it college admissions FOMO; fear of missing out — and *falling out* of the upper class as a result. Consider the alarm a movie critic raised about the casual acceptance of cheating in high school, exhibited by the heroine in the Oscar-nominated film *Lady Bird*, as a socially normalized way to get to the front of the admissions line at a prestigious East Coast college. (Smithey 2017) Could it be that the corruption of student attitudes toward cheating reflects their implicit assumption that the entire elite admissions process is corrupt in any event, and that they might as well play the game on its terms?

This book will explore many high school students' working hypothesis that elite college admission is a rigged game. Even some of the harshest critics of admissions practices and outcomes nonetheless wind up agreeing with college admissions directors who insist that they do not intend to be causing the stress and unfairness that result from college admission processes and standards. Those are simply the unavoidable consequences of colleges' understandable desire to assure the appropriate mix in their entry classes that will meet each of their distinctive academic and social objectives. We will examine, however, whether the overriding objective is not so much academic and social but essentially a financial, bottom-line goal, and whether that goal is deliberately advanced by the stress, anxiety, and unfairness built into the application system.

Unprecedented Student Stress Is a National Phenomenon

Constant striving for admission to elite colleges is, of course, not the only possible explanation for the increase in teenage stress, depression and anxiety, nor is such stress the only or even primary cause of the increase in suicidal ideation and execution among our children, whether in Palo Alto or across the nation especially in similarly advantaged communities. High-performance, knowledge-driven business cultures like Silicon Valley and elsewhere have lately been successfully disrupting and changing whole industries: phones, music, automotive, rental cars and taxis, lodging, travel, energy, health care and diagnostics, advertising, cable and network television, movies, news media, et cetera. If so, why could they not also be changing and disrupting the entire teenage experience?

Indeed, social media now literally defines teen identity, and academic achievement has now become a status symbol rivaling athletic prowess. It has produced its own distinct anxiety patterns. Listen to the closing lyrics of 21 Pilots' 2015 hit song "Stressed Out": "Wake up, you need to make money!" The highly successful 2017 film *Lady Bird* uncritically depicted the teenage heroine played by Saoirse Ronan deliberately cheating by erasing her math test score, then lying about her actual grades and cheating on another test, all to improve her chances of getting in to a big-name college —and she succeeded! (Frye 2018) The head of an admissions consulting firm called College Essay Mentor (which charges $3,000 for its "essay package" with guidance proceeding from brainstorming topics to final drafts) has acknowledged that his industry's growth (more fully addressed in chapter 4) has been driven by a cycle rooted in anxiety. (Anderson 2017)

Sylvia Matthews Burwell, president of American University and former senior Walmart executive and President Obama's Secretary of Health and Human Services, called attention in her article

"Generation Stress" to the student anxiety specifically stemming from "the pressure on young people to constantly present a curated version of their lives on Instagram, Snapchat and other platforms." She compared this pressure to what adults would feel if they were forced to update their resumes daily to keep their jobs. As in the song quoted above, however, she also honed in on the economic challenges today's college students confront: "fear that they will end up jobless, unable to pay off their debt, and forced to live with their parents.... As a result, many students worry they will do no better than their parents, and with good reason: in the United States, the likelihood that a child will earn more than his or her parents has dropped from 90 percent to 50 percent over the past half century." (Burwell 2018)

Students' economic anxiety, in turn, translates to even more stress about college admissions, especially as the most elite colleges are reputed to be the most reliable ticket to a golden zip code in later life. Their reputations are to some considerable degree due to the way elite colleges market themselves — especially their *selectivity*, as well as the unmistakable presence of wealth in a large percentage of their enrollment. These and other stress factors cited by Burwell (including campus safety and technology) led her to conclude that the US higher education system "must be a part of resolving today's mental health crisis" among our young people, "which presents a broad challenge to American competitiveness and productivity." (Ibid.)

Evidence of that crisis includes a 2015 report from the Center for Collegiate Mental Health, cited by President Burwell, which revealed a 30 percent increase from 2009 to 2015 in the number of college students visiting counseling centers, while total enrollment grew by only 6 percent. The problems college counseling professions must deal with include the growing number of students experiencing thoughts of suicide, which require a capacity for 24/7 rapid response in the face of expanded waitlists for even initial appointments. Burwell also noted that 39 percent of college students in a recent poll reported symptoms of depression and anxiety. They need *someone* to listen to them

At one university, however, the administration actually threatened a student with disenrollment who shared with trusted peers her personal thoughts and feelings about possibly committing suicide. The student was suffering from depression, but the university (Northern Michigan) warned her against such behavior and required her to sign an agreement barring her from discussing suicidal thoughts even with her dorm mates and friends. That student and others filed complaints with the US Justice Department's Office of Civil Rights. Another received an email warning that if "you involve other students in suicidal or self-destructive thoughts or actions, you will face disciplinary action" — a policy Northern Michigan asserted was "followed by many universities and colleges." (Mangan 2018) Northern Michigan, however, wound up paying a total of $175,000 in settlements to students under an agreement reached with the Justice Department, which also required the school to implement a training program for faculty, staff, and administrators, with specific steps for accommodating students with disabilities, including mental health issues, and to change the way it addressed "behavioral concerns" in its messaging to students.

A 2017 Associated Press survey found that most big public colleges do not formally keep track of student suicides: forty-nine of the one hundred top state colleges do not track student suicides, and only twenty-seven others had consistently done so over the prior ten years, despite the fact that such data would clearly assist in formulating localized prevention strategies. (Binkley 2018) The University of Texas at Austin, which has tracked suicides since the 1990s, was moved to install iron barricades at an iconic campus tower where multiple suicides have occurred. The US Centers for Disease Control do not track college student suicides specifically;

the same goes for the National Institutes of Health. The known youth suicide data, however, reveals the seriousness of the problem occurring during the college prep years and, alarmingly, even in the years just before. A David Brooks column around the same time as Burwell's article hit mailboxes noted that while the suicide rate has been dropping in Europe in this century, it has climbed 30 percent in the United States. Among those moving through middle and high school, when our children now start thinking about college and submitting their applications, it jumped for white children by 70 percent and by 77 percent for black children between 2008 (just after the start of the Great Recession) and 2016. (Brooks 2018)

Suicide clusters at high schools have been occurring across the country in other high-expectations communities besides Palo Alto. And this sad phenomenon is trickling downward in age — the cohort with the fastest-growing suicide rate in the United States is ten to fourteen, covering the middle school years. (Margolin 2018) CNN reported in April 2019 that data from the National Hospital Ambulatory Medical Care Service showed that the number of children through teenage years coming to emergency rooms because of suicidal thoughts and attempts doubled between 2007 and 2015. During the same period, the rate for girls ages twelve to fourteen increased threefold. (Holmes and Almendrala 2016) Girls are also catching up with boys in terms of their "success" rate in suicides attempted, according to a four-decade study published in JAMA Network Open and cited in *Time's* Health Brief column. For teens aged sixteen through nineteen, the average annual increases in suicides were 8 percent for girls and 3.5 percent for boys during that period. In 1975, boys ten to fourteen years of age died by suicide 314 percent more often than girls the same age, but by 2016, that gap had narrowed to 180 percent. A Centers for Disease Control study found that young girls have been shifting their suicide attempts from more "recoverable" methods like poison to more effective means such as hanging. (Ducharme 2019)

The Netflix serial *13*, which reverse-chronicled a fictional high school girl's path to suicide, purporting to show the specific triggering events, itself triggered an increased level of curiosity about suicide methods and means on Google and other sites. (Teenage suicides increased across the nation after that series began streaming.) Along with the increase in successful teenage suicide attempts and recurrent suicidal thoughts, a potential new diagnostic category emerged generally termed *academic dysmorphia*. Used originally in connection with classroom anxieties of first-year college students who realize early on they are no longer the smartest kids in the room despite their 4.5 and above weighted high school GPAs, the term reflects by analogy the more established diagnosis of body dysmorphia disorder. Each such disorder refers to a psychologically overwhelming state of anxiety due to an imaginary sense of shameful imperfections or defects — bodily on one hand or intellectually on the other — that in each case must at all personal cost be kept hidden or at least disguised. Dealing with academic dysmorphia is a terrible way to live in high school, and to the extent that the chase for admissions gold plays a triggering role, the elite college leaders should be ashamed of themselves for exploiting it, as we shall see in chapters 3 and 4.

The elite college admissions criteria (real or imagined) has become what Silicon Valley might call the "source code" for the parental checklists of schooling and activities deemed essential for their offspring in pursuing what author Julie Lythcott-Haims (*How to Raise an Adult*) has termed the "checklisted childhood." (Lythcott-Haims 2014, 7, 29-42) Those children, mostly of affluent parents, seem to be programmed from birth (and even before, in terms of pre-school applications) to win the elite college admissions game. In early 2019, however, four years after Ms. Lythcott-Haims' critique of this form of child-programming as amounting to "unrelenting pressure to be perfect" (Ibid., 102), the *New York Times* published an op-ed by Pamela Druckerman that helicopter parenting works. Druckerman cited research by economists at

Northwestern University and Yale University to the effect that "high-octane, hardworking childrearing has some pointless excesses but nonetheless "done right it works for kids," which the op-ed affirmed would produce "life-changing" benefits.

The op-ed traced the emergence of helicopter-style parenting to the sharpening income disparities that began in the 1980s, replacing the more permissive style of the preceding decade. Upper- and even middle-class parents began focusing on gaining admission to fast-track preschools and spending after-school family time monitoring homework or driving the kids to enrichment activities. As the *Times* headlined in boldface: "[Parental] Hovering gives kids a real leg up in a competitive, unequal economy." Druckerman also conceded, that parents "who can afford to helicopter are probably making things more unequal for the next generation." (Druckerman 2019)

Another term for intensive parental oversight in terms of the admissions process has been coined by James W. Jump, a private school college counselor quoted in the *Chronicle of Higher Education* — "curling parents"— named for the sport in which the players strive to sweep the tiniest obstacles on a slippery surface from the desired path their disks are traversing to the winning target. (Supiano March 13, 2019) In the same article, Jessica Calarco, author of *Negotiated Opportunities: How the Middle Class Secures Advantages in School*, describes parents who "see their own self-worth in term of their kids' success…defined in narrow terms: 'Can you get in to Harvard'…Even if they're super rich, they're not a good parent unless their kid is successful." (Calarco 2019)

The *New York Times* columnist Frank Bruni has perceptively labeled the whole parental chase for the necessary leg up on an elite college admission a literal "mania." (Bruni 2016, 7, 10) Decrying as "madness" the tendency to view "getting into a highly selective school…as the conclusive measure of a young person's worth [and]….an incontestable harbinger of the successes or disappointments to come," Bruni pointed out that "For one thing, the admissions game is too flawed and too rigged to be given so much credit." (Bruni 2016, 8-9) Attempting to make sense of, let alone come out ahead in, a process that is truly maniacal might be considered suicidal by definition. Perhaps this explains why there is so much parental, student, and community trauma and insecurity even among those who have the upper-class background and economic wherewithal to play the admissions game to the hilt. One would expect more fear and loathing among those middle-class-and-below families who are being denied a fair chance to compete.

The numbers in this chapter and in chapters 2 through 6 tell a story, extending well beyond Palo Alto across America, of the intense stress on families and children of all income categories (for different reasons) caused by entrenched income disparity and growing gridlock in college graduation rates and socioeconomic mobility. This anxiety is triggered in no small part by the admissions practices of our most elite academic institutions. As Tom Bartlett, a senior writer for the *Chronicle of Higher Education,* concluded shortly after the admissions bribery indictments in March 2019: "I think the bottom line is that what has happened with elite colleges is that they've democratized anxiety far more effectively than they've democratized opportunity." (Bartlett 2019)

It is apparent that the elite power colleges have designed their admissions systems first and foremost to keep *themselves* on the right side of any "income disparity" scales within higher education, with scant regard for the emotional and psychological well-being of applicants, or for their traditional assertion that higher education deserves special status, including a significant degree of immunity from public regulation, because it serves as an indispensable engine of upward mobility in America. Among our most elite colleges, that "engine" is barely operating, replaced by a more self-interested "business model" strategically aligned with entrenched privilege.

CHAPTER 2

Amid Applicants' Fear of Missing Out, Elite Colleges Run a Seller's Market, Admitting Their Chosen Few Mainly from the Upper Class While the "Un-Hooked" Face Relegation to the Student-Debtor Class

Strategically Rationing Their Purposely Limited Admission Opportunities Creates Huge Market Value for Elite Colleges

Let's begin with the basic matter of supply and demand: there are far more qualified applicants for admission to elite colleges in America than there are seats available, and the prize of a degree is worth more than ever before in our economy. After the Great Recession, from 2010 through 2016, 11.6 million new jobs were created, but fewer than 100 thousand jobs went to persons with just a high school diploma. Think of it: 99 percent of new jobs in this period of recovery went to those with at least some college education. (Sherman 2016) 8.4 million high-skilled jobs were filled by individuals with a bachelor's degree or higher; low-skilled jobs were the only area of growth for those with at most a high school diploma. *(Insurance Journal* 2016), citing Georgetown University Center on Education and the Workforce: "America's Divided Recovery: College Haves and Have Nots," 2016.)

Consensus estimates among economic researchers have indicated that upwards of 75 percent of all new and replacement hiring will require more than a high school diploma. And, according to a 2019

McKinsey Global Institute report, jobs held by those with a high school diploma or less will be four times more likely hold a job easily replaced by automation than those with at least a bachelor's degree. (Blumenstyk 2019) By 2016, the percentage of the U.S. workforce with undergraduate degrees or higher had surpassed that of workers with only a high school diploma. (MarksJarvis 2016, citing Georgetown University Center on Education and the Workforce, ibid.) The former group's employment and compensation advantages are growing ever wider, as the requirement for college degrees to qualify for even entry-level living-wage jobs also continues to prevail among job openings. Meanwhile, graduate school degrees have become the "gold standard" for exceptional lifetime personal income opportunities, and admission to elite undergraduate colleges is increasingly but wrongly perceived as the only sure gateway to that pot of gold (a perception that elite colleges, which control the supply side, do little to discourage).

In addition, one of the most powerful demand factors is the palpable (and measurable) fear among upper-class parents that their children may wind up living in a lesser-class zip code. A *Wall Street Journal*/NBC survey found that twice as many Americans felt "not confident" than "confident" that life for their children would be better than for them. (Dunn 2019) That conclusion is supported by the increasing income disparity and the importance of a college or master's degree from an elite institution to get on the right side of that disparity. In his book *Dream Hoarders*, Richard Reeves observed that as more ordinary folks earn college degrees, upper-middle-class families have sought to up the ante for social advancement by concentrating on hoarding access to postgraduate education. (Reeves 2017, 11)

Frank Bruni observed that higher education in America is "forbidding to students of limited means" who often start behind their wealthier classmates because of poor K-12 schooling. Bruni concluded that four-year college has become "the new high school" but that, as Paul Tough, author of *The Years That Matter Most: How College Makes or Breaks Us*, told him, "'[w]e're not responding the same way'" to make college degrees broadly available to the poor in our age of technology as our nation did with respect to high school in the early 20th century age of industrialization. Instead, Tough said, the attitude is "'you figure it out, you pay for it, and we're going to make it hard as possible.'" (Bruni September 3, 2019)

Families with middle-class incomes, meanwhile, also share upper-income parents' demand for excellent higher education opportunities for their kids, but increasingly lack sufficient means to finance college without threatening family solvency. Concerns about rising income disparity in America between the top quintile and everybody else are, in fact, forcing constant redefinition of which dollar-denominated parameters exactly constitute the middle class. But most economists conclude that the middle class, however defined, is shrinking from both the top and the bottom in terms of absolute numbers of families who fit within a common-sense measure of that category. In terms of higher education, families in the bottom 80 percent are becoming a new debtor class.

Paying for College Has Begun to Look Like a Sub-Prime Mortgage

Economists question whether, without taking on staggering debt loads, the middle class can any longer afford ever-increasing college tuition not only at well-endowed, elite private colleges, but also at flagship public universities essentially being privatized by state governments facing hard budget choices and baby-boom taxpayers' revolts against funding the very systems that provided them cheap bachelor's degrees. *Forbes* magazine reported that between 1989 and 2016, the average cost of a college degree doubled after accounting for inflation, growing at a rate of 2.6 percent per year, while the average wage was increasing by only 0.3 percent. In short, college costs were growing at eight times the rate of workers' pay. (Maldonado 2018) A New York Times editorial, citing a federal Consumer Finance Protection Bureau study reported that the number of Americans 60 or older with student loan debt outstanding had grown by 400% between 2005 and 2015. (Editorial Board February 13, 2017).

The cost of this debt forces more students to work while in college and slow their path to degree completion. This delay could add even more debt by the time they finish, leaving a lifetime burden that, unlike other debt, cannot be discharged in bankruptcy. In total, at mid-2019, upwards of forty million Americans carried $1.5 trillion in student debt. A quarter of a million federal student loan borrowers go into default for the first time every calendar quarter, and twenty to thirty thousand more default on even their restructured loan terms, which often lead to additional total indebtedness in the long run. Average student debt per person is $34,000, which is more than the average of $30,000 that the U.S. spends per person on higher education programs. Meanwhile, American taxpayers stand to lose $31.5 billion on student debt defaults over the next decade, as colleges have no liability for the failure of their students to graduate and earn enough money to pay off their federal borrowings. (Mitchell 2019)

Notably, the student debt load is not just a student and parental problem — it's also a burden on the grandparent class! Total student debt for the over-sixty generation stood at a stunning $86 billion by early 2019. Some of this elder debt tracks to the now nearly universal practice of lenders (begun in the years after 2008) requiring parents to cosign their children's student obligations. Note that Social Security income can be legally captured to force repayment. One such debtor cited by the *Wall Street Journal* who, at age sixty-six, still owed $29,000, saw his entire $1,600 monthly

Social Security payments garnished by the federal government to apply to the loan debt. Parents burdened by long-term student debt also face credit rating downgrades inhibiting their ability to borrow for anything else in support of a middle-class lifestyle except at exorbitant cost, like the 400 percent annual interest rates for rolling payday loans due in two or four weeks. (Andriotis 2019)

In her recent book *Squeezed: Why Families Can't Afford America*, journalist and poet Alissa Quart described how America's middle class is being wiped out by relentless cost of living increases and automation, while salaries in even traditionally secure professions are not even keeping up with what is needed to service student debt loads, which, for example, can exceed $140,000 among recent law graduates. At the same time, teachers work shifts as Uber drivers to meet the rising cost of housing and raising a family, with ostensibly middle-class families now spending 20 percent of their incomes on childcare — not including their student debt loads from ever-rising tuition levels. (Getlen 2018, citing Quart 2018)

Ever-Inflating Tuition Puts a Permanent Lien on the Futures of the Most Economically Marginalized Students

At the turn of this century, average college tuition in America still amounted to less than 2 percent of median family household earnings. But by 2013, it had risen to greater than 40 percent, and climbing. Meanwhile, the lack of a college degree has been relentlessly reducing the chances for the average working-class individual to catch up with escalating college costs! The *Chronicle of Higher Education* reported that in the year 2000 it took 250 hours of work in by a typical private-sector employee to pay for an average year of tuition and fees at an American college, but that by 2017, 447 work hours were needed to pay for a year's tuition. (Patel 2019) A 2015 report from the Social Security Administration based on its own data determined that the median lifetime income spread between high school and college graduates had increased to $900,000 for men and $630,000 for women. In their 2018 *Foreign Affairs* article "How to Save Globalization," Kenneth F. Scheve and Matthew J. Slaughter point out that even a community college associates degree increased the median lifetime earnings as compared to high school graduates by four hundred thousand dollars. (Scheve and Slaughter 2018)

Economist David Autor, cited in the book *Our Kids*, found that hourly earnings of male college graduates rose in a range from 20 percent up to 56 percent from 1980 to 2012, while those males with high school diplomas saw their earnings decline by 2 percent. Meanwhile, 47 percent of earnings in the US went to the top ten percent of earners in 2018 (versus only 3 percent in 1980). Estimates also indicate that roughly three-quarters of students admitted and enrolled at the 200 most highly ranked colleges and universities come from families in just the top quartile of income. (Putnam 2015, 38) These data also have profound implications in terms of racial disparities in lifetime outcomes. Although median wealth also rose between 1992 and 2013 by 20 percent among white college graduates, it declined by about 56 percent among college-educated African Americans. Median black household income in 2016, per the Census Bureau, was $39,490 versus $65,000 for white households and $81,000 for Asians, although overall median income was up 3.2 percent to $59,032, a new high.

Before the Supreme Court's decision in *Brown v. Board of Education* that racially segregated public schools are inherently unequal and violate the Constitution's requirement of equal protection of the law, a combination of Jim Crow rules and restrictions on availability of veterans' benefits did not allow African Americans to use the GI Bill to support college achievement to the same extent that whites veterans could. Black students were specifically precluded from attending many public universities. This discrimination choked off educational opportunities for black veterans. One study showed that, among white veterans who turned eighteen from 1941 to 1946, 28 percent enrolled in college, while among their black peers, the rate was only 12 percent. Even in today's world, black students remain at a collegiate disadvantage. Among elite private schools, despite the emergence of need-blind admissions policies, the percentage of black students among entering classes has remained a virtual constant high single digit. State school results are higher, but there are alarming differentials in state funding for schools that are predominantly black. (Carlson 2016)

Nicholas Hillman, an associate professor of educational leadership and policy analysis at the University of Wisconsin at Madison, analyzed the balance between state appropriations and tuition revenue at more than 450 public colleges. Those that served primarily white students got more of their money from the state, while the colleges that served minority students relied more on tuition. He points to a striking, if lopsided, comparison between the University of Tennessee at Knoxville and Tennessee State University, a historically black institution. State funding per undergraduate at Knoxville, where 7 percent of students are black, is $19,500; at Tennessee State, where 71 percent of students are black, that figure is $5,600. (Ibid.)

Because colleges with a high percentage of black students must rely more on full-tuition revenue to stay alive, many black students who do attain college admission tend to borrow more than whites to pay for college. A January 2018 report by the Brookings Institution exposed how loan default rates are at crisis levels for students of color, in part because these students are often first in their families to attempt entry to college and vulnerable to high-pressure marketing by for-profit colleges. Many of those schools jumped to exploit low-income college aspirants disadvantaged by nonprofit college admissions practices and campus cultures.

Families of color and in the lower quintiles of income will find their children further disadvantaged by moves to convert standardized admissions testing venues from physical to online, as well as by the shift to streamed classes, as colleges have adjusted to the potential or actual outbreaks of Covid-19 on their physical campuses. The National Association for College Admissions Counseling (NACAC) concluded that plans for offering SAT, ACT and Advanced Placement tests primarily online for the 2021 admissions process would "further jeopardize educational equity and raise legitimate questions about the fairness of admission practices in this cycle." NACAC took the unusual step of directly urging all colleges to reassess their standardized testing policies, and its president reminded them that not every high school student "has a computer, at home, a network that's stable, or a quiet place to take a test." (Hoover April 29, 2020)

Low-income minority students, however, are not the only losers in the admissions game. Many low-income white parents who have themselves never completed or even entered college have also suffered grievously in terms of affordable access to higher education for their children, in large part as a result of the long-term decline in jobs that require only a high school education and lack of effective job retraining despite the myriad number of programs intended to address that issue. Income disparity and lack of access to college were among the factors that drove non-college-educated white voters to the polls in 2016 and elected President Trump. (Selingo February 16, 2017)

Children from poor white families also often lack internet and computer access and will be equally disadvantaged whenever colleges not only are forced to turn to online teaching by campus Covid-19 outbreaks, but also to curtail need-based tuition discounts due to dramatic funding shortfalls. (Anderson April 23, 2020) Cutbacks due to the Covid-19 impact may also include reductions in outreach to both rural and urban under-resourced local school districts to attract more qualified applicants from those communities (See Chapter 6 for more details on the effects of the coronavirus pandemic on both the collegiate learning environment as well as the admissions process.)

In the present-day American higher education universe, the only families that can readily afford to repay the increasingly severe student debt burdens brought on by increasing tuition costs are precisely those who don't need to borrow to fund college in the first place and whose children also have the best chance to get in, all other factors being equal. We shall see in chapters 4 and 5 that children in those families are the ones elite colleges seem most ardently to recruit and admit. Everyone else is essentially a beggar at their tables, whatever their academic and intellectual qualifications, desperate to gain admission to the best college possible as their perceived main chance to move ahead in life (or at least not move down), debt load and all.

Elite Colleges Reputedly Hold the Keys to the Top Ranks of America's Economic Kingdom — Their Business and Admissions Models Relentlessly Exploit That Reputation

In the American economy as it stands, it has never been more important financially to graduate from college in terms of economic and social prospects, and it has also never been harder financially to do so for children in most families. But there is a deeper philosophical and cultural problem underlying this bleak view of our future than just dollars and cents

In her provocative June 2020 *New York Review of Book* essay ("What Kind of Country Do We Want?") the distinguished author Marilynne Robinson focused on how the Covid-19 experience has exposed an economy that has enshrined at its core an "eager deference of profitability" and "an unembarrassed opportunism" has produced "arrangements that have been highly profitable for some people but gravely damaging to the world." She decried the ascendant "Theory of Everything" that "subordinates all other considerations to some form of "cost-benefit analysis" where "personal advantage...is seen as the one thing at stake in human relations" and discredits "ideals like selflessness and generosity...as inefficiencies that impede the natural economy of self-interest."

Robinson excoriated U.S. higher education for "bending the knee" to the newly predominant thinking that "the share of national wealth distributed as wages must be kept as low as possible to prevent the cost of labor from reducing national wealth" — where such wealth is not seen as a "broadly shared prosperity....but rather as "closely held" and "privatized" in part by suppressing wages and thereby making certain goods and services (including higher education) unaffordable for most working class families." (Robinson 2020)

> This richest country has been overtaken with a deep and general conviction of scarcity...that has become an expectation, then a discipline, even and an ethic. The sense of scarcity instantiates itself. It reinforces an anxiety that makes scarcity feel real and encroaching, and generosity, even investment, an imprudent risk....[S]tudents and their families ...are given to understand that higher education is crucial to their financial prospects and also that the costs and debts involved may be financially ruinous. Worse, the press speaks of elite universities as if there were only a dozen or so institutions in the country where an excellent education can be had. (Ibid.)

What Marilynne Robinson has labeled as a pervasive psychology of scarcity — driven by and in turn driving an economy featuring unembarrassed self-opportunism — places America's most elite colleges and universities in the driver's seat in what amounts to the definition of a seller's market. The *Chronicle of Higher Education* quoted Stanford economist Caroline Hoxby's assertion that the

United States is unique in having "'arguably the only true market for higher education....Market forces still dominate this market...and that really sets us apart.'" (Reeves December 3, 2017) Elite college admissions may, indeed, represent the last *free market* in American enterprise in terms of the paucity of regulatory interventions in the admissions process that might otherwise be expected in such a structurally unbalanced market as between buyers and sellers. The elite colleges are in a position to shape and exploit increased admissions demand while they ration admissions supply for their own purposes.

The elite college business model suggests analogies to orthodontia: a particularly high-skilled, knowledge-based professional service delivered over a consecutive period of several years intended to produce an outcome (a winning smile) that will help open the door to social acceptance and economic opportunities leading to a successful life. At least the similarly high cost of orthodontia is marginally insurable. But, like an elite college education, it has become essentially a luxury option rarely affordable for lower middle class and poor families.

Higher education is essentially a knowledge-based service enterprise in common with businesses that are driving much of the economic growth in America. Despite some similarities, however, elite colleges have distinctive characteristics that find few pure analogies in the commercial world. Microsoft and Netflix do not require you to gain their permission to purchase and download their work product: just agree to the dictated terms and pay. Law firms, investment banks, and consulting firms do systematically employ screening committees to vet erstwhile clients (although the more prestigious the client the more likely they are to negotiate the bill down, which also goes on at elite universities).

Some colleges and universities, including public universities, can sometimes even resemble elite executive search firms that can collect fees even if they do not bring forward the successful job candidate, or even if no one is hired for the position. Similarly, universities collect tuition and keep it even if the student never graduates. Of course, the schools bear the expense of the effort to educate. But if failure to graduate on time or at all means the student's federal loan debt goes into default, the US taxpayer bears the full risk, and the college bears none because it has no skin in the game except reputation. Elite colleges, however, assiduously manage and market their generally excellent graduation rates.

Colleges and universities in general offer the goal of a certain destination (graduation day) but have no accountability if that day never comes, and they can raise prices throughout the four-to-six-year duration of that journey. Imagine an airline that offers an around-the-world ticket but reserves the right to raise the price at each leg of the journey, and even to leave the passengers hanging at the last leg if they cannot fill the plane or don't have enough pilots. But colleges get away with postponing a student's path to graduation if they overbooked or under-budgeted and do not have enough teachers for the course requirements their students need to earn a degree. Recent measures show that only about 58 percent of all collegians graduate even within six years, and the schools don't give any refunds for their failure to provide enough classes within a traditional four-year schedule for a student to graduate. The US higher education system as a whole (not to mention the economy) suffers considerably from this graduation gridlock. Moreover, despite recent increases in enrollment rates, only about 40 percent of eighteen- to twenty-four-year-olds in America even begin two- or four-year college education. As Jamie Dimon, CEO of J. P. Morgan Chase, pointed out early in 2019, 40 percent of Americans earn income at the rate of $15 per hour or less, and the same percentage do not have savings sufficient to cover a surprise bill of only $400. (Dimon 2019)

It would be inconsistent with elite colleges' business models, however, to expand enrollment or reduce tuition and other charges across the board to accommodate well-qualified demand among historically disadvantaged applicants. Their reputations for maximum selectivity as measured in the annual *US News* college rankings would certainly suffer. Their aura of exclusivity, in turn, underwrites their ability to increase tuition prices annually, far in excess of the prevailing consumer price index rate, while accumulating massive endowments (i.e., retained earnings) based on tax-advantaged donations from wealthy stakeholders, where the "stake" is often admission for their children to the disadvantage of those whose parents cannot afford the sticker price. As we shall see in subsequent chapters, even the discounts on stated tuition prices increasingly go to families of above-average wealth. As a result, tuition-dependent colleges with modest endowments and taxpayer-dependent state universities lacking sufficient research contracts or big sports franchises are forced to compete for high-quality applicants on the elite colleges' terms. This situation has led to institutional debt levels and tuition discounting practices that adversely affect their own financial flexibility, credit ratings, and even their viability, which we shall further explore in chapter 6.

Secret and Unregulated Rationing of Enrollment to Preferred Groups at the Core of Elite Colleges' Competitive Business Models and Admission Strategies

America's elite colleges have arrived at a highly successful business model and strategy for an admissions system. These colleges limit and then ration their supply of admissions by assuring privileged status for the wealthiest applicants with "hooks" to the campus via legacy status, specific athletic attributes, faculty or staff parentage or as major donors' relatives. A kindly IRS even looks the other way in the case of such donor-related admissions made "in return," as one admissions dean put it, for the "value" those beneficiaries bring to the college. If an admission is really in return for a donation, the value of such a gift should not qualify as a tax-deductible charitable contribution under the law as *written* but not as *enforced* — a questionable outcome challenged in chapters 5 and 8. Meantime, "well-hooked" families can legally avoid being snared by the tax and other authorities — unless outright fraud or bribery is involved, and exposed!

Alumni and other donors with applicant children, as well as legacy children of alumni, have been effectively converted to something like college shareholders under this business model, with an untaxed "special dividend" in the form of extra-credit admissions preferences for their children. Meanwhile, current college costs and fees and resultant debt loads can easily exceed the typical middle-class family's mortgage, car loan, and credit card debt. (Maldonado 2018) As yet, however, there is no authority like the Consumer Finance Protection Bureau when it comes to the college admissions processes and practices, or the lending practices associated with tuition loans, and particularly the forced restructuring of student indebtedness.

Admissions officers of the most desirable colleges function as both salespersons (before application deadlines) and gatekeepers (after those deadlines). They are somewhat like the door guardians at the hottest new nightspot or the membership committee of a trendy and expensive country club. They are happy to attract a crowd and a long line "wait listed" for entrance, but they only let in those that most epitomize the special brand of trendiness the club wants to be known for. Some hopefuls perhaps make it in, but the majority of the chosen few are demonstrably able to pay as well as play — although at elite colleges, they may even wind up paying less by way of merit aid allocated to ward off competition from other clubs. Analysis by Stephen Boyd at New America has concluded that merit aid has, as chapter 5 will further show, become a vehicle to attract the "right" kind of applicants — those with parents who can actually afford to pay full tuition. (Reeves December 3, 2017)

When an enterprise is able to make its best customers a key part of its own brand, it has achieved marketing nirvana. Consider the essence of a typical Apple ad: beautiful, intuitive devices for beautiful, intuitive individuals. (The *I* in the I-Phone does not really refer to the *Internet*.) Even before Apple, elite colleges smartly brought their customers into their core brand: *The chosen few who choose the chosen few.* Private and some elite public schools have amassed endowment resources that collectively rival Apple's retained earnings hoard that at times has reached over $200 billion. Moreover, the elite colleges' caches are accumulated with the help of direct federal tax exemptions rather than the complex but legal tax avoidance practices employed by for-profit enterprises.

The Unmistakable Pattern: Admissions to Elite Colleges Reflect the Relative Shares of Income and Wealth of Applicants' Families

In a 2014 *New York Times* article, Peter C. Dreier and Richard D. Kahlenberg reported that at the top 193 colleges and universities considered selective, students from the richest 25 percent of the population outnumber students from the poorest quartile by a ratio of 14 to 1. (Dreier and Kahlenberg 2014) At the most highly selective schools, the Jack Kent Cooke Foundation's "True Merit" report on admissions found that children of the top quarter of income earners accounted for 72 percent of students, while those from families in the bottom income quartile make up only 3 percent of enrollment. (Giancola and Kahlenberg 2016)

A comprehensive 2017 study, led by Raj Chetty of Stanford and colleagues from Brown, UC-Berkeley and the U.S. Treasury, was focused on the back-and-forth relationship between college access and economic status and mobility. Among other things, it revealed that thirty-eight of America's top-ranked colleges, including five in the Ivy League, had *enrolled more students in their entering classes from the top 1 percent of income earners than from the bottom 60 percent.* The research by Chetty's team was developed through the Equality of Opportunity Project located at Harvard University, renamed and expanded as Opportunity Insights. It was conducted under an IRS contract, funded by several prestigious foundations, and built on data used for the U.S. Department of Education's 2015 College Scorecard covering enrollment data from over two thousand colleges and universities as well as anonymous data from millions of federal tax returns. (Chetty et al, "Mobility Report Cards: The Role of Colleges in Intergenerational Mobility," 2017 — hereinafter Chetty et al. 2017)

The Chetty team's analysis has inspired and informed multiple books, scholarly articles, research papers, media essays and investigative reporting on both college access as it related to income and its consequence for economic mobility. The latter subject will be dealt with extensively in chapter 6 of this book, particularly on the correlation of college attendance with parental income history and students' post-college earning outcomes. At this point, however, the focus will be on the data beneath the headlines establishing the correlation between parental income and college access, particularly to the most elite schools. We will see Chetty's access data has very significant consequences in terms of reinforcing patterns of income inequality across generations. (Gao 2017) Data from Chetty's work published by the National Bureau of Economic Research showed that the degree of income segregation across all colleges looks like the degree of income segregation across neighborhoods in the average American city. In terms of income disparity as it affects access to the most elite colleges, it found that children with parents in the top 1 percent are 77 times more likely to attend an Ivy League college than those of from families in the bottom income quintile. (Chetty et al. 2017; Ratsenar 2019)

A report in the *Chronicle of Higher Education* by Audrey Williams June during the Harvard Asian American discrimination trial also disclosed a wide gap in the percentages of Ivy League undergraduate enrollment between the highest and lowest household income quintile. The following data from the Chetty et al. 2017 study show for each Ivy League school its undergraduate enrollment from the top 1 percent of household incomes ($630,000 or more) first; next from the top 20 percent ($110,000 or more); and finally from the bottom 20 percent ($20,000 or less):

Brown: 19 percent; 72 percent; 4.1 percent
Columbia: 13 percent; 62 percent; 5.1 percent
Cornell: 10 percent; 64 percent; 3.8 percent
Dartmouth: 21 percent; 69 percent; 2.6 percent
Harvard: 15 percent; 67 percent; 4.5 percent
Penn: 19 percent; 71 percent; 3.3 percent
Princeton: 17 percent; 72 percent; 2.2 percent
Yale: 19 percent; 69 percent; 2.1 percent.

Jennifer Morton pointed out in her 2019 article on "The False Promise of Elite Education" in the *Chronicle of Higher Education* that Chetty's work also revealed that four in ten students from the top 0.1 percent of US incomes attend an Ivy-plus college (the eight Ivies plus MIT, Stanford, and Chicago). The median household income of Ivy-plus students' families ($171,000) ranked at the ninety-second percentile nationally. (Morton 2019)

The Ivy League schools, however, were not even at the top of the list in terms of the spread between enrollments from the top 1 percent and the bottom 60 percent of family income levels. In order, the top ten were Washington University of Saint Louis, Colorado College, Washington and Lee University, Colby College, Trinity (Connecticut) College, Bucknell University, Colgate University, Kenyon College, Middlebury College, and Tufts University — all elite, highly ranked colleges in their own right. Overall, the share of elite college students in lower-income categories had remained relatively stable over the ten-year period the Chetty team studied: the bottom 10 percent at less than 2 percent, the bottom quintile at less than 4 percent, the bottom 40 percent at roughly 7.5 percent.

Days after the admissions bribery indictments were announced, the *Economist* cited a survey by Yale's student newspaper finding that twice as many students there come from families in the top 5 percent of income distribution than from the entire bottom half. *(Economist* 2019) The *Harvard Crimson* reported that the median family income for Harvard undergraduates was three times the national average. (Flanagan and Xie 2017) The federal district judge presiding over the sentencing of Felicity Huffman after her guilty plea in the admissions bribery case took note of the "incredibly high percentage of spots" that go to families in the top 20 percent of income brackets, while also decrying legacy admissions and the high rate of additional test taking time granted wealthy versus low-income students. (Weintraub, Renstrom, and Anderson 2019)

Research on the socioeconomic stratification in higher education by Jon Boeckenstedt, a former admissions officer and a prominent blogger on the college admissions process, was cited in Paul Tough's extensive 2019 *New York Times* magazine article: "What College Admissions Offices Really Want: Elite schools say they're looking for academic excellence and diversity. But their thirst for tuition revenue means that wealth trumps all." Boeckenstedt compared data from over 1,000 colleges across three variables: average freshman SAT scores, the percentage of freshmen with Pell grants, and the percentage who are black or Latino. He found that the schools with high average SAT scores, low acceptance rates and high endowments admitted very few black and Latino students. There was also nearly perfect correlation between those colleges' level of selectivity and their students' average family income — namely, the lower the schools' admission rates, the higher their family income averages. (Tough 2019)

The emerging pattern of economic disparity in the student bodies of elite colleges is not limited to private colleges. The Chetty team research cited above also found that, over the most recent decade they measured (2000 to 2011), the University of Michigan, as an example, enrolled just 16 percent of its undergraduate students from families in the bottom 60 percent of earners, while fully 10 percent of students came from the top 1 percent group. Even though the number of disadvantaged students attending college has increased in recent years, the share of all bachelor's degrees awarded in the United States to students from the lowest income quartile declined from 12 percent in 1970 to 10 percent in 2014, despite many well-publicized programs introduced during that period that somehow failed to improve those results.

The following three chapters will reveal exactly how elite colleges effectively reserve the bulk of their admissions space for their legacies, their highest donor-bidders, and those who can afford to commit in advance to accept an early decision admission with little or no tuition bargaining power. This arrangement works to the distinct advantage of those colleges and of families most anxious to preserve for their children their upper-class economic and social status. It also works to the clear disadvantage of those first in their families to aspire to higher education and those seeking to gain a foothold up from the bottom of the economic ladder or to avoid slipping off the middle rungs.

The highly self-interested outcomes of elite college admissions practices for both the colleges themselves and their benefactors, however, raise the question whether intelligent design and strategic purpose are, in fact, at work in those practices. Are the best and the brightest at our most intellectually respected universities who shape admissions policies and practices to be considered but lucky amateurs who simply stumble unintentionally into the financially outstanding results they achieve through their admissions policies year after year for themselves and the rich clientele that their focus on exclusivity attracts, to such an extent that some have been willing to bribe their way in? If collegiate admissions are indeed purposely biased to the rich and famous, should freedom of association concepts any longer preclude legislative action to reform a garden-variety rigged market that threatens the well-being of the children who must participate in it, as well as the access to socioeconomic mobility that America has always promised?

To answer these questions, we need to look more closely at the dark side of the elite college admissions process in order to understand exactly how its tilt to the rich has been accomplished. As chapters 1 and 2 have shown, college admissions are simply too important to our national future to leave to the elite colleges themselves and their enablers.

Part II

The Dark Side of Admissions: Exploiting Anxiety, Concealing Criteria, and Favoring the Wealthy Boost Elite Colleges' Rankings and Revenues at the Expense of Most Applicants, Other Colleges, and the American Dream

CHAPTER 3

Rigging Already Unreliable College Rankings with Slippery Data and Employing Slick Marketing Tools to Create an Aura of Exclusivity That Attracts the Wealthy and Well-Connected

Admissions Corruption Starts with the Rankings Game

The most affluent and intellectually gifted college applicants from the most privileged, high-performance communities in America compete largely with one another to be the chosen few selected for admission to the most prestigious colleges. Those from less-fortunate circumstances, even in the same communities, compete with everybody just to be chosen by a decent school. Yet, as we know from chapter 1, the more affluent seem to suffer the most anxiety and stress despite their better odds of success — perhaps because their identity and idea of success will be measured by the relative prestige of the college they will attend. Missing out is an option that induces much fear and shame lest they fail to live up to expectations of parents, their communities, or even their peers. For less well-positioned applicants, missing out has a much lower definitional bar, as do their expectations. Colleges likewise compete to be among the chosen few who win consistently the favor of the most gifted and prestigious applicants, who will ultimately bring much glory and gold to their alma maters. The primary (but not the only) scoreboard for this mutually reinforcing dual competition that the aspirational students and the aspirational colleges pay most attention to is the annual college rankings published by *US News*, which, in fact, no longer publishes anything else.

In his book *Where You Go Is Not Who You'll Be*, Frank Bruni asserts that most of the educators he knows cite the *US News* ranking as the "major culprit in the admissions mania." (Bruni 2015, 92) Certainly, it was at the forefront in terms of creating the rankings industry, dating back to the 1984 acquisition of the *US News* magazine by the publisher Mort Zuckerman. It was he who decided to expand the nascent rankings and issue them annually with great fanfare to illustrate the magazine's branding as "the news you can use."

The *US News* college rankings criteria, devised by Robert Morse, quickly became public knowledge, and elite college admissions departments were quick to understand them and use (and even lobby for change) for their schools' best advantage. Other colleges of course needed to do the same or be left out of the running. Another book, *Engines of Anxiety: Academic Rankings, Reputation and Accountability*, by Wendy Nelson Espeland of Northwestern University and Michael D. Sauder of the University of Iowa, has concluded that the *US News* rankings undermine sound decision-making and encourage destructive practices by both schools and students. The authors cite years of student interviews showing how relative rankings alone often determine their decision between the schools they are admitted to. (Espeland and Slaughter 2016) University admissions deans and other officers, aware of the rankings' impact on student decisions, feel trapped into making decisions about how they run their institutions for the effect each will have, positively or negatively, on the numbers driving each of the rankings' criteria. And why wouldn't they worry when the bond-rating agencies on Wall Street take movement in relative ranking into account when assessing a college's creditworthiness and the soundness of its debt obligations? (Harper 2016)

Other commentators, however, have questioned whether those numbers-driven ranking criteria might provide a fundamentally false sense of objectivity for students, parents, high school counselors, and Wall Street analysts, while masking the subjectivity underlying the choice and weighting of each factor considered by *US News*. Of course once *US News* has its anxiety-driven teenage readers (and their parents) hooked on reading up on its free online college ranking, it will then offer a deeper dive into its data and analytics as well as webinars on subjects like "How to Impress Admissions Officers With Your Extracurricular Activities" — all for an annual fee of $39.95, plus another opportunity to capture more personal data from the registration.

US News has asserted that its methodology "focuses on academic excellence, with schools evaluated on hundreds of data points and up to 15 measures of academic quality." (Morse, Brooks, and Mason 2019) The specifics of the criteria and the relative weightings used for determining the *US News* 2019 college rankings were applied to 1,400 participating colleges and universities in four categories: national universities, national liberal arts colleges, regional universities, and regional colleges. *US News* changed the weights of multiple indicators and dropped one indicator from the 2018 edition. (Nietzel 2019) The indicators and their weights in the

US News rankings formula for 2019 were as follows:

Outcomes (35 percent) Success at retaining and graduating students within 150 percent of normal time (six years) (22 percent weighting), measures of social mobility (5 percent), and graduation rate performance (8 percent).

- Graduation and retention rates: The average six-year graduation rate is weighted 17.6 percent, average first-year retention rate 4.4 percent.
- Social mobility: Measured by graduating students who received federal Pell grants who graduated, weighted at 2.5 percent; Pell grant graduation rates compared to all other students are weighted at 2.5 percent.
- Graduation rate performance: Compares each college's actual six-year graduation rate to what *US News* predicted for its relevant fall entering class.

Faculty Resources (20 percent) Five factors used to assess a school's commitment to instruction: class size, faculty salary, faculty members with the highest degree in their fields, student-faculty ratio, and proportion of faculty who are full time.

- **Class size** is weighted at 8 percent. Schools receive the most credit for the proportion of their fall term undergraduate classes with fewer than twenty students. Classes with twenty to twenty-nine score second highest, thirty to thirty-nine third highest, and forty to forty-nine fourth highest. Classes that have fifty or more receive no credit.
- **Faculty salary** is weighted at 7 percent: The average faculty pay, plus benefits, during the preceding two academic years, adjusted for regional cost-of-living differences.
- *US News* also factors in the proportion of full-time faculty with the highest degree in their fields (weighting 3 percent), student-faculty ratio (weighting 1 percent), and the proportion of faculty who are full time (weighting 1 percent).

Expert Opinion (20 percent) Survey of top academics, including presidents, provosts, and deans of admission, to rate the academic quality of peer institutions with which they are familiar on a scale of 1 (marginal) to 5 (distinguished) (weighting 15 percent). Survey of nearly 24,400 counselors at public, private, and parochial high schools from all fifty states and Washington, DC (weighting 5 percent).

Financial Resources (10 percent) Average spending per student on instruction, research, student services, and related educational expenditures in the previous two fiscal years. Spending on sports, dorms, and hospitals does not count.

Student Excellence (10 percent) *US News* asserts that a college's academic atmosphere is influenced by the selectivity of its admissions. Simply put, students who achieved strong grades and test scores during high school have the highest probability of succeeding at challenging college-level coursework, enabling instructors to design classes that have great rigor. They emphasized that colleges' acceptance rates have been completely removed from the ranking calculations to make room for the new social mobility indicators. Standardized test results of entering students are weighted at 7.75 percent. Schools sometimes fail to report SAT and ACT scores for students in these categories: athletes, international students, minority students, legacies, those admitted by special arrangement, and those who started in the previous summer. For any school that does not report all scores or that declines to say whether all scores were reported, *US News* reduces its combined SAT/ACT percentile distribution value used in the ranking model by 15 percent. If the combined percentage of the fall entering class submitting test scores is less than 75 percent of all new entrants, the combined SAT/ACT percentile distribution value used in the rankings is discounted by 15 percent. The average class rank of entering students is weighted at 2.25 percent.

Alumni Giving (5 percent) Average percentage of living alumni with bachelor's degrees who gave to their college in the previous two years. Giving measures student satisfaction and postgraduate engagement.

The reader can judge the degree of quantitative versus qualitative, objective versus subjective, and assumed versus verified information reflected in the categories comprising the composite rankings in the annual *US News* surveys. *US News*'s recent decision to remove any weighting for participating colleges' acceptance rates is a major concession to the reality that those rates, as we shall see later in this chapter, have been subject to egregious marketing and data manipulation as well as outright lying. Yet the *US News* website continues to prominently publish a separate selectivity ranking measured solely by such acceptance rates: "Top 100 Lowest Acceptance Rates...The 100 colleges and universities listed here are among the most selective..."

Six senators (all Democrats) wrote to *US News* in late 2018 requesting that the publication "use its influential platform to better align its rankings with...improving college access, supporting student success, and providing every talented student a pathway to economic stability and meaningful participation in our country's economic, social and civic life." The senators acknowledged the "modest improvements" the publication had made in its ranking formula but urged that more needed to be done. "We fear *US News* continues to create a perverse incentive for schools to adopt or maintain policies that perpetuate social and economic inequalities." (Quintana 2018) As we will see in chapters 7 and 8, Congress has power o address how the *US News* criteria encourage and facilitate serious inequities in the college admissions process.

US News Rankings Exert Influence Beyond Their Relevance

and Reliability by *Appearing* to Quantify Colleges' Relative Exclusivity

Frank Bruni of the *New York Times* has called attention to the inherent circularity of the highly weighted reputational aspects of the *US News* ratings, noting that since one of the principal engines of reputation is the *US News* publication itself, "[t]here's a self-fulfilling prophecy at work" where schools rated highly for reputation before are rated similarly again and again. (Bruni 2015, 95) This reality is particularly troublesome because the matter of academic reputation is weighted most highly in the *US News* calculations. The author of another admissions guidebook, *The College Solution*, in its chapter 37 titled "What's Wrong with *US News and World Report*'s College Rankings," has made the same point, somewhat less delicately:

> What could the provost or president at Vanderbilt or the University of Connecticut possibly know about the academic quality of Hofstra University and the University Oregon, as well as all the other schools the *Us News* bumped together in this category? If this sounds crazy, I'm not making this up!…[It's] also nuts…Faced with an impossibly ludicrous task, administrators stuck with completing the survey will turn to *US News*' past college rankings to assess which schools are exceptional and which ones are simply ordinary (O'Shaughnessy 2015, 171-72)

Not surprisingly, given the tendency to simply reiterate prior years' assessments of the heavily weighted "reputation" variable, the annual *US News* rankings have changed very little year over year, especially at the top, where Williams College has held *US News*'s top national liberal arts rankings for fifteen years straight, and Princeton has been number one among national colleges and universities for seven years in a row. Single-digit moves up or down are common. Although this relative rigidity underscores the unreliable subjectivity in major elements of the rankings, the lack of volatility also means that even minor changes up or down become a very big item in an admissions department's in-box (and another business opportunity for college enrollment management and marketing consultants). When UCLA tied Berkeley for a position recently, it prompted a headline as far away as the *Washington Post*. (Anderson, September 12, 2018) We will encounter the consequences of such minor blips in *US News*'s rankings when we examine how admissions officials have come to terms with them, and turned to strategies for what website gurus might term *rankings optimization*. But first, a deeper dive into the *US News* criteria will reveal how there are enough ambiguities that create not only room for skepticism, but also actual incentives for manipulation and outright cheating, even by the most elite colleges.

It is unclear to many educators how some of the variables as defined by *US News* contribute to the actual quality of education: are faculty salaries worth their weight in terms of students' interests as compared to other expenditures not even listed by *US News*, such as scholarship and other financial aid resources? (And don't for a moment think that university officials have not been forced to choose between these two spending options in calculating the best interests of their educational mission as compared to their best interest in terms of the *US News* rankings.) In a 2011 *New Yorker* article, Malcolm Gladwell, assessing just what college rankings really tell us, observed that "it's an act of real audacity when a ranking system tries to be comprehensive *and* heterogeneous" (Gladwell 2011) — which is exactly what *US News* tries to do.

Gladwell used the example of a *Car and Driver* survey attempting to pick the best sports car using the same extensive set or ranking factors and weightings that it used for all cars it tests, from SUVs to economy models, where styling and looks count for only single digits, whereas they probably count for more for sports car enthusiasts. Trying to come up with a heterogeneous system that is broad enough to rate all vehicles with the same methodology, they ended up with a system ill suited to a *particular* class of cars. If a heterogeneous grouping were to be subjected to just one dimension of ranking, like acceleration or driving pleasure, that would be credible. But, according to Gladwell, if *Car and Driver* also wants to rank on a comprehensive basis "using twenty-one variables…weighted according to a secret sauce cooked up by the editors…it will break down when the field is in fact heterogeneous, leaving an impossible task in terms of how to weight each variable" for radically different kinds of vehicles. Gladwell observed that *US News* tries to cover a relatively heterogeneous class of schools within each of its four broad categories of schools, while at the same time attempting to be comprehensive and not limited to ranking only one dimension like test scores of freshmen. "It cooks up an algorithm that tells us with apparent certainty that Penn State is a better school by one point than Yeshiva University." But those two schools would otherwise be impossible to compare because of their extreme mission-based differentiation.

Gladwell concluded that there is no "direct way to measure the quality of an institution" — how well a college manages to inform, inspire, and challenge its students. He pointed out that "the *US News* algorithm relies instead on proxies for quality — and the proxies for educational quality turn out to be flimsy at best." The percentage weighting for faculty resources, for example, does not come close to measuring the elusive but vital matter of student satisfaction with their engagement with faculty, which educators find has much to do with greater learning and progress to graduation.

Yet there is no real need for *US News* to rely merely on proxies to measure student engagement, as demonstrated by the National Survey of Student Engagement (NSSE) based at Indiana University, which asks actual students direct questions about their classroom experiences and how they spend their time interacting with faculty outside class around topics like their classroom performance, course topics, and career plans. The NSSE also asks directly whether, overall, students would make the same enrollment decision if given the chance for a do-over. Most elite schools, however, do not participate in the NSSE. *US News* ignores the option of student polling and relies on its proxies — that's their story, and they're sticking to it. As *US News*'s rankings guru put it, as quoted by Gladwell, "We're not saying we're measuring educational outcomes. We're not saying we're social scientists, or we're subjecting our rankings to some peer-review process. We're just saying that we've made this judgment...We've developed these academic indicators, and we think these measures measure quality schools." (Ibid.)

Elite colleges seem to agree. They play the rankings game to the hilt to defend and enhance their high ratings, especially their reputations for maximum selectivity. But there are better emerging sources of data and analysis of admissions practices and outcomes. Even the common nomenclature describing elite college admission results are sanitized with socially acceptable verbiage. "Admissions" offices would far more correctly be labeled "rejections" offices — they do much more of the latter than the former. "Selectivity" rankings would best be framed as "exclusion" rankings. For example, the special admissions lane reserved by elite schools for legacies automatically excludes any applicant whose parents did not graduate from that particular college, or any college. The same with the special lanes reserved for their own faculty members' children or children of major donors. As chapter 5 will detail, elite college admissions are steeped in deliberately exclusionary preferences.

Consider how many of the selectivity-stoking hopeless applications enticed by misleading marketing practices that we will explore later in this chapter might be dissuaded if *US News* and others published the admissions results in terms of percentages rejected instead of the reciprocal chosen few numbers: Stanford would show 95 percent rejected, Harvard 94 percent rejected, Princeton 93 percent rejected, and so forth. And that would not even be giving effect to the high percentage of legacy, early decision, and other wealth-related admissions that effectively take places off the table for those who are born or raised without such hooks.

The COVID-19 pandemic will likely have continuing adverse financial impact on both the overall number of entering class seats available and the number of applicants available to recruit and financially able to enroll. By the spring of 2020, major state flagship universities were estimating calendar year losses ranging in the hundreds of millions up to a billion dollars due to the pandemic. McKinsey analysis concluded that more than 800 private colleges would experience 20 percent or greater budget shortfalls in their 2021 budgets. (Friga April 20, 2020)

A reputation for educational exclusivity may counter-intuitively have less value in the wake of the Covid-19 experience – and be harder to quantify as US *News* attempts to do. SAT and ACT scores used by *US News* as its key selectivity metric may prove useless in a world of test-optional applications. As noted in chapter 2, adoption of such a policy was suggested by the leading association of admissions officers and counselors to take account of the inability of lower-income students lacking broadband access to take those tests to the extent they shift to online formats. (Hoover April 29, 2020) Colleges experiencing dramatic funding shortfalls due to COVID-19 may no longer be so willing to disclose to *US News* data like faculty salaries and other academic spending levels, as well as alumni giving and student retention and graduation rates. With even less relevant and reliable testing and financial data available during the COVID-19 outbreak, future *US News* rankings could turn primarily on what has been viewed as its weakest element: namely, its "expert opinion" survey of a college's reputation among top university officials at other schools. Moreover, in a pandemic-affected period, evaluations of colleges will likely become even more important **to** based more on student *outcomes* rather than institutional *inputs* applicants **and** their families. Fortunately, there are credible sources of college data beyond *US News* already poised to provide some of those measures even in the pandemic environment.

US News **Is Not the Only Rankings Game in Town: Other Sources Already Offer Better and More Relevant Data for Applicants**

Despite its focus on ranking heterogeneous colleges against a quite comprehensive list of variables, *US News* conspicuously chooses to omit any consideration or comparison of price, affordability, or value for money. Other institutions, including business organizations looking to employ college graduates and other journals that focus on the concerns of business, have stepped into the breach left by *US News.*

- Although *Money* magazine's college rankings use metrics similar to *US News*, like test scores and graduation rates, in assessing a school's quality, they also include a measure of affordability, taking into account not just tuition levels but also the amount of financial aid and the relative length of time to degree completion.

- *Forbes* magazine's rankings attempt to measure return on investment in college, including data on success in getting jobs after graduation, salaries, and the levels of student debt carried into working lives, as well as the four-year graduation rates and post-graduation awards like Rhodes and Fulbright scholarships. The *Princeton Review* publishes an annual in-depth summary of data relevant to applicants and their families (without rankings) but with statistics comparable across several hundred leading colleges). So does the *Fiske Guide to Colleges*. Books such as *The Hidden*

Ivies and *Colleges That Change Lives* focus on characteristics and data of selected schools deemed by the authors to deliver the particular value reflected in their titles, again without relative rankings.

- The *New York Times* began publishing its own college access list in 2014, assessing and ranking schools based on the percentage of their students who qualified for Pell grants (and make it to graduation), as well as their discounted college cost for families that are otherwise not affluent. The list focuses on colleges where the five-year graduation rate is at least 75 percent. The *Times*'s financial columnist James Stewart produced his own ranking in conjunction with the Brookings Institution to measure the value added by colleges through comparing precollege expectations for earnings based on test scores and family situations to what the same students, in fact, earned in the years after graduation (adjusted for science-related degrees). In 2015, no Ivy League school made the top twenty in Stewart's Brookings-Common Sense ranking.

- Not to be outdone, the Gallup organization announced a plan in 2017 to certify colleges based on the well being of their graduates in terms of social, financial, and community connectedness as well as physical health. This undertaking will include not only a major survey of graduates but also an intensive up-to-three-year evaluation of the effects of efforts to improve student well-being by the colleges that sign up to participate.

- The *Wall Street Journal* and *Barron's* also produce annual college rankings that add specific focus on value for money considerations. And *Washington Monthly* produces rankings intended to measure colleges' relative contributions to the public good.

- Individual actors such as media and polling entities have also taken leading roles in assessing college quality. Edwin B. Fiske, a former *New York Times* education editor, annually publishes the *Fiske Guide to Colleges,* which the author of *The Gatekeepers* (a detailed study of the innermost workings of Wesleyan University's admissions department) has described as "thumbnail sketches of dozens of institutions, based on small surveys of students and administrators. (Steinberg 2002, 285) A group of college leaders created an online search tool, BigFuture, now hosted by the College Board, that contains far more particular data for applicants than the *US News* rankings (for example, average net price). (Lythcott-Haimes 2015, 137)

- The Department of Education's College Naviance also has a price calculator and information on the range of accepted ACT and SAT scores per college. The Naviance site shows (self-reported) admissions results and score ranges for an applicant's high school classes from previous years. Websites like Niche (formerly College Prowler) and College Confidential share anecdotal evidence from applicants on their admissions results and likely admissions criteria, and, in the latter case, estimations of a national applicant's chances of admission based on his or her test scores, grades, and other relevant characteristics. Unigo does the same on its website, along with anecdotal reviews of a particular college's academic quality, social scene and physical plant, along with a raft of statistics similar to those found in *US News.*

President Obama was very critical of the published college rankings systems, which he thought encouraged colleges to raise costs. His administration created its own college rating system, the College Scorecard, which sought to cover major aspects of a college's attributes and outcomes not addressed by *US News,* including costs, loan default rates, average amount of student loans, and employment results. (Zhou 2015) The federal Scorecard has been continued by the Trump administration, a rare exception to

President Trump's multiple actions reversing Obama-era initiatives, but with significant alterations that removed such important contextual data as net price as well as whether each school's results were higher or lower than the national medians for those measures. (Kreighbaum 2018) Trump's Education Secretary Betsy DeVos, however, also acted in 2019 to expand the Scorecard's information about graduation rates, including for both first-time and non-full-time college students, as well as the percentage of students who transferred from and were still enrolled in school. Loan debt rates have been added for particular academic programs as well as at the institutional level. Data from 2,100 non-degree-granting institutions (such as those offering certificate programs in particular vocations) have been added to the figures from 3,700 degree-granting institutions. But the amended Scorecard does not include any direct consumer ratings of schools or programs.

Another good source of information about particular colleges — without any type of ranking involved, is the Common Data Set, which is a collaboration among participating colleges and publishers (including *US News* and the College Board, who use some of the data in their own websites). The schools provide an agreed set of data points each year relating to admissions and wait lists, along with midrange test scores and other data for those who actually enrolled. (Springer, Reider, and Morgan 2010, 115-16)

Some economists have investigated the feasibility of developing a more consumer-based, Yelp-like ratings system allowing alumni to comment directly on their college experiences and outcomes for the benefit of potential applicants and enrollees. A June 2017 study, based on data gathered by Gallup and the Strada Education Network's Education Consumer Pulse research platform, compared alumni comments with data from their colleges and found that those alums who rated their colleges more highly tended to have higher incomes and other indicia of personal well being. These data, in turn, were found to correlate with certain metrics about their colleges like alumni income levels and graduates with doctorates. The study's principal author (Jonathan T. Rothwell, a visiting scholar at George Washington University Institute of Public Policy) suggested that a Yelp-type survey limited to a simple question such as "Would you recommend your alma mater to others?" could offer reliably helpful information to college applicants. (Chan 2017)

The multiple efforts by respected private institutions and the federal government to move away from mostly proxy measures of the relative value of education at particular colleges toward more precise metrics of efficacy and outcomes put the flaws of the *US News* rankings into sharp relief. The failings in their rankings are somewhat reminiscent of the faulty judgments of bond rating agencies that misled investors with rosy scenarios in the lead up to the subprime mortgage finance scandals. Despite the many ambiguities and the other weaknesses in the *US News* rankings, however, college officials have found themselves in a "can't live with them, can't live without them" position because those deeply flawed rankings nonetheless remain very important factors influencing student decisions about where to apply and where to enroll. Elite colleges, despite their earned academic reputations, are as sensitive to their *US News* standings as their lesser-ranked competitors; they will go to the hilt to defend or enhance their rankings, and *US News* is ripe for gaming.

US News Rankings: Too Big to Ignore, but Too Easy to Game

A recent survey of college-bound students undertaken by Art & Science Group LLC found that 72 percent of traditional students consider published rankings when choosing where to apply. Despite the availability of other more relevant data sources, the survey also found that students most commonly rely on the *US*

News rankings, although *Forbes* Top Colleges, the *Princeton Review*, and Niche are also being frequently consulted. About the same percentage of students agreed that rankings are important in sorting out differences between colleges and agreed with the proposition that graduates of higher-ranked schools obtain good jobs more easily; 7 percent of students surveyed reported that they talked about rankings with others, and higher-scoring students are most likely to do so. (Student Poll 2016)

Given the mindshare the annual *US News* college rankings publication has captured, it is understandable that university executives generally have pursued strategies to make those rankings work for their admissions goals. College boards of trustees are certainly looking over their shoulders in terms of where their schools place in the annual *US News* rankings. A Harvard Business School study in 2011 found that each notch in the *US News* rankings leads to a 1 percent increase in applications. (Marcus 2014) Remember that 1:1 relationship. Submissions of the various admissions data points are not audited or certified. And the pressure on an admissions dean to move up in the rankings can be as intense as that on a football coach.

There can be a fine line between a winning rankings strategy and a cheating one, however, especially where no form of "honor code" seems to apply. Some otherwise reputable colleges have crossed the line in order to move up or hold their place. As Raymond Brown, Texas Christian University's dean of admissions, observed: "We on the inside have a pretty good idea of who is reporting accurately and who is not. And quite a few schools appear to be cooking the books" in terms of their submissions of ratings-related data. (Marcus 2013)

Inside Higher Ed's Survey of College and University Admissions Directors found that 9 percent of them believed that some other institutions had provided false data on test scores and other factors relevant to college rankings although they all denied doing so themselves. (Jaschik and Lederman, editors 2017) Several highly ranked and well-regarded schools, however, were caught and/or admitted falsifying admissions data sent to the US Department of Education, their own accrediting agencies and *US News*. (Perez-Pena 2012; Kutner September 2014; Zahneis 2018; Svrluga 2019; Gee 2019)

- Claremont-McKenna lied about admissions test scores.
- Bucknell University for years inflated its mean SAT scores by an average of 16 percent.
- Emory University submitted the much higher SAT test score averages of those who applied instead of the required (but lower) average of those who ultimately enrolled.
- George Washington University misrepresented the number of entering freshmen from the top 10 percent of their high school classes.
- Tulane University's business school gave *US News* inflated figures on the average test scores and total number of its applicants.
- The University of Illinois law school provided false data to the American Bar Association in connection with its accreditation review.
- Baylor University offered some applicants $300 in bookstore credits to retake their SATs and another $1,000 in aid per year if they increased their scores by fifty points or more.
- Clemson University submitted false financials and strategically lowballed its peer ratings for competitor schools' academic reputations.
- Iona College submitted false test scores and acceptance and graduation rates.
- The University of Oklahoma was forced to publicly apologize — and forfeit its *US News* ranking — after

submitting inflated alumni-giving data to the survey and now faces a lawsuit brought by disgruntled students.

- Several business programs at Temple University submitted falsified data to *US News*, including the number of entrants providing GMAT scores, the average undergraduate GPAs of entrants, the number of admissions offers extended by the programs, and how much debt the students incurred. Some of these false submissions apparently contributed to very high rankings for these programs by *US News*. The federal Department of Education also probed whether Temple used related deceptive marketing practices for its Fox Business School online programs.

Even a handful of outright cheating cases per year are troubling, especially because so many of the professionals in the field think much more cheating is going on than has been uncovered. Lately more college admission departments have been acknowledging their own false data submissions that advanced their rankings when they have discovered the errors themselves, including the University of California-Berkeley, Scripps College, Johnson and Wales University and the University of North Carolina-Pembroke. *US News* publicized these disclosures on its own website and revoked these schools' 2019 rankings. (Morse, Mason, and Brooks 2019) As a purely statistical matter, the outright, deliberate falsification cases on record might be dismissed as outlying situations that were eventually caught out. More indirect methods of subtly influencing outcomes of the *US News* variables, however, are probably more troublesome overall because the rankings themselves seem to invite such gaming.

A former president of Northeastern University, Richard Freeland, realized when he took over the financially challenged school in 1996 that "There's no question that the [*US News*] system invites gaming." (Kutner September 2014) He embarked on a systematic ten-year effort to break the rankings codes (generally well known now but not then) and then to do what was necessary to move up under the formulas his researchers had reverse engineered. Northeastern lowered class size caps to nineteen, switched to the Common Application to increase their totals and thus enhance selectivity, spent $1 billion on a new dorm complex they believed would improve retention, personally lobbied peer institution officials for higher reputational ratings, and met with *US News* officials to convince them not to count Northeastern's co-op students (who took regular job placement breaks from classes) in their enrollment totals so that their rating for financial resources per student would improve. It all worked: By the time he retired in 2006, Freeland's program had met its target of reaching the top 100 ranks at number 98. Northeastern broke no rules and did not cheat, but its efforts are a remarkable example of *US News'* influence on college priorities and, by analogy, a prime case of "teaching to the test" in terms of university policy decisions. (Kutner August and September 2014)

More recently, the extraordinary and unprecedented rankings-related actions of Mount Saint Mary's College in Maryland were not nearly as arguably benign as what Northeastern University did. The student newspaper exposed the plans of university president Simon Newman to use a misleading and intrusive survey to identify entering freshmen who might for family, emotional, or academic reasons be prone to dropping out and then push them to withdraw ASAP so they would not be counted as dropouts when the school reported the government and thence to *US News* and other rankers. He went on to criticize those who opposed this plan: "'[T]his is hard for you because you think of the students as cuddly bunnies, but you can't. You have to drown the bunnies...put a Glock to their heads." (Svrluga 2016) Shortly after the story broke, the president fired faculty members who challenged his plan, demoted the provost, and tried to silence the student paper. Fortunately, the university's accreditor intervened, the president and five trustees resigned, and faculty members were reinstated.

But the case shows that the *US News* ranking game can even corrupt the leaders of a religiously affiliated college (Wells 2016)

Stuffing the Applications Channel, Intrusive Data Mining, and Other Tricks to Inflate College Rankings and Reputations for Selectivity and Low Admission Rates

By far the most pervasive effects of the *US News* rankings on college admissions practices, among the many college quality factors *US News* attempts to measure, are associated with relative admissions selectivity as measured by student excellence and the well-publicized separate ranking of acceptance rates. Focusing on any data that purports to reveal a college's relative selectivity tends to reward at the margin the most elite private colleges and religiously affiliated universities with the mostly homogeneous enrollments from well-off families at the expense of even the best state-supported and other schools that choose, or are required to choose, more diversified student bodies both economically and socially.

The temptation for colleges of all types to submit false or misleading selectivity data regarding their enrollees' average SAT and ACT test scores and class ranks, which contribute most to the student excellence 10 percent weighting in the *US News* rankings, has already been illustrated in the outright cheating scandals cited above. There are also many ways to fiddle with the test score and class rank data by exclusion of lower-testing athletes, legacies, or children of important donors or celebrities (which *US News* has, to its credit, lately recognized and discounted). Because *US News* counts the scores only of the freshmen who enter in late summer or early autumn, however, some elite schools have moved to admitting certain lower-testing admits including legacies and athletes to their spring term. There are even more consequential effects of test-optional and early decision admissions policies that are difficult to integrate into the reported test score mix without major distortions in terms of selectivity ratios, discussed more fully in chapters 4 and 5.

In terms of the class-ranking indicator of selectivity, many high schools have moved away from class rankings, reducing the overall scope for manipulating that data but also making it hard to maintain valid comparisons among students from different high schools. This, unfortunately, means that *US News* incentivizes admissions departments to pit applicants from each particular high school primarily against each other rather than in comparison with all applicants with similar actual test results and grades, increasing the level of student stress at the most local and intense level.

ACT and SAT test results, however, remain widely utilized and are particularly simple to present and understand in terms of medians, means, and standardized range, and can appear, on the surface, to be objective measures of enrolled student quality (although that is now widely disputed). These scoring data fit easily into the colleges' own data website dashboards and brochures, as well as on scatter-grams on otherwise quite useful and student-friendly independent data sites like Naviance, as well as the US government—published Common Data Set for all schools receiving federal education funding. Chapter 4 will cover the extent to which the Data Set and other such resources are (or are not) able to discern the actual baseline screening criteria and preferences of elite colleges hidden in their admission black boxes.

A college's admissions rate (the ratio of admits to total applications), however, remains the most readily recognized attention-getter in the media coverage of the annual *US News* rankings and in the minds of admissions departments. The admissions rate is the speedometer on the selectivity dashboard: a one- or two-digit number. It's simple, clear, and to the point, a shorthand definition of selectivity all by itself. Despite excising this number in calculating its overall rankings, *US News* continues its practice of publishing a ranking of the one hundred schools with the lowest acceptance rates. (*US News* 2020; Moody 2019) Other college admissions ranking publications like Niche predictably follow suit, and college admissions departments have accordingly continued to calculate, massage, and fudge admissions data for promotional purposes.

Acceptance rates weren't always an issue. From the founding of Harvard in 1636 to the 1920s, most colleges admitted all comers who could demonstrate mastery of clear (and clearly disclosed) admissions standards. Even the most prominent Ivies had no stated limits on entry-class size — if you could pass the entrance exams, you got in — until "too many" Jews began to gain admission that way. This unanticipated outcome triggered a resort to the first forms of "selectivity-based" admissions focused on assessing "personal character" and setting aside reserved seats for less academically qualified legacies who were obviously from the "right" families and religious and ethnic backgrounds. (Larson, in Kahlenberg, ed. 2010, 169-70)

The heads of college admissions departments understand that the acceptance rate cited in the *US News* publication is the *one* number that moves the *entire* market. It dominates the headlines about the schools, particularly at the top of the categories, sometimes even more so than their overall numerical rankings. It is a neon sign of exclusivity; it purports to show exactly how hard it is (in many cases, even harder than it appears, as chapter 5 will show) to win a place in the most elite colleges' entering classes. This aura of exclusivity is intended to create an indelible market perception that both the school and its admitted students are member of America's "chosen few."

The overall selectivity brand is so significant that it has been further refined by commentators and advice books like *Admission Matters* into distinct tiers:

- *Ultra*-selective: less than 10 percent of applicants are admitted
- *Super*-selective: less than 20 percent
- *Highly* selective: less than 35 percent
- *Very* selective: less than 50 percent.

Unfortunately, for all its simplicity, the ratio of admissions to applications can be "adjusted" by inflating or deflating one of the numbers making up the ratio. The temptation is to inflate the denominator with applications knowing only a fraction will ever be admitted. (Springer, Reider and Morgan 2013, 12) Public and ranking focus on the raw number of applications received virtually invites manipulation. That invitation has been broadly accepted by the ranks of college admissions departments, including the most highly selective schools. "Colleges want to appear to be highly selective in who they accept. They yearn for *US News & World Report* to label them as a school that is hard to get into. This is accomplished by inflating the number of students who apply so that they can reject more of them and appear to be pickier....Some colleges even waive the application fee to this end." (Brenoff 2016)

This practice of stuffing the applications channel with hopeless submissions in order to game the reputational rankings is not limited to what might be considered the fringe of the elite college group in its broadest definition. Harvard's own expert witness in the federal trial of charges that it discriminates against Asian Americans in its secretive admissions policies testified under oath that three-quarters of Harvard's undergraduate applicants are "out of the money" — meaning they have no chance of getting in. (Hoover October 31, 2018) If such a perennially highly-ranked, ultra-elite school for some reason needs to stuff its black box with hopeless applications to secure its prestigious reputation, what choice do lesser elites and all other colleges have but to compete on the same pumped up terms?

In terms of the *numerator* of the admission rate fraction, most elite colleges have no business plan interest in either inflating or deflating the size of their incoming class: rather, their priority is to hit their "yield" (and associated tuition income) targets from the admissions they offer. Thus, all the rankings-related manipulation occurs with the application totals. Enrollment management professionals are consulted to develop the most finely honed strategies in terms of how admissions are rationed to provide the optimal yield and tuition outcomes. (Springer, Reider, and Morgan 2013, 120) Indeed, the better a college manages the yield of newly-enrolled as compared to the number admitted, by selecting only those most likely to come, the lower its application acceptance number needs be, and therefore the stronger its selectivity reputation will be. (Ibid.) We will examine in chapter 5 how certain wealth-focused preferential application "lanes" and especially the option of early decision — ironically marketed as an anti-anxiety palliative for stressed-out applicants — actually are strategically powerful elements of these schools' business models designed to achieve their optimal yield ratios and tuition revenue targets, as well as assure a continuing flow of wealthy and grateful donors.

Fortunately for the elite colleges' business plans, the increasing focus on selectivity in recent decades since the emergence of the *US News* rankings coincided with the emergence of the Common Application and its online format, now adopted by the vast majority of colleges and universities in the United States as at least one of the ways to submit an application and often the only way. The Common Application eliminates duplication of fundamental statistical information about students and their track records, leaving only individuated essay questions to be submitted on a school-by-school basis. While it first appeared in 1975, the real growth in usage began in the midst of the Great Recession fallout, doubling in the five years from 2009 to 2014. (Bruni 2015, 51)

The number of applications in all forms to most colleges and universities has soared since the Common Application became truly common, as has the number of schools that the typical student applies to, moving from a single digit in the 1980s into low double digits at the present time and ranging up to as many as twenty or more among those families that can afford the services of certain types of admissions consultants (see chapter 4). In 1990, only 10 percent of college students applied to seven or more colleges by 2015 about one-third did so. (Bruni 2015, 52) Even elite colleges like the University of Chicago, Oberlin, and Washington University Saint Louis have been significantly extending their traditional early January deadlines for regular admission submissions to garner even more applicants, not only to buttress their selectivity reputation but also to assure a financially respectable enrollment yield. Through 2017, the average yield for all colleges had fallen from 48 percent to 34 percent over the preceding decade in the face of mounting competitive pressure in the admissions game. (Korn November 29, 2019) Financial markets know all about the importance of the "search for yield" — and so now do *all* colleges, and the agencies that rate the quality of their bonds!

Even the Common App has been supplemented, in service of the goal of inflating application numbers at some schools, by so-called snap apps — online applications that the colleges themselves send to students, already filled out and often waiving the application fee: all the high school kid has to do is click, and he or she is automatically another addition to the school's applicant denominator. (McGinty 2016) Admissions departments have not left the opportunity to ramp up applications to chance. As Frank Bruni pointed out in his book, citing the admissions director of an elite college, "emissaries from colleges will fan out across the country, extolling the magic of their schools and exhorting students to come aboard even as their very exhortations lengthen the odds against any one student getting in...ginning up desire only to frustrate it...In other words, their come-on is successful if it sows more failure." (Bruni 2015, 48)

Colleges and their enrollment management consultants also long ago recognized that they could purchase from the College Board the names and direct mail and email addresses of students who take their SATs and other standardized tests on a bulk basis, targeting those who achieved a score range above basically any level that the colleges chose to designate (without getting the exact scores themselves, which the students submit). And they did, in huge numbers, to their own very specific ends. As described in 2015 by Eric Hoover in his article ("College Admissions, Frozen in Time") in the *Chronicle of Higher Education*: "for colleges aspiring to greater selectivity, the system's undeniable inefficiency is by design."

> Each year, four-year institutions everywhere spend a fortune buying tens or hundreds of thousands of high-school students' names from testing and other companies, and bombard those "suspects" with letters and emails. The hope is that, as they move through the recruitment funnel, enough of them become interested "prospects," then, ideally, applicants, at which point the bulk of colleges, tuition-dependent and not world famous, scramble to admit and enroll a certain number (to meet their enrollment and revenue goals), while the wealthiest, choosiest institutions use elaborate criteria to whittle down the vast numbers in an intensive exercise known as crafting a class…Application inflation is, in part, a result of colleges' own marketing prowess. (Hoover 2015)

In addition to the data revealed by students filling out the surveys associated with standardized tests, literally millions of high school students' personal information is for sale in a data-brokering market based on forms filled out by those students when filling out one or another of the many surveys like the My College Options questionnaire. Students readily get into this pattern of giving away their data unwittingly, despite the fact that such uses may be disclosed in the survey's fine print. The My College Options survey, for example, discloses that it may sell such data to student loan services and test prep companies.

Despite the well-known issues around Facebook users' data being shared with Cambridge Analytica and other data privacy concerns emerging in social media, there is no federal regulation of online data brokers. Public schools are themselves responsible for controlling access to student data, not the venders or test services and student surveys they may engage. The US Department of Education, however, has at least urged public schools to make clear to students and their parents that detailed testing service surveys are entirely voluntary and not required to take the test and get a score, but there has been no follow-up enforcement action.

Meanwhile, admissions departments at elite colleges and the "lesser" schools trying to keep up with them with special on-campus summer study programs to introduce a curated campus academic/social environment to high school students whose parents can afford to pay for the privilege. More importantly, they continue to be aggressive buyers of whatever personal data potential applicants have revealed as they work their way through the application mania. Just how aggressive? Data for the three million or so high school seniors and juniors who took the ACT, SAT, and PSAT in 2018 went for 43 to 45 cents per name, and there were many scores of buyers for the same data sets, given the level of competition in the *US News* lowest-acceptance-rate sweepstakes. (Singer 2018) The number of individual contact details purchased varies, but the lists can top 100,000 names per college according to the *Wall Street Journal.* (McGinty 2016)

All this teen-age data mining effort seems to have been worthwhile. Growth in overall college application volume has been humming along at a 4 percent rate annually. (NACUBO 2018) Until very recently (due to stricter US immigration policies), international applications had been running at an annual growth rate of 8 percent. Elite colleges, where consistent success in recruiting and enrolling wealthy applicants has led to the financial capacity to support large marketing budgets, have a clear bidding advantage in the data market.

Another really big cost (and related advantage for elite colleges) relates to the production of slick, stylized brochures and other promotional mailing materials, as well as state-of-the-art professional websites, email, and social media marketing operations to flood those purchased names and addresses with seemingly nonstop invitations to submit their applications. As Bruni put it, the college admissions office "is no longer a mere screening committee. It's a ruthlessly efficient purveyor of Ivory Tower porn." (Bruni 2015, 48) In addition, prospects are bombarded with text messages pressing them to connect with the admissions office and "demonstrate their interest" (more on this topic in chapter 4) by visiting in person, or at least on the colleges admission offices' websites. (Gardner 2017)

"Always Be Closing" — Elite Colleges Use Peer Media and Pressure Marketing to Drive Applications into the Stratosphere, and Do the Same with Their Reputations for Selectivity

In their adoption of the most commercial hyper-marketing techniques, elite colleges also have recognized that the most used communication platforms for teenagers today are online social media, including Instagram and Snapchat as well as Facebook and Twitter. Admissions offices now hire social media specialists to engage with as many potential applicants as possible using devices like Snapchat's geo-filters and multimedia aspects like letting followers hear the roar of a basketball crowd, or watch video clips of tasty-looking food disappear from a plates in well-appointed dining hall. They have also engaged current students (like Duke

University's "Devils Advocates") to staff attractive social media platforms to connect with and encourage prospects for admissions and enrollment. (Dried 2016)

Social media applicant recruiting is now a "24/7" line of work for admissions departments, which can also quickly frame explanations regarding controversies that emerge on campus regarding issues not related to admissions decisions, but which affect the day-by-day social-media reputation of the school. The University of Michigan maintains over a thousand social media accounts, and NYU has that many on Facebook and Twitter alone, many of which serve interests beyond those linked directly to admissions but are within online reach of applicants in terms of forming their impression of the schools. (Chan 2017)

College students acting on their own initiative (and sometimes in coordination with admissions offices) have taken to digital media to vlog on YouTube about their day-to-day lives as they settle in to their dorms, meet their roommates, and go to classes and parties. (Nguyen 2019) These online testimonials to "real life at XYZ College" are an emerging critical element in viral marketing to potential applicants that accrue an authenticity over and above student quotes on official school websites or even independent "inside scoop" aggregators of college "factuals" because applicants may be inclined to view those sorts of commentaries as contrived or untrustworthy. This author personally observed the same student headshot appearing next to two different student testimonials regarding two different colleges on one admission tip sheet.

Potential applicants also experience direct telemarketing by student ambassadors engaged by admissions offices to encourage them to get their paperwork in and visit the campus. Colleges also have learned lately that texting is a far more effective way to actually get the attention of teenagers, and their admissions processes deliberately require potential applicants to disclose their text addresses as a preliminary step in accessing their admissions systems. Often the application invitation letters contain a unique ID code to access a personalized web form to get on the mailing list, as well as the emailing and texting list, with the all-caps promise that "YOU WILL BE OUR PRIORITY." Others offer personalized websites literally named after the potential applicant as a faux-private channel for direct communications with the admissions office. Some colleges also, as the *Chronicle of Higher Education* put in its headline, "Consult the King of Clicks: BuzzFeed" — and *BuzzFeed* is more than happy to offer its platform and ideas to college admissions offices. Temple University garnered nearly 800,000 views, and for every ten views, three others saw the posts because they were shared, which *BuzzFeed* calls "social lift." For the college or university, this network effect can lead to the desired application lift. (Hesse 2017)

None of the glossy marketing brochures that usually commence the standard elite college mass-recruiting campaigns (or the emails, social media, phone calls, and text messages) are subject to any truth-in-advertising rules mandating some degree of honest disclosure to consumers, as are in place regarding food, drugs, credit cards, and mortgages. Nor are there any legally enforceable prohibitions against material omissions and deliberately misleading material in securities offerings. So it is relatively painless for college to make themselves look, in certain but not all respects, more selective than they really are.

For example, typical ranges of previously enrolled entry class test scores, GPAs, and even sometimes high school class rank are often made available in their hard and soft marketing materials, given that such data are now readily obtainable online from independent sites. The actual unaudited form of disclosure, however, is subject to definitions privately set by the schools themselves. Some schools have been found by *US News* and others to have omitted data for categories of students whose results might negatively skew the range numbers and thus indicate a lesser degree of selectivity in terms of the test scores and grades portion.

One might think that such omissions, which indicate artificially high bars for acceptance in terms of grades and test scores, would scare off more applicants than it would attract. But the same colleges' marketing materials counteract that by framing their message as a direct and very personal invitation to apply, even over the signature of the admissions dean. This sort of letter or web message usually starts off with a phrase something like "Congratulations on your academic success," intended to leave the impression that the recipient, regardless of whatever the school has "disclosed" about its admissions standards, would in the eyes of the top admissions officer, stand a good chance of being one of the chosen few to gain admission. This message becomes especially powerful when it comes from a school that is itself one of the chosen few in the most recent *US News* rankings.

This sense of being potentially one of the selected is reinforced in an opening paragraph inviting the high school student to visit the campus in person and to be sure to attend any road show the school is taking to the recipient's high school or a neighboring venue. The road shows further drum up applications but often with a hint that the college may be keeping track of website visits, log-ins, and especially in-person visits in order to assess the demonstrated interest that will be a consideration in assessing applications. More on this practice in chapter 4, especially in terms of how it establishes a clear advantage for applicants from wealthy families that can fund the college road trip.

Even the most highly ranked universities resort to sending out potentially misleading marketing letters inviting applications for particular types of students on their admissions shopping lists. The recent court case challenging Harvard University's undergraduate admissions standards and practices as prejudiced against Asian students revealed a white student in a state that was underrepresented in Harvard's admissions data would get a recruiting letter if he or she scored 1310 or better on the PSAT, whereas students with Asian names would get the same letter only if they scored 1350 (for men) or 1380 (for women). But scores in that range, if repeated in the final SAT submissions, would actually be in the bottom range of actual Harvard admits.

Rarely if ever do any of the elite college recruiting letters or mass-marketing messages indicate the actual baseline admissions standards of the schools concerned so that a potential applicant might know exactly what his or her real chance of earning admission is. This practice of opaque or misleading disclosure come-ons sometimes also occurs during the in-person high school road show presentations admissions staffs make during the early autumn "hunting and gathering" season. Sometimes their less than transparent presentations reportedly weigh on the consciences of staff who know they must soon switch roles: from very cheerful salespersons tasked to generate a surfeit of nominally qualified applicants to highly selective gatekeepers who will briskly weed out many or even most of those they encouraged to apply.

There is also a variant of this game where the traveling recruiters tell a roomful of potential applicants that they need to take a lot of advanced placement courses and get A grades in all of them to make it to the admissions finals — sometimes an exaggeration designed to convey an aura of extreme *academic* exclusivity that the college deems more important than simply padding its application totals by telling everyone they have a real chance of getting in without such sterling academic standing.

In *The Gatekeepers*, Jacques Steinberg, who was given access to follow and memorialize the activities, deliberations, and even individual decisions made by the admissions department at a highly ranked Northeastern liberal arts university, explored the doubts of one particular admissions officer who was "like a politician wading into a room full of strangers" but who also knew that he was inviting most of his listeners to pay an application fee solely for the "privilege" of being rejected.

> You realize that, further down the line, a lot of these kids will end up applying and being denied…[b]ut you can't really think about that at this stage," the staff member told the author. He knew he was in a competition with other elite colleges and universities ….to assemble an entry class that would be at least a little better than the previous year's, and better than his competitors would attract, a goal so worthy "that it justified the difficult and sometimes cruel practicalities that were required to make it happen. (Steinberg 2003, 5)

What the recipient will learn for sure is the art of manipulation. One recent elite college brochure starts off with a cover reading as follows: "DON'T READ THIS." Why not? It's a whole lot of marketing blah blah blah. Is this some kind of reverse psychology? Maybe. Another suggests the recipient may be up to snuff for admission because "ALREADY you know you're more interesting as an outlier than a pack member." Another: "Don't come here because we're great. Come here because you are." The letters often contain a reference like "Your strong grades and standardized test scores" indicate that our university "may be a good fit for you" — even though the recipient has yet to submit either test scores or grades to the school in question. (The test scores were purchased unless the student happened to notice the opt-out option on the test and checked it…and sometimes even that doesn't work.)

One admissions dean's letter, sent in early June just after a potential applicant had finished her junior year in high school and her ACT, told her, "You're on my list of candidates…and I'm reaching out to you now so that when application time comes around [our university] will be included in your list of top schools! In the meantime, I invite you to get to know us better by visiting our campus...I can't wait to consider you for admission and send you a decision as soon as possible." The letter had everything but a formal RSVP address, despite the fact that all the school knew about the recipient at the time was her ACT score.

Another elite college letter, sent near the end of the process as admissions deadlines neared for a potential applicant who had already been deluged with blanket multimedia marketing took the following final approach (supplied by a disgusted parent):

> We've been at this for a while now. Us sending you brochures and emails. You reading them briefly and giving an occasional nod of approval or disdain before shuffling them into the recycling bin. (We are realists....)

> May we assume that one of the following is true?
> 1. You are planning to apply to...you like us. You *really* do.
> 2. No way, no how you're applying to....You loathe intellectual stimulation and shudder at the thought of life in an actual arboretum. The thought of graduating from a surprisingly affordable college with strong financial aid policies is somehow distasteful to you.
> 3. You are on the proverbial fence. You might say tom*a*to or you might say to*mah*to. You may apply. Or you may not.
> If 1, hurrah! We look forward to reading your application.
> If 2, we totally get it. No one college (however extraordinary and esteemed) is right for all people. (know that we will miss you....)
> But if 3, let us offer the following observation: Applying to...is not more arduous and taxing than clicking an additional box when you create your Common Application list.
> And clicking an additional box is no more arduous and taxing than putting an extra pickle on your burger or doing

an extra jumping jack (even when you're already kind of tired).*

Which is to say, click that box. Have that extra pickle. Keep your options open.

Sincerely,

The various people of the…admissions team

P.S. If you want that extra pickle, get yourself over to the Common App website and do something about it.…

Okay, so you will also need to submit a short statement telling us why you want to go to…. But this is no more arduous and taxing than telling us why you want to have a jet pack or win the lottery.

The last-minute sales pitch quoted above is an example of how one of the most elite colleges embraces the *Glengarry Glen Ross* sales mantra: "ABC — always be closing." The apparently contradictory twin goals of attracting a high enough number of applicants (hopeless or not) to assure the desired low acceptance rate for ranking purposes and, at the same time, pitching the marketing material to assure the highest possible test score results for the admitted class to support the other *US News* measure of selectivity, make for a robust enrollment management consulting industry. The wealthiest colleges, of course, have the brains and the bucks to attract the best professionals in the field.

To suggest that the elite college admissions departments somehow do not realize they will be attracting doomed applications to suit their admits ratio and other selectivity targets or that the vast majority of their applicants will fail to qualify under their actual secret algorithms for screening academic performance can only be proven by knowing the cutoff-score levels they use for purchasing their marketing lists. But that information, like those screening algorithms, is preposterous.

What makes matters worse is the fact that virtually all of the elite colleges keep to themselves the actual number and percentage of admissions places effectively reserved for, or ultimately allocated to, several categories of high-affluence applicants. Those with such admissions hooks include the legacies (descendants of the college's alumni) previously referred to, children or other close relatives of major donors or public figures in a position to help the college with treasure or talent or both, athletes (brawn for the money sports, lineage for the upper-class sports), and faculty members' children (at heavily discounted rates) or even faculty kids from similar schools — a cousin to country club reciprocity.

Moreover, the test scores of students who get these secret preferential admissions do not always measure up to the colleges' baseline screening benchmarks and sometimes are not included in the official test score averages submitted for the *US News* rankings. As a result, the published selectivity statistics for elite colleges actually may dramatically overstate the test-taking quality of the freshman class as well as the odds of "ordinary" applicants with no associated preferential "hooks" ever gaining admission, regardless of their fine academic records. If 25 percent of a college with a published 10 percent admissions ratio is reserved for the applicants with hooks, the real odds for anyone else are at best 7.5 percent, and so on down the line. Yet the invitational mass brochure mailings and emails will not mention that reality, ever. If the regular applicants are not ready to take the option (and the risk) of an early decision (which is also tilted toward wealthy applicants), that 7.5 percent chance will be diluted even further because an additional 20 to 40 percent of the entry class will already be captured in early decision admissions, which are set up as binding on the applicant. *Powerball* lotteries offer more transparency than the publicly stated odds of winning an elite college admission ticket!

The Real Admissions Winners

The indisputable victors in the admissions marketing game are elite colleges themselves, achieving their goal of amassing tens of thousands of applications for only a few hundred or a few thousand places in their freshman classes, with the upshot being secure *US News* rankings in the single or low double digits and ultra-selective or at least super-selective status, which will, in turn, beget even more applications the next year, and so on. Frank Bruni captured the absurdity of this competition in his "College Admission Shocker" column purporting to reveal how Stanford University had secured distinction as "the most selective institution in the country" by choosing to admit exactly none of the record-setting number of applications it had received for the upcoming freshman class.

> News of Stanford's unprecedented selectiveness sent shock waves through the Ivy League, along with Amherst, Northwestern and at least a dozen other elite schools where, as a consequence, there could be substantial turnover among underperforming deans of admission…At first blush, Stanford's decision would seem to jeopardize its fund-raising. The thousands of rejected applicants included hundreds of children of alumni who'd donated lavishly over the years…But over recent years, Stanford administrators noticed that as the school rejected more and more comers, it received bigger and bigger donations, its endowment rising in tandem with its exclusivity, its luster a magnet for Silicon Valley lucre. (Bruni 2016)

It is noteworthy that at least one elite university (Stanford) has to some degree recognized (after the admissions indictments) that the prevailing admissions-rate Olympics "helps fuel the madness," as the *New York Times* put it reporting record low elite college admissions rates in 2020. Stanford's 2019 entering cohort had crept close to Frank Bruni's satirical zero admission rate outcome with a 4.3 percent acceptance rate, and thereafter announced that it would no longer promote its admissions rate directly to the general public, and simply provide the related data as required to the federal government. (Hartocollis and Taylor 2019)

Nonetheless, the vast majority of high school students and parents remain caught up in the admissions mania and what Julie Lythcott-Haims in *How to Raise an Adult* called the "meaningless distinctions people make to feel superior to those who are exactly like them," citing "the narcissism of small minds" from William Deresiewicz, author of *Excellent Sheep: The Miseducation of the American Elite.* (Lythcott-Haims 2015, 131) Another critic, former Yale University Dean of Admissions Jeffrey Brenzel, condemned the college ranking process as "a business enterprise that capitalizes on anxiety about college admissions." Business writers have also explained how companies in general are "becoming adept at identifying wealthy customers and marketing to them, creating a money-based caste system…a degree of economic and social stratification unseen in America since the days of Teddy Roosevelt, J. P. Morgan and the rigidly separated classes on the *Titanic* a century ago."

> What is different today, though, is that companies have become much more adept at identifying their top customers and knowing which psychological buttons to push. The goal is to create extravagance and exclusivity for the select few, even if it stirs up resentment elsewhere. In fact, research has shown, a little envy can be good for the bottom line. (Bruni 2015, 92-93)

What can be added is that business has also taken full advantage of the massive trove of personal information and the data analytics capability of social media platforms to even more precisely refine their targeting of specific wealthy audiences. And elite colleges, well enough connected to the business world with or without business schools, have followed the corporate lead with extraordinary enthusiasm. No wonder dean Brenzel characterized the admissions "arms race" as essentially a "business enterprise" for attracting and building wealth, where wealth is attracted by exclusivity, and is ultimately the university's prize!

Stanford admitted only 5.01 percent into the entry class of 2019 out of then-record total of 42,487 applicants, earning the lowest elite college acceptance rate. Moreover, its "yield" (the number of enrollments from those admissions) was also among the highest in the nation. Some commentators have suggested that measuring the ratio of yield rate to admissions rate (YTAR) would be a much more illuminating and useful measurement of the quality and efficiency of an admissions department's operations achievements. Focusing on yield could possibly cut against the headlong and corrupting competitive rush for low admissions selectivity. There are two problems with that, however. As *College Confidential* has pointed out, a university like Stanford, with a yield of about 80 percent and an admissions rate likely approaching 4 percent, would have a 20 percent YTAR, but so would a very specialized college like the Curtis School of Music. Moreover, simply replacing a deeply flawed measure of selectivity with another, more complex measure would do little to enhance admissions transparency and would just give the top 100 *US News* colleges something else to compete over.

Moreover, yield can be managed up by increasing the number of early decision applicants who are admitted, since they have agreed in advance to accept. Relying on yield rate or yield-related derivatives instead of the *US News* admissions rate as a measure of admissions efficacy would only invite even greater reliance on the early decision admissions process, which strongly favors wealthy applicants. The selectivity strategy is working to mimic the emerging winner-take-(almost)-all trend of the US economy. Universities like Southern Methodist University that have allocated increased marketing money specifically to recruit students with high SAT scores (disproportionately from wealthy families that can afford tutoring and private high schools with low student-faculty ratios) have jumped in the *US News* rankings. Schools like Georgia State University, on the other hand, that have focused on graduating more low- and moderate-income students have fallen significantly (by thirty spots, in GSU's case).

In a report by *Politico*, former chancellor Carol Christ of the highly ranked University of California Berkeley, decried the "mind-boggling" extent to which the *US News* Rankings motivates colleges to pick wealthier students. And a Stanford sociologist has characterized the rankings as a "peculiar form of governance...of higher education in this country because schools essentially use them to make sense of who they are relative to each other. And families use them basically as a guide to the higher education marketplace." (Wermund 2017) *Politico* referred to interviews with university presidents and other educators who affirmed that several of the measures used by *US News* work to the benefit of more affluent applicants. The test score selectivity factor was shown to disproportionately benefit students from wealthy families (per a *Psychology Today* study); even the SAT scoring rewards children from the top income bracket, who average 130 points higher than those from the bottom. While many college leaders are skeptical of the predictive value of standardized tests, according to *Politico*, they are compelled to pay close attention to these score levels to protect their rankings.

Paul Tough's 2019 article in the *New York Times* referenced near the end of chapter 2 cited the research of a former admissions officer (Jon Boeckenstedt) illuminating the link between admissions decisions, money and the *U.S. News* rankings, as understood by admissions officers themselves. That research found 87 percent of them think the rankings cause universities to do things that were counterproductive to their educational missions. Boeckenstedt told him that admissions "'for us it's not a matter of turning down students we'd like to admit. It's a matter of admitting students we'd like to turn down.'" (Tough 2019.)

The former admissions officer explained, as Tough put it, that "the easiest category of student for you to admit are below-average students from high-income families. Because their parents can afford tutoring, they are very likely to have decent test scores, so they won't hurt your US News rankings. They probably won't distinguish themselves academically...but they can pay full tuition." Boeckenstedt told Tough that "[t]hese are kids who will gladly pay more to move up the food chain... I call them the C.F.O. Specials, because they appeal to the college's chief financial officer. They are challenging for the faculty, but they bring in a lot of revenue." Boeckenstedt and Tough further explained that the *U.S News* algorithm rewards colleges for spending a lot of money, not cutting expenses so they can admit more low-income students, which would cause the college's ranking to decline. To keep spending high, "you need a lot of tuition revenue, which means you need to keep admitting lots of rich kids." (Ibid.)

Berkeley's Chancellor Christ noted the simple mathematical fact that the rank weighting of spending per student pushes schools to admit more of the wealthy because they need less financial aid and thus leave more funds available for other *US News* rankings factors like hiring more faculty to reduce class size, which then, in turn, requires tuition increases, which, in turn, requires more wealthy full sticker-price admits. (Wermund ibid.) This is a prime example of purposeful, strategic-fit thinking in elite admissions practices. Manipulating the *US News* rankings for selectivity and other factors, however, is not the only or even the most significant way that the elite college admissions black box is secretly tipping the admissions scales toward the wealthiest applicants.

CHAPTER 4

Rewarding Demonstrated Interest, Favoring "Feeder" Schools, Pushing for High Test Scores and More APs, and Hiding Actual Selection Criteria in a Black Box Process Give Wealthier Applicants a Leg Up

We know that most of the power colleges and universities generally use that power to require applicants to submit SAT or ACT test scores, understandably as a way to provide a common standard for evaluation over and above the variety of grading practices at our nation's high schools. As the previous chapter revealed, they also use their power to purchase the names and other personal information supplied to the SAT and ACT by students taking the test so they can target broad groups of test takers with promotional brochures and other marketing efforts to pump up their application numbers and their ultimate *US News* rankings for low acceptance rates, even though many who receive these materials will have little or no chance of surviving the first-cut screening of applicants in terms of minimum grades or test scores. Colleges not among the elite ranks (or those fearing a loss of such status) also buy the same data, but more in an effort to assure that they will be able to have enough applicants to meet the yield goals their operating budgets require for solvency.

Elite colleges will receive far more applications from students whose records not only far surpass their minimum standards for admission and who would fit well within the top-quartile test and grade quadrants of those ultimately admitted and enrolled yet will not be admitted because there are not nearly enough spaces available. Having secured their selectivity goals by encouraging grossly excessive application numbers, elite college admissions offices are left with the problem of how to find some ostensibly rational basis for choosing among the overwhelming number of well-qualified candidates. Evaluation of essays and extracurricular activities can help, but with only a few minutes at best to review each of the thousands of applicants, something quicker is also desirable, giving rise to the focus on "demonstrated interest" (beyond merely applying) on the part of each applicant.

Demonstrated Interest Often Demonstrates Wealth

Perhaps heeding Woody Allen's observation that ninety percent of life is just showing up, these admissions offices are able to create check-a-box scorecards, which can be scanned though artificial intelligence software to spare human time (and expense), capturing and ranking various data points: in-person and virtual visits to campus; online visits to various campus websites, chat rooms, and social media sites maintained by admissions offices; submitting questions to the admissions office via texts and emails; responses to same; and, of course, showing up when campus representatives come calling in their communities and at their high schools and personally connecting with the admissions office personnel who are recruiting at those events. Colleges can even capture and compare the exact amount of time applicants took to open texts or emails from their admissions offices and the number of times they opened college webpages on their cell phones. In the algorithmic rubrics that are employed to measure and weight each such demonstration of interest, every conceivable touch point is statistically encoded: but on-campus visits have the biggest impact. A headline in *The Boston Globe* of August 21, 2017, advised: "Want to get into your first-choice college? Better book a plane ticket."

> On university campuses, a summer tradition has unfolded: High school juniors and their parents are inspecting dormitories, checking out libraries, and visiting classrooms…Such visits have become increasingly mandatory for students looking for an edge in the highly competitive admission process. As colleges try to winnow large applicant pools, many use a student's interest in the school as an important factor in admissions. But the practice has some counselors and researchers worried that low-income students who can't afford to travel or those who aren't savvy about the importance of the college tour may lose out. (Fernandez 2017)

As Robert Scherrer, a professor at Vanderbilt, observed in a *Wall Street Journal* op-ed: "When did looking for a college turn into a modern version of the 18th-century 'Grand Tour?'" (Scherrer 2015) Although the precise timing of when this phenomenon emerged is uncertain, the general answer is when enrollment consultants and their admissions office clients hit upon the demonstrated interest criteria to justify late-round admissions decisions that would otherwise lack a coherent explanation. Elite colleges were quick to add this point of emphasis to applicant recruiting messaging — for example, as one elite college recruiting brochure advised, after noting its highly selective admissions policy: "Campus visits are strongly encouraged." (Vassar College 2018)

Special admissions committee focus on in-person campus visits by prospective students gives an edge to those fortunate applicants whose families can afford to fund such travel, including across multiple time zones. These visits also create valuable opportunities for interviews and less formal introductions to admissions staff with the advantage of putting a face and personality with a mere name on applications. Such direct on-campus connections are especially relevant in terms of influencing the opinions of staff assigned to assess applicants from high schools in a particular geographic area.

Dr. Jennifer Glynn, author of "Opening Doors," a Jack Kent Cooke Foundation 2017 report on low-income access to college, pointed out that nearly half of high-achieving (3.8 or better GPA) low-income students do not visit any of the colleges they apply to, a situation she said would be "'unfathomable for a wealthy student.'" The Cooke Foundation reported that when these students were asked what their biggest challenge in the college application process was, campus visits topped the list. (Nadworny 2017, quoting Glynn)

Admissions offices justify, in understandably self-interested terms, their use of demonstrated interest as a material factor in determining which applicants at the margin among all those academically qualified actually are given offers. They have been strongly advised by their enrollment consultants (and have found correlations based on their own records) that such data analytics provide one of the most reliable predictors of which applicants will mostly likely accept an offer so that admissions slots are not wasted and ultimate yield-per-acceptances numbers reach their goals.

The kind of admissions savvy needed to provide an applicant with a high quotient of computer-readable demonstrated interest can be purchased early on (like the services of a good travel agent) from private admissions consultants. To be sure, word of the demonstrated interest scoreboard spread through to prep school college counselors, then more broadly into the public school districts that can afford right-size college counselor staffs, and finally through the multiple online admissions advice platforms as well as the colleges' own websites.

The long list of ways to demonstrate interest has become broadly known (albeit not broadly practically available) to most applicants. For example, *The College Solution* offers the following basic list, most of which is now within the capacity of any applicant with reliable access to a computer:

- Go on the college's website;
- Visit the college's booth at a local college fair or if it sends representatives to your high school;
- Visit the college's virtual open house, including on the website CollegeWeekLive;
- Chat live with a current student at the college through its admissions website;
- Check out and follow the college's Facebook, YouTube and Twitter posts;
- Make contact with the admissions officer assigned to cover your school or locale;
- And, of course, arrange a college tour. (O'Shaughnessey 2015, 88)

The admissions advice website College Factual perhaps unwittingly exposed just how much the demonstrated interest criteria tips to the rich when it suggested enrolling applicants in special summer programs on campuses because colleges "understand how tough it is for families to get away during the school year." Of course, many of these programs involve costs that, on a pro rata basis, are equivalent to private high school tuition. Basically, this sort of option is limited to children in upper-income families.

A full-page advertisement by and in the *New York Times* illustrated that even media companies that cover college admissions practices critically are getting into the business of sponsoring special summer educational programs that can serve as application sweeteners by demonstrating a student's special interests that may align with a particular college's programs. This one touted "Summer Travel

Programs for Middle & High School students" guided by the *Times'* experts to Ecuador and the Galapagos Islands, Eastern Europe, Iceland, Ireland and the U.K., Israel and Jordan, and Russia, as well as Los Angeles and Nashville in the U.S. The travel "would inspire students as they delve into a new or existing passion." The ad might as well have been accompanied by an "old-media" version of a webpage chyron: "Soon to be a part of your college application!" (Advertisement, *New York Times* 2019)

Most applicants cannot afford any such adventure travel, or even visit any campus that attracts their interest but would require getting on a plane, whether in the summer or during the academic year. Some are working in their only free time between school times and cannot attend college fairs because they lack transportation; many cannot afford to cut class for an admissions official's visit to their high school, even though not attending may count against them under demonstrated interest metrics.

Many lower-income families cannot provide their children access to a computer or a smart phone to make inline contact with schools they might like. And some communities make it hard for children of undocumented parents to gain access to their libraries' online resources by requiring them to produce a parent's government issued identification. (Sanchez 2017) Applicants in these situations are clearly playing from behind in the demonstrated interest sweepstakes. Bear in mind that a typical high school district serving a predominantly low-income and minority community may be financially challenged when it comes to providing students with computers to use for classes and homework, and even if they do, a majority of the families they serve may not have home access to online technology or connectivity, if they even have a home!

As Frank Bruni observed in *Where You Go Is Not Who You'll Be*, "certain applicants may have the knowledge, incentive and time to make sure they signal 'demonstrated interest,' even if it's a total fiction, where others don't." (Bruni 2015, 65) But elite colleges, which are spending more dollars lately on big data analytics to help them predict who among those who show such interest will actually accept an offer, are willing to take the risk of mistaking manufactured interest for the real thing because the broader reality is that focusing on demonstrated interest has helped underwrite the level of yield data that *US News* will value and that, in turn, will make their school look even more desirable to the rich.

Even elite schools that have dropped the practice of allocating a level of admissions places for descendants of alumni like to emphasize the demonstrated interest angle. They believe that the legacies they still want to attract (see chapter 5 for the reasons, one of which is money) will be in a better position to work the demonstrated interest route. One admissions official at Texas A&M (which had abandoned legacy admissions preferences) told one of the authors of *Affirmative Action for the Rich,* in referring to on-campus applicant visits with academic advisors: "Sons and daughters of former students know that academic association is the replacement for legacy." (Golden, in Kahlenberg, ed. 2010, 95)

A May 2018 cover story in *Atlantic* ("The Birth of a New American Aristocracy") identified dominant socioeconomic power as residing not only in the usual suspects — those families in the top 1 percent of household income or wealth — but also in the top 10 percent group. As evidence, the authors state two key facts: (1) the top 10 percent holds most of the wealth in the United States (nearly 60 percent while the top 1 percent and bottom 90 percent hold about 20 percent apiece); and (2) the top 10 percent also do the best job at assuring that their offspring "apples" do not fall far from the tree in terms of economic status. (Stewart 2018) As it happens, the children of the bottom 10 percent tend to wind up closer to their parents' income tree as well.

The statistical measure for this phenomenon is technically known as intergenerational earnings elasticity (IGE). A zero IGE means no correlation between parents' income and their offspring, whereas an IGE of 1 means their children are highly likely to end up where they started in terms of wealth. And one of the ways the top 10 percent does so well at this game of preserving economic status is by getting their kids into the most selective colleges. We will explore in chapter 6 the deeper effects on higher education of the reality that, as the *Atlantic* reported, "economic mobility in the land of opportunity is not high, and it's going down." (Ibid.) It is important to understand, however, how some apparently benign elite college admissions practices like the emphasis on demonstrated interest indirectly but very effectively help the upper classes hoard preferred pathways to admissions for their children, while keeping the children of others in their place.

Many elite admissions college offices are, in truth, attempting to solve a burdensome admissions office time-management problem they created themselves by their aggressive marketing efforts to inflate their applicant pool and thereby secure their desired rank on any selectivity list. But even in pursuing legitimate yield objectives, their admissions officers must surely realize that using demonstrated interest as a tiebreaker will reduce the chances of the most economically and socially disadvantaged applicants who are found to be fully qualified for admission, but for the limited number of slots available to the huge pool of applicants, they must sift through with minimal time for assessing qualitative distinctions.

The well-endowed elite schools, it would seem, have access to the talent required to control or otherwise adjust the outcomes of such algorithmic demonstrated interest rankings for family income and access to high-end resources. There is, after all, a well-recognized digital divide that especially isolates many high school students living in rural areas (a sore spot for admissions to elite colleges) as well as low-income minority inner-city residents. If admissions departments can fine-tune distinctions down to split seconds on how fast texts or emails or Snapchat messages are opened by tech-savvy applicants, surely they could figure out how to balance the deck for those applicants who face major obstacles to personal or virtual visits and other forms of contact with the colleges that truly interest them and whose offers they would be thrilled to accept. By and large, however, the elite colleges are obviously satisfied with the enrollments they achieve through their new data analytics, which just happen to lean toward the higher end of family incomes.

Curating Elite Applicants from Feeder Private Prep Schools and Public School Districts Serving Wealthy Zip Codes

Writing in the *Cornell Journal of Law and Public Policy*, David Orentlicher observed that, while upper-income families have multiple reasons for carving out exclusive residential enclaves with excellent local schools, college admissions policies play an important role, and have done much to accelerate residential segregation by income in America. He also took note of how enclaves of families wield their political and economic power to gain greater public funding for their school districts, and set up private foundations to funnel tax-exempt donations to supplement the government dollars (a practice dealt with at length in *Dream Hoarders* by Richard V. Reeves, cited in chapter 2)

> When thinking about their children's prospects for admission…upper income parents recognize they are better off with a two-tiered educational system in which their children attend a small number of high-performing schools that the Ivy League and other elite universities rely on as 'feeder' schools. …The parents' children will be better prepared for the SAT or ACT exams, and selective colleges will dig deeper into the schools' senior classes in making offers of acceptance. (Orentlicher 2016)

Accordingly, the starting gun in the race to be among the select few academically qualified applicants chosen for admission goes off when the elite colleges focus their recruiting primarily on those who are *already* among the select few in terms of the economic status of their communities and high schools. This front-end bias toward the rich also gives those students a most convenient opportunity to establish the demonstrated interest that the colleges are now demanding by simply cutting a class at their own school or taking a night off from homework to go to a nearby recruiting fair.

Analysis of 130,000 applications to "name-brand" colleges over a ten-year period by Human Capital Research Corporation found that only 18 percent of high schools accounted for 75 percent of applications and 79 percent of admissions! (Selingo 2020) Top college admissions departments do in fact shape their travel schedules for high school recruiting and admissions fairs to concentrate mostly among high schools and communities characterized by two central factors: they are predominantly affluent and predominantly white. Researchers from UCLA and the University of Arizona for the Enrollment Management, Recruiting and Access Project "scraped" the travel itineraries of admissions departments posted on the websites of 150 private nonprofit and public colleges and matched them with demographic data about the high schools visited or the neighborhoods of public schools. They found that the majority of schools and communities visited were toward the higher end of the income scale, and primarily Caucasian. Although only about one-third of all US communities have average family incomes over $100,000, over half of these colleges' events and school visits were to such locales.

In addition, the many private school visits on these recruiting schedules were also to communities high on the average-income scale. (Jaschik April 1 and 16, 2019) Some elite colleges have lately touted their expanding outreach to highly qualified high school students in areas of poverty through local recruitment fairs and the like, but these visits somehow aren't yet showing up on enough of their published recruitment travel schedules to shift the balance materially.

The admissions offices' outreach bias toward visits to wealthy neighborhoods is not limited to well-endowed private colleges. Public universities trying to find students from wealthy families to make up for the funding withdrawn by their state governments over the past few decades have also focused their recruiting trips more on out-of-state (full-tuition payers) than in-state locations, and even more so on affluent private schools and neighborhoods. (Mangan March 26, 2019) Two of the authors of the 150-college study who surveyed for the Joyce Foundation the travels of high school recruiters for 15 flagship state universities summarized their findings in a *New York Times* op-ed. They concluded that although those schools visited rich and poor neighborhoods nearly equally when recruiting in their own states, "they visited the same affluent high schools targeted by private colleges when recruiting elsewhere." (Jaquette and Salazar 2019)

In an example the authors cited, when Colorado Boulder admissions team came to the Boston area public high schools, they chose to visit mostly those in wealthy communities but skipped even schools in poorer districts that had higher numbers of students scoring proficient in math. They also noted that public universities were more likely to visit predominantly white rather than nonwhite schools with comparable levels of academic achievement. They pointed to the Boulder team visit to a 88 percent white public high school with "about 154 students with proficient math scores …. [but] did not visit… [another school] where just 21 percent of students are white but about 622 students have proficient math scores." (Ibid.)

This recruiting bias toward wealthy and white neighborhoods reveals its most specific and institutionalized expression in the semi-official admission "feeder school" relationships between many selective private high schools and America's most elite colleges — one of the several reserved admission lanes for applicants from wealthy and well-connected families. The feeder prep school relationships long established in the admissions programs of elite private colleges formalize this pattern of special access for the children of wealthier families that can afford prep school tuition, room, and board (and are therefore good bets to afford those charges at the college level as well). Wealthy families spend tens of thousands of dollars to send their children to expensive private schools that offer a deep college preparatory curriculum or provide added tax-deductible contributions to public schools in their wealthy neighborhoods to do the same. In the private high schools in particular, the funding also supports a robust college admissions counseling program where the ratio of counselors to students is substantially lower than even the most advantaged public high school. (Schmidt, in Kahlenberg, ed. 2010, 36-37; Steinberg 2003, 113; Golden 2006, 59)

Some public high schools in wealthy school districts are a close match for private prep schools in terms of resources available to support a high-performance curriculum, and enjoy nearly equivalent pipelines to elite college admissions offices. Parents in wealthy zip codes are able to subsidize enrichment activities and a strong AP or International Baccalaureate curriculum through contributions to local non-profit foundations to position their children at the front of the line for admission consideration. The main drawback persisting even in these schools is usually the level of individual college counseling resources, especially in the larger high schools with enrollments upwards of two thousand students. But wealthy families can afford to supplement school resources by hiring private counselors and tutors. Richard Reeves in *Dream Hoarders* pointed out that those families can also use their political influence over zoning laws to create attractive and exclusive one-family housing enclaves, which then socially dominate, and promote the high-achievement agendas of, those neighborhoods' high school districts. "Almost 40 percent of top-quintile families live in areas with public schools ranked in the top fifth of their state in terms of test scores and almost one in four are near a school in the top 10 percent....Every researcher that looks at the question finds that teacher quality is higher in schools in more affluent areas." (Reeves 2017, 47)

New research also shows that students enrolled in private and suburban public high schools achieve relatively higher GPAs than their urban public school counterparts with no less academic proficiency and potential; it's not that those students are getting smarter — their standardized test scores have generally been declining while their school grades have been, shall we say, inflating! The College Board found that such grade inflation is accelerating particularly in schools attended by higher-income Americans. Parents in those districts are well known to use their professional skills and political power to directly nag teachers to raise their children's grades, especially if another teacher or neighboring elite generally grades higher, so the result is inflation contagion. Quoted in the *Atlantic* magazine, Andrew Nichols, director of higher education research at The Education Trust, called this phenomenon "just another systemic disadvantage that we put in front of low-income kids and kids of color." (Marcus 2017)

University of Virginia researchers who conducted a longitudinal study of more than one thousand high school students, found that all the academic and social advantages presumed to be offered by elite private high schools came to naught once the data was controlled for socioeconomic factors. As the lead author, Dean Robert C. Pianta, reported in an interview: "You only need to control for family income and there's no advantage. So when you first look, without controlling for anything, the kids who go to private schools are far and away outperforming the public school kids. And as soon as you control for family income and parents' education, that difference is eliminated completely." The study "found no evidence that private schools, net of family background (particularly income), are more effective for promoting student success." Assuming that is the case, then the strategy of elite college conferring multiple admissions advantages on graduates of elite prep schools, as a logical matter, makes no sense in terms of assuring the academic quality of their entering classes. Indeed, it only makes sense in terms of successfully recruiting a large number of students from wealthy families. (Strauss July 26, 2018) Nationally recognized prep schools of this type, private or public, have sometimes been specifically invited by elite colleges to nominate individual students for admission with prestigious merit scholarship awards like the Morehead Scholars program at the University of North Carolina, which is more generally reserved for local state students. Only 2.2 percent of US students graduate from nonsectarian private high schools, yet they account for 26 percent of students at Harvard and 28 percent at Princeton.

The 2017 federal Tax Cut and Jobs Act created further advantages for families of prep school students by allowing individuals to use up to $10,000 annually for private school tuition from the state-based, already tax-advantaged 529 college investment plans. These plans allow after-tax contributions to grow untaxed over time and then to be spent tax free to pay tuition and many other college-related expenses, although not travel. These 529 advantages accrue mainly to families that can afford to set aside regular substantial amounts from their income over several years. (Strauss November 8, 2017) The Obama administration tried to eliminate this special tax benefit because of its inherent subsidy of parents in the upper middle class and higher (and contributing grandparents) but quickly withdrew the proposal in the face of fierce opposition from the investor class, its bankers, and their lobbyists.

Students at most selective private prep schools enjoy a very low college counselor to student ratio. Compared with those attending poorly funded public high schools where individual counselors carry caseloads that approach 500 students a piece. (Levy and Tyre 2018) This impossibly burdensome caseload prevents real familiarity with any one student's attributes and aspirations, resulting in vague, brief recommendation letters. A reader in the University of Virginia's admissions department referred to public schools' "harried guidance counselors…writing hundreds of recommendations," often not knowing any applicant very well, and contrasting that with the advantageous situation of "applicants attending private schools, where the rate of college acceptances is an important recruiting tool," and where counselors have time to prepare "four-page tomes" to send to admissions staff like herself. She went on to acknowledge, as quoted in the advice book *Admission Matters*, that "[f]airness demanded that I factor in the inequity, but invariably I was told more — though in hyperbolic terms — about the private school student than I ever learned about the public school one." (Springer, Reider, and Morgan 2015, 33-34)

Inside Higher Ed surveyed four hundred senior admissions officers to rank the relative effectiveness of informational and counseling resources available to their applicants: ranked first overall were college counselors at private high schools; public high school counselors did not even make the top five. Independent private college admissions consultants ranked fourth. Relatively few public school students can afford such services, if they are even available in their own communities. Later in this chapter, we will explore how college admissions practices, especially commercial-level secrecy about their actual baseline admissions screening criteria, have facilitated the growth of this estimated $2 billion consulting industry that primarily advances the admissions interests of families of above-average wealth.

Elite prep school headmasters cultivate personal relationships with admissions deans, and prep counselors also have the time and the travel budgets to establish close and mutually beneficial relationships with elite college admissions offices, often using code phrases in recommendation letters to signal that certain applicants come from families that have been especially strong contributors to the prep school's endowment (signaling potential for more of the same for the college that admits their kids), and, in turn, the college admissions staff often gives the prep counselors a heads-up on which students they are likely to admit. The book *The Price of Admissions* also notes that elite college admissions offices sometimes work with prep schools to ameliorate the effects of taking a lower-performing but especially wealthy student from a particular high school class by balancing that choice with a high-achieving student whom the college otherwise would not need to admit for its own purposes in order to mollify that student's wealthy parents, who have been generous donors to the prep school. (Golden 2006, 59) Pass the back scratcher!

Children in elite private high schools are coached on effective interview techniques and strategies, essay writing, and standardized test tactics more or less as part of those schools' standard offerings. (Boland 2016) Wealthy families often take a belt-and-suspenders approach and hire independent admissions consultants to assure the highest likelihood of admission to elite colleges, especially if they do not possess the hook of legacy or big-donor status already. Private admission advisors function as the unofficial decoders of the black box admissions criteria at elite colleges: but, as we shall see later in this chapter, their services often come at a price only the upper economic class can afford.

Ambiguity and Secrecy Are Hallmarks of the Elite Admissions Process: Special Test Score Screening Rubrics and Previously Undisclosed "Tips" for Certain Kinds of Wealthy Applicants

Most applicants below the top income level do not easily become aware of, or fully understand, the secret admissions criteria the elite colleges use or the actual rejection odds they are up against. Thus, they cannot take them into account before making up their target lists, investing their limited time and money, and filling out their applications. Above all things, the secrecy of admissions criteria is the key ingredient of the elite colleges' admissions business plans. Elite colleges, like commercial businesses, claim that secrecy is needed to protect the confidentiality of their marketing plans and objectives. But that is not the only, or the most important, reason for keeping their selection criteria and particularly their first-cut screening algorithms close to the vest.

In chapter 3, we observed how the ease of submitting multiple applications (which also constitutes an income stream to the colleges) has led colleges to purchase thousands of names and addresses from the admissions test firms and unleash slick marketing machines to stimulate a swell of applications from even marginally qualified students, thereby enhancing selectivity. In turn, this swarm of applications drives part-time admissions staffs and budgets ever larger (at least until artificial intelligence takes over), with less application reading time — sometimes down to thirty seconds — and more reliance on screening algorithms that quite obviously must be kept secret lest applications from those who will not make even the first cut be discouraged and thereby reduce selectivity rankings. Despite their pubic disclosures of the cutoff benchmarks for the top and bottom quartiles of previous entering classes, keeping most applicants guessing about the *minimum* GPA and test score requirements for further consideration beyond initial screening remains a core characteristic of an enrollment management strategy intent on attracting an overwhelming number of applicants to assure more favorable *US News* selectivity placement. This black box practice obviously adds to higher levels of stress and anxiety among college applicants generally.

Standardized tests were originally conceived as a method to drive a more meritocratic admissions outcome than either reliance on breeding and inherited privilege as the most important criteria for entry into the most elite colleges, or reliance on high school grades that notoriously lack a common standard of assessment from one school to another. The original Scholastic Aptitude Test was first used merely as a screening device for *scholarship* applicants at Harvard. As use of the SAT expanded to become one of the central criteria for all admissions decisions, however, complications arose. Some applicants performed substantially better than others despite having high school grade profiles indicating lower intellectual aptitude, scoring better than peers who had demonstrated outstanding academic prowess. Along came a competitor called the ACT, designed to focus on learning attainment in the same subject matter covered by the SAT, and the high-stakes financial competition between the formally nonprofit testing enterprises began in earnest. Each fought college by college to be accepted as the official standardized test accepted by the admissions departments and state by state to win contracts valued in multiple millions of dollars each to administer their tests to each state's high school students. The SAT responded to the ACT with several revisions and structural options to its format, intended to focus similarly on actual academic subject mastery rather than the original concept of measuring aptitude.

Applicants now generally have the option of taking either the SAT or ACT route, but these test sponsors' duopoly also means high school students have yet another admissions riddle to solve with few if any hints from the colleges — whether one or the other choice represents their best chances to get admitted at each particular school. The ACT and SAT folks early on saw this dilemma as an opportunity to introduce (for a fee, of course) the chance to take preliminary versions of the tests that produce results that don't count toward admission but trigger the process of awarding National Merit Scholarships and the deluge of application marketing materials sent to the names of practice test takers that colleges buy to support their selectivity campaigns. The "better take both" solution has brought riches to the two non-profits that produce and harvest the proceeds of these tests, with their combined total revenues reaching past $1 billion. (Gray 2015)

Most elite colleges publicly profess neutrality regarding which test best fits into their actual selection criteria, but data concerning the number of enrollees taking either the ACT or the SAT for each school, which can be derived from the colleges' general public disclosure and reporting, suggest a degree of leaning toward one or the other that, in turn, becomes self-reinforcing. Colleges commonly disclose, one way or another, what the middle 50 percent of SAT and ACT test scores have been for previously admitted classes, sometimes even at the level of individual high schools. This type of disclosure is at least more transparent than merely showing the average scores because it automatically also shows the top 25 percent and bottom 25 percent benchmarks: if an applicant's score fits well within either of those quadrants, it will be somewhat easier to assess the likelihood of a favorable or unfavorable admissions decision, either way. But even that data cannot be taken at face value.

For example, colleges vary in terms of whether they are disclosing test score data only for fall and not winter or spring admissions. The latter two are particularly convenient cohorts in which to place those with lower test scores who may have been admitted through wealth-related preferences: *US News* asks only for the scores relating to the fall entry class. Some schools that have established test-optional applications may not make this material fact clear in their general disclosure of prior classes' test quadrant. Such an option, however, will likely induce applicants to submit their scores only if they are on the high side, skewing the score ranges (and selectivity ratings) higher. *US News* has even caught some schools misleading them precisely in that way.

Elite colleges also do not break out the SAT/ACT test score

averages and ranges for special admissions preferences like legacies, children of faculty, donors' children, and athletes. These scores, on available anecdotal evidence, are often lower than the general averages and ranges, and their absence will distort the figures for an entire entering class. This means that applicants without such hooks will, on the whole, be secretly held to higher standards than suggested by the published scatter-grams or other standardized test quintiles disclosures.

Confusion about just how much those scores weigh in the overall admissions criteria abounds because the weighting assigned is kept in the black box. Many colleges, both elite and non-elite, disclose a list of factors considered in their admissions decisions, with generalized and non-quantified information with respect to the *relative* importance of each. They also make those factors known to the publicly-available Common Data Set, which is an effort among those colleges and publishers to provide a sense of what is considered in admissions decisions, along with related and standardized statistical data, especially about the composition of their incoming freshman classes. The data includes nineteen factors considered in admissions decisions: six academic (like class rank, GPA, test scores, high school curriculum rigor, and essays) and thirteen nonacademic. The latter include interviews, talent (including athletic), alumni relationships, religion, race, residence, work and volunteer experience, and level of interest.

As to each factor, participating schools are asked to reveal whether it is deemed very important, important, considered, or not considered in admissions decisions — but we get the answers only if a particular school is participating and answering all the questions. (O'Shaughnessey 2015, 86-88) Moreover, no disclosure of *minimum* acceptable levels, or specific *weighting* algorithms regarding any of these factors, is made available. Nor does the Common Data Set reveal whether college admission processes provide special preferences and lesser screening benchmarks on the listed factors for early decision applicants, legacies, non-scholarship athletes or children of donors or faculty members — or whether early decision applicants are given special consideration or benefit from somewhat lower test score or GPA requirements.

The Common Data Set also provides, for the freshman class, their standardized test score ranges and other data relating to the number that submitted SATs and ACTs, GPAs, and class rank percentiles. But note that these particular data relate only to students who actually enroll, and only in the fall cohort, so in themselves they are not especially accurate guides to actual *admissions* benchmarks. Multiple admissions-focused publications and online services like Naviance (with its SuperMatch function), College Confidential, Unigo, and College Access offer to rate a student's chances for admission (based on that student's actual record) against the data published by the colleges. These sites are doing the best they can, but the results are inherently imprecise particularly in terms of understanding what algorithms are in place to screen out applications at the outset of admissions office reviews, merely on the basis of test scores and GPAs or even "demonstrated interest" markers.

Indeed, a sales pitch on the College Confidential website makes clear that they know even the college data they themselves publish does not tell all, offering a seminar to "learn what admissions officials discuss behind closed doors" but "may not tell you in an information session." The 2009 book *The Gatekeepers* revealed much about those inside discussions through the author's special access granted by Wesleyan's admissions department to a year's worth of deliberations among admissions counselors and their committees. The application processes in those "pre-algorithm" days were meticulous, assigning numerical codes for rating all assessed categories of academic and nonacademic factors, with guidelines on how to assign those ratings. The author concluded that "for all the appearance of scientific rigor, such ratings were obviously and unabashedly subjective," and, as a result, admissions officers "were instructed to consider them as only one of many factors they were to include" in admitting a class. (Steinberg 2003, 96) As the author traced the process from beginning to end, these numerical ratings continued to play a role, taking on a life of their own as a composite stand-in for the real person. This was especially true in close cases and where the desired class mix, economic considerations regarding the total amount of financial aid available to the class, and even the maintenance of good relations with feeder prep schools, alumni, or donors posed some hard choices among virtually equivalent applicants.

Most colleges and universities, like Wesleyan, have definitive internal rubrics that allow for certain automatic admit and deny decisions based on weighted numerical scoring and perhaps an initial screening by an experienced admissions officer. Recently, more schools have been using computerized algorithms for early screening decisions to save time and effort, so that admissions officers can spend more time reading ·the entire remaining applications, essays and all, but often for only ten minutes or less. (Hoover February 1, 2018) The admissions offices, however, remain reluctant to disclose publicly the automatic early screening algorithms, although that would save time, effort and wasted application fees for many applicants. To do so would, of course, hurt the marketing objective to drive up applicant numbers to earn high selectivity status: better to be fuzzy than forthcoming. Data analytics students at one elite college or another are likely pursuing efforts to reverse engineer and then reveal these critical criteria, as a public service!

Elite colleges also do not disclose much about the practice of installing tracking software on the admissions office websites to discover the web browsing patterns and personal information of potential applicants (who increasingly hit those admissions sites to show "demonstrated interest"), in the process generating a secret score on a 1-to-100 scale as to the likelihood of an applicant student accepting an offer of admission even before an application is submitted! (MacMillan and Anderson 2019) Applicants are being secretly pre-screened by digital "black cookies" before their applications are preliminarily screened in the admissions black box.

The legal controversy about alleged discrimination against Asian-American applicants at Harvard University has also provoked a petition campaign to elect a new slate of five candidates (under the banner "Free Harvard/Fair Harvard) - to the university's board of overseers. The slate proposed to lift the *veil of secrecy* shrouding Harvard's admissions standards, by seeking disclosure of exactly how its freshman class is selected. The petition (which did not succeed) urged Harvard "to provide much more detailed information on how they select the very small slice of applicants receiving offers of admission, in order to curb the huge potential abuse possible under the entirely opaque system." They argued that more transparency could show that Harvard bypasses better-qualified Asian American candidates in favor of whites, blacks, Hispanics, and children of wealthy and well-connected parents. A similar complaint was filed with the civil rights division of the US Justice Department. (Saul 2016)

A 2017 *Wall Street Journal* editorial ("What is Harvard Hiding?") generally supportive of the plaintiff's cause in the Harvard case noted that prevailing Supreme Court precedent allows race to be considered as a plus factor in admissions but not as a minus, whereas research from a Princeton sociologist had observed that "[a]ll else being equal, an Asian-American must score 140 points higher on the [SAT] than a white counterpart, 270 points higher than a Hispanic student and 450 points higher than a black applicant." A leaked Justice Department memo also cited by the *Journal* suggested that it would consider a broader investigation of potential race-based admissions discrimination. The *Journal* editorial asserted that "the admission books at Harvard and elsewhere are ripe for a closer look" and that discovery in the legal case would be "instructive." (Editorial 2017) The editorial was prescient in that respect, although the initial ruling by the federal District Court judge in October 2019 held that Harvard was not intentionally discriminating against Asian applicants. The case is on appeal, which may ultimately reach the Supreme Court. (Anderson October 1, 2019)

The *New York Times* reported that documents relating to a review of more than one hundred sixty thousand admissions candidate records submitted in the lawsuit consistently rated Asian applicants lower than others in terms of their personal characteristics like positive personality, likeability, courage, and being widely respected, which dragged down their chances of admission despite their higher scores on tests, grades, and extracurricular activities. (Hartocollis October 25, 2018) Harvard, not surprisingly, defended its "whole-person" admissions analysis, which it was forced to disclose more fully than ever before in court. Harvard scores applications in five categories: academic, extracurricular, athletic, personal, and overall, ranking each 1 through 6, with 1 being the best. On the surface, this sort of focus seems reasonable enough, but the lawsuit revealed that there is much more to the admissions game at Harvard than first appears.

> Generations of high school students have applied to Harvard thinking that if they checked all the right boxes, they would be admitted. But *behind the curtain*, Harvard's much-feared admissions officers have *a whole other set of boxes that few ambitious high school students and their parents would know about* — or could check even if they did. The officers speak a secret language — of "dockets," "the lop list," "tips," "DE," the "Z-list," and the "dean's interest list" — and maintain a culling system in which factors like where applicants are from, whether their parents went to Harvard, how much money they have and how they fit the school's goals for diversity may be just as important as

scoring a perfect 1600 on the SAT. (Hartocollis, Harmon, and Smith 2018) (Emphasis added.)

Tips, as it turns out, means admissions weighting advantages for five specific groups: legacies, relatives of donors to Harvard, children of faculty or staff, recruited athletes, and racial or ethnic minorities. *DE* relates to a candidate's distinguishing excellence, or lack thereof. Asian applicants apparently often submitted records that were so uniformly excellent that it worked against them as they were frequently characterized as not showing a DE. The term *dockets* refers to a practice of sorting applications by geographic areas assigned to separate admissions subcommittees and given distinctive relative weightings.

The *dean's interest list* does not refer to a particular academic dean's interest in a potential student, but rather to a list the admissions dean maintains to check up on during the process because he or she happened to meet them at a recruiting event or because they are related to big donors or have other connections with Harvard. The Harvard admissions dean testified that candidates on his dean's list could receive a separate admissions rating, based not on the applicant's particular credentials but the level of interest that other people at the university (the development office, for example) have in this applicant's admissions outcome. At other elite colleges, this may be called the watch list or the like and may also get a tip in the right direction at the right time.

The term *lop list or lopping* relates to the endgame of the process, where candidates tentatively ticketed for admission have their status changed to "deny" or "wait list" based on the targeted admissions number. But before the list is final, it is scrubbed with particular reference to four factors: ethnicity (ETH), athlete (ATH), financial aid need (HFAI), and lineage (LIN), another word for *legacy*, which can also incorporate children of donors, celebrities, or public officials. We will explore more fully in chapter 5 how the

LIN factor plays a most important role in determining the entering classes at elite colleges like Harvard and tilts their economic profile decidedly up the family income scale.

And yet, after all these boxes are checked, there remains at Harvard another admissions lane, this one called the *Z-list*, which refers to a special path to admission for an applicant who is borderline academically but whom Harvard wants to admit in respect to connections the student's family may have with the university. For Z-listed applicants, the admissions office guarantees admission on the condition that the student defer enrollment for one year. (Gluckman November 2, 2018; Zauzmer 2010) Z-listing obviously reduces the number of spaces available to more qualified applicants in the next year's entering class and also allows Harvard to maintain a very high level of benchmark SAT scores for the initial year and potentially also the later year since the test scores of such marginal z-list admits would not be counted in the data posted and sent to the various ranking publications. Other elite colleges have been known to defer such well-connected but academically sub-par admissions to the second semester, since *US News* only counts data for fall-entry classes.

The lawsuit also revealed that Harvard had commissioned an internal study that found its admissions process could be biased against Asian Americans, but kept that study and its results under wraps and did not take any specific action in response prior to the litigation. (Hurtado, Lawrence, and Maki 2018; Korn October 17, 2018) An internal admissions department directive issued during the litigation, however, for the first time contained guidelines for its admissions staff on consideration of an applicant's race, to the effect that it could be considered only as one of many factors and only in connection with the overall rating and (by omission) not in connection with the more specific personal assessment that had been alleged to be particularly harmful to Asian-American applicants. (Gluckman October 26, 2018; Hoover November 1 and

4, 2018) Around the time of its internal study of potential racial bias against Asian applicants, Harvard had also provided a guidebook for alumni who conduct interviews of applicants, including advice on guarding against their own personal biases in conducting and evaluating the interviews and encouraging them to become familiar with minority life but not to ask questions that could suggest applicants were being ethnically screened though a special admissions process.

An extensive *BuzzFeed News* article revealed that Princeton University's admissions officers also had repeatedly expressed racially focused comments about particular applicants, which were made available through a federal investigation of that university's practices, including multiple references to Asian applicants being "hard to differentiate" or otherwise spoken of as "having very familiar profiles." Black, Hispanic, and Native American candidates were also spoken of as having unusually impressive standardized test scores for their respective racial backgrounds. The investigation was concluded without any action against Princeton, but a group has sued for release of the entire set of admissions records from the case. (Hensley-Clancy 2017)

Racial discrimination in elite college admissions, although it to some degree reflects a bias toward wealth, is not the primary focus of this book. Despite elite colleges continuing passion for secrecy about actual admissions standards and internal communications, the disclosures of previously secret goings-on at Princeton and Harvard revealed in discrimination litigation have invited further investigation, including by federal enforcement agencies, relating to racial discrimination in admissions. The testimony of Richard Kahlenberg regarding how Harvard's admission outcomes closely reflect America's growing income disparity, as well as the forced acknowledgement by the University's officials about "tips" in favor of legacies, donors' children and athletes in sports most available to relatively wealthy participants have opened an intriguing but still limited peek into the elite colleges' secret admissions biases. Harvard argued strenuously to keep what it called "granular" admission process details — including statistical snapshots of entering classes — under court seal. (Hoover June 24, 2018) The judge in the case ultimately drew a line that offered Harvard some continued privileges regarding its admissions secrets, including by way of an analogy between admissions secrets and soft drink secrets; "You don't need to put the recipe for Coke in your motion. But you can allude to the fact that there is a recipe for Coke." (Anderson April 10, 2018)

The revelations about Harvard's admission practices and preferences, however, have basically outlined (but not quantified the relative weighting of) the various "black box" preferences elite colleges can use to tilt the *economic* characteristics of entering classes in favor of the wealthiest applicants. We will explore several specific preferences tied to wealth in chapter 5, and later in this chapter examine how the deliberately opaque and subjective nature of intentionally opaque application screening criteria create economic opportunity for professional consultants to provide black box *decoding* for families that can afford to pay for inside guidance in traversing the elite college admission maze.

Obscuring Special Admission Pathways and Screening Criteria in a Black Box Triggers Grade Weighting Games, and Applicant Stress

The emergence of private admissions data search engines and social network chat sites, partially standardized consolidated reporting from colleges about their actual entering classes (but not their admits), big-data analytical scrutiny, and even lawsuits seeking to compel disclosure through document disclosure and deposition does suggest that the black box days of college admissions may at some time come to a forced end. For now, however, the black box remains firmly in place. As one guidebook somewhat charitably put it: "purposely vague but not intentionally misleading." The available picture of the admissions system established by the elite colleges and followed necessarily by most other schools is like looking at a roadmap that has all the town names correct and directionally related but leaves out any means of calculating the actual mileage from point A to point B. One admissions dean, quoted in *Admission Matters,* summarized the situation with respect to the actual internal weighting of SAT and ACT results: "At most institutions, standardized test scores count less than students think and more than colleges are willing to admit." (Springer, Reider, and Morgan 2015, 128)

Clean and clear SAT and ACT admissions data sets, and the actual first-cut screening minimums for considerations, are not the only selection criteria that elite colleges are not willing to reveal. They are also less than forthcoming about how they view, and actually score and weight, applicants' grade point averages and other quantitative measures. GPAs, as noted, are not standardized across the nation's public, private, and charter schools, so admissions departments have a real comparability problem, as with respect to class rank comparison. Many high schools have opted out of that practice altogether.. The upshot is that admissions departments emphasize comparisons among applicants from the same school, whatever the relative weighting factor is, and the students know this, in part because this is one instance where most admissions departments have been quite candid. Their representatives make this clear in visits to individual high schools and in their on-campus presentations to visiting high school students and their parents and guidance counselors. The predictable result is an increase in stress and anxiety as juniors and seniors realize they will be competing with some of their BFFs for the same precious elite college brass ring that their parents have groomed them to grab for themselves.

As if this level of increased student anxiety were not enough, the College Board was also quick to seize the (financial) opportunity presented by admissions departments' GPA "comparability" problem by developing and aggressively marketing its own solution — the standardized advanced placement (AP) curriculum and tests, which are scored against a common set of national grading rubrics that college admissions departments rely on in evaluating and comparing applicants from across the country. The financial opportunity proved significant for the College Board. For example, in spring 2020, college applicants around the world took a total of 1.64 million AP exams at home online rather than in-person and on paper at monitored testing sites, due to social distancing requirements relating to the coronavirus. The Board took in $94 from each domestic student and $124 from those outside the U.S.

It is worth noting that, although those AP exams were marred by multiple technical glitches that prevented thousands of students from successfully entering their answers, those affected did not get their money back, only a chance to retake their tests. The Board blamed the students for having outdated web browsers – which even if true would have more likely occurred among lower income households. (Hoover May 15, 2020)

Aside from their money-making value to the nonprofit College Board, the AP courses were intended to replicate actual entry-level college courses to a sufficient degree so that solid 4- or 5-level performance on an AP exam would qualify a student to skip some of their general ed and major field prerequisite courses. This result could be a very useful benefit at a time when fewer than 70 percent of US college students finish even after six years of studies because in many cases they have to wait in line to get into the classes they need to graduate. Many elite college academic departments, however, have recently pushed back against awarding actual advanced placement in the form of college credit hours for high school AP courses. As Julie Lythcott-Haims pointed out in her excellent book *How to Raise an Adult*, Stanford's English, History, Psychology, and Biology departments ceased recognizing such AP credits in the 2006-2007 academic year, which was also the last year AP credits for micro- and macroeconomics were recognized. (Lythcott-Haims 2015, 65)

The key to the spread of AP curricula across the nation's high schools, however, was the fact that school board members, high school administrators, students, and their parents realized that admissions departments would now be able to sort applicants according to the degree of rigor of the courses they signed up for. Having no APs available at a school would mean that its students would fall behind in the elite college admissions game. And at schools offering APs, taking on a rigorous AP subject and getting a B for that course could ruin an otherwise perfect 4.0 GPA even if (or at least before) an applicant could inform a college about a great result on the College Board's separate AP test!

The next move in the admissions chess game, therefore, came from the high school side. The problem with APs in terms of college applications is that not all the AP courses in the curriculum could reasonably be completed before the end of junior year so that the related College Board AP test results could be reported along with college applications. The Common App form does not expressly provide a space to self-report those results. But colleges typically invite students to self-report AP test results taken in any high school year, and applicants find multiple ways to disclose them — unless they are disappointing.

The limitation on effectively reporting AP tests scores from senior year courses, however, remained a problem for the applicants who can afford to apply for early decision, which must be done before their first-semester senior courses are completed and graded, and well before their senior AP tests are taken. The only universally reported AP-related results for application purposes would be the classroom grades reflected in students' GPAs. High schools under pressure, especially in upper-class, high-performance districts, to earn a reputation of getting their students into elite colleges, proceeded to adopt forms of "weighted" GPAs. A wide variety of "extra-point" systems emerged, intended to give extra GPA credit to students who "risk" taking the more challenging AP courses, most commonly by providing an additional one-point weight above the standard four for an A, three for a B, et cetera. And yet, this type of weighting in fact meant giving those risk-taking students what my Wall Street colleagues would call the "downside protection" of knowing that even a full house of Bs in AP courses would result in a weighted version of the gold standard 4.0 GPA. High schools with weighted AP grades are actually safeguarding students from the dreaded "B = 3" in an AP course, which would automatically spoil the perfect 4.0 that would practically guarantee passing most colleges' first-cut screening algorithms.

Despite the inherent contradiction in providing risk takers a form of safety net, weighted GPAs have caught on broadly, led by private high schools and upper-income public school districts and followed by other lesser-resourced school districts to the extent they can keep pace. Even pluses and minuses can be assigned special weightings, like a 5.25 for an A+, while an A- would earn only a 4.75, and so on. Many small, poor, or rural schools have not been able to afford the costs of supporting any AP courses, disadvantaging their students in the admissions game. Some upper-class public school districts like Scarsdale, New York, and seven prominent private schools in the Washington, DC, area, however, have abandoned APs, taking a stand on principle against hyperinflation of grades and in confidence in their own curricula as solid preparation for elite college studies. (Anderson June 18, 2018)

The next big move in the grading assessment wars was made by college admissions departments. Confronted with incomparable GPA weighting systems that wind up as incomparable as un-weighted GPAs, they responded by simply doing more of what they were already quietly doing anyway — namely, their own weighting of high school transcripts, based on critical assessments they would undertake of particular high schools' quality of curriculum and teaching and the academic track records of their prior enrollees from those high schools. As *Admission Matters* pointed out: "It may be disheartening for students to learn that some colleges recomputed each applicant's GPA in un-weighted form, including only the years (usually tenth, eleventh, and twelfth) and classes (usually academic 'solids' such as English, foreign language, math, science and social studies) they consider most academic." (Springer, Reider and Morgan 2015, 26) Bad luck for those with talent in art, music, and theater that colleges purport to value but can't find ways to show that as they do for athletic prowess. But this is hardly the only instance where admissions departments engage in double-talk and mixed messaging that keeps the admissions black box at least a reliable shade of opaque.

The colleges are also keeping their particular high school course-weighting algorithms secret. Meanwhile, their admissions staffs, in their autumnal sales-force mode on the roadshow trail, pitch openness to a diverse range of talents but simultaneously advise high school students to sign up for the most demanding program available (translation: take a lot of APs) while pursuing impressive extracurricular and summer engagements to best secure consideration for admission as compared to their own classmates.

As if high school students don't have enough angst from the admissions mania, being pressed to take APs to have a chance at elite admissions most likely means substantial additional homework of up to five hours a night in the most high-performance public and private schools. Efforts by school district professionals to create some limits through homework limitation policies usually have failed utterly when it comes to APs, as the high school teachers assigned to those classes are often determined to demand college-level intensity of effort to best assure that their charges can score high on the College Board's standardized AP tests, and

135

thereby lock-in those teachers' choice assignments to classes with the brightest kids.

Elite college admissions departments, despite their passion for secrecy regarding admissions criteria, have added to the stressful high school environment by their own emphasis on doing well in AP curriculum courses as the best way to get to the front of the admissions line. For example, here's what the publication *PrepScholar* was able to discern and communicate about highly ranked Williams College's admissions standards:

> [T]he school is **extremely selective**. Meeting their GPA requirements and SAT/ACT requirements is very important to getting past their [the admissions officials'] first round of filters and proving your academic preparation. If you don't meet their expectations, your chance of getting in is nearly zero. After crossing this hurdle, you'll need to impress Williams College application readers through their other application requirements, including extracurricular activities, essays and letters of recommendation...The GPA requirement that really matters is the GPA you need for a real chance of getting in. For this, we look at the school's average for its current students, [which is] 4.05. (*PrepScholar* circa 2016) (Emphasis in the original.)

Given that a weighted grade point average *above* 4.0 is necessary for a meaningful chance of admission, it would behoove an applicant to excel at AP courses (with their weighted credit) so that achieving an A grade would result in a numerical weighting above 4, typically all the way up to 5. *PrepScholar* pointed out that with a GPA below 4.05, an applicant would "**need a higher SAT or ACT score to compensate**." (Ibid.) (Emphasis in the original.)

The publication then calculated, as an example, that an applicant with a weighted GPA of 4.05 and an SAT score of 2160 (out of

2400 possible) or an ACT of 34 (out of 36 possible) would have an 18.34% chance of acceptance by Williams. *PrepScholar* went on to offer its consulting and tutoring services to those with initial SATs below 2300 and ACTs below 34 (and the financial resources to pay the fees) to help such applicants retake the test to get higher scores.

Williams College's recruiting brochures have urged applicants to take as many APs as possible: "To be competitive, applicants should pursue the strongest program of study offered by their high schools, taking whatever honors or advanced courses are available." (Springer, Reider and Morgan 2015, quoting Williams College brochure, 24) A Harvard admissions officer likewise reported that students and parents "sometimes ask if it is better to get an A in a regular course or a B in an AP course. My answer is that it is best to get an A in the AP course." This writer has personally heard essentially the same answer in multiple college-recruiting presentations: for example, by a representative of Carnegie-Mellon University to a student-parent audience in a San Francisco hotel meeting room. As the well-known admissions advice book *The College Solution* stated succinctly, "Unfortunately, college admissions reps don't often level with teenagers about their chances for admission or receiving financial assistance." (O'Shaughnessy 2015, 76)

Applicants to elite colleges are confronted with confusing messages about test scores and APs that are intended to attract applicants on the basis of the school's academic exclusivity without actually lying about the chances of the garden-variety, unhooked applicant to actually get in. An op-ed on the topic of affirmative action in the *Wall Street Journal* of October 27, 2017, helpfully suggested:

> One way schools could make admissions less "unfair" and a bit less stressful is to be more transparent about their scoring rubrics — the combinations of GPA, SAT and course selection that get an applicant into the "possible" pile. Colleges could say: to be a serious candidate for

admission, you need a 3.2 GPA and a 1200 SAT scores. Of course, if you are a potential All-American athlete, an all-state flutist, or have a family income under $15,000, we'll probably make allowances. But importantly, once you've met that threshold, we really do not care if grades or SAT scores are higher. At that stage we're looking for interesting, nice kids with a passion. (Katzman and Cohen 2017)

No elite college, however, has as yet taken up the *Journal's* transparency challenge. They have nothing to gain and (they perceive) too much to lose by opening up their admissions black box. Eric Hoover, the distinguished reporter on admissions affairs for the *Chronicle of Higher Education*, interviewed a former admissions officer Noble Jones, author of a paper entitled "Inside the Black Box: The Garbage Can Model of Decision-Making in Selective College Admissions," who explained that "garbage can model" terminology was intended to capture the "fluid participation of actors" in and out of meetings during the admissions review process, producing a degree of "variability" in applying specific evaluation standards to individual cases that "astounded" him. (Hoover December 12, 2018)

A decision to admit one applicant often adversely affects another's chances for reasons that neither the applicant who was accepted — nor the one who was not — could reasonably anticipate and counteract. For example, if one admitted applicant happened to be a trombone player, and the school only needed one more for the band, another trombone player might lose out as a result. Similarly, Hoover referred to terms like "good fit" and "intellectual fire" that admissions officers use without any "way to objectively measure those perceived virtues." (Ibid.) Admissions officers do have a very tough, energy-intensive job with little time per applicant to discern differential characteristics. Mr. Jones told Hoover how the best of them used their humanity — as well as their awareness of how their own biases and experiences could affect their choices — in order to bring integrity to the process. This burden on admissions personnel, however, is essentially triggered by application overload due to elite colleges' obsession with proving they are more selective every year, as well as strict internal limits on the size of their entering classes, due not only to reluctance to deplete endowments, but also to the strategic objective of projecting an aura of exclusivity that in turns attracts applications from rich families.

Lesser-endowed tuition-dependent colleges have their own problem in terms of sizing their entry classes while seeking to compete with elite schools for the best students. Like the elite colleges who set the terms of such competition, they also apparently believe they dare not open up their own admissions black boxes, lest they expose themselves to even lower rankings, lower admissions, and lower donations or state funding as a result. Colleges looking to improve their *US News* rankings and move into its top 100 selectivity group will put even highly qualified applicants (who they fear are using them as a safety school) onto their wait lists, so they do not waste an admissions offer that will cut their yield. We also know from sociological research referred to in an opinion piece in the *New York Times* by Rebecca Zwick, senior researcher at the Educational Testing Service and author of *Who Gets In? Strategies for Fair and Effective College Admissions,* that "the fuzzier the admissions criteria, the greater the disadvantage suffered by low-income students and others who are less familiar with university culture." (Zwick 2017)

The somewhat wistful *Wall Street Journal* op-ed quoted above notes that admissions officials are well aware that, despite their normative value vis-à-vis comparing high school grades alone, standardized tests are "very responsive to focused preparation...And less useful at predicting whether an applicant will be an academic star in college." (Katzman and Cohen ibid.) It seems there must be something about the SAT and ACT requirements that most colleges still like to hold on to. Could it be that they know that the best focused preparation (as offered in the example above from *Prep Scholar* and similar tutoring services) is something only the upper middle class and above can afford? Continuing to ratchet test performance requirements higher and higher assures a steady flow of applicants and enrollees whose families can afford full-price tuition and perhaps become endowment-level donors.

There is well-documented controversy surrounding standardized testing itself as an admissions criterion, based on research showing a strong correlation between test scores and the socioeconomic standing of students' families. Research by Sean Reardon at the Stanford Graduate School of Education and featured in the *Stanford Alumni* magazine revealed that, over thirty years' time, the difference in test performance between students from the ninetieth percentile and the tenth percentile of family income has grown by about 40 percent, which is double the gap between white and black students that has been more frequently focused on. (Scott 2016)

Elite college admissions departments (as well as the test providers) know that the SAT and ACT test scores are better guides to applicants' socioeconomic status than to their scholastic aptitude. (Hoover May 26, 2015) Even the College Board has conceded that scores on its SAT test can be coached-up significantly with enough tutoring. (Strauss 2017) The Board also found that students whose parents earned over $200,000 per year were 35 times more likely to score above 750 on the SAT's critical reading test than students whose parents earned less than $20,000. (Markovits 2019) Bond-rating agencies that evaluate the quality of college debt, however, see higher test scores as evidence of a reliable margin of safety in terms of the school's ability to collect full sticker-price tuition, as well as eventual donations to their endowments. (Lythcott-Haims 2015, 135) No surprise then that their own economic interests have led elite colleges to continue to push their benchmark test scores higher and higher despite what they know about their highly questionable predictive value in terms of academic success. Is it possible that such business interests and their related quest for higher *US News* rankings and enrollees from higher-income families is taking precedence over any professed focus on increasing enrollment for highly qualified but economically and socially disadvantaged applicants?

Even the opportunities for elite education across the learning-style spectrum have been complicated by the corrupting power of wealth. The indictments of rich parents who stooped to purchase false medical certification of learning disabilities so that their children would have more time to complete standardized rests has of course made it harder going forward for students with legitimate needs for such accommodations. Lindsay E. Jones, head of the National Center for Learning Disabilities, told the *Chronicle* of *Higher Education* that "it's really going to hurt the people who need help the most....We work with individuals with learning disabilities and attention issues and they fight stigma and discrimination every day to get the accommodation on tests just to show what they know." (Mangan March 13, 2019)

Recent research at the University of Virginia has suggested that the best way to expand opportunity across the full range of family incomes for admission to that states' public universities would be to offer *free* SAT and ACT college admission tests to all high school graduates. Specifically, according to the study as cited in the *Washington Post*, "the pool of prospects for the highly selective University of Virginia and the College of William & Mary would expand nearly 20 percent...and as much as 40 percent for broader access public universities." The increase would be most notable for students of poor families "who otherwise might not think about signing up to take the SAT or ACT." (Anderson June 25, 2019)

The study analyzed academic data of 32,000 high school graduates that had not taken the tests, and concluded that there were upwards of 8,000 with real potential to do well enough on the tests to earn admission to Virginia's state universities but were overlooked by university recruiting efforts because none of their names or addresses were on test score lists the school had purchased. Virginia had not as yet adopted universal testing but the next-door state of Maryland, among others, had done so at an annual cost of $450,000. That state's educators found that doing so was helping to remove barriers associated with entrance exams. In tie, the Virginia state superintendent of public instruction acknowledged that offering free admission testing to all high school students would indeed "'be beneficial in providing students with equitable academic opportunities.'" (Ibid.)

It would also be advantageous for students from disadvantaged backgrounds to sign up for the Pre-SAT, SAT and ACT tests as early as possible in high school so that they have time to re-take them, even more than once, to gain the advantage of so-called super-scoring by most admission departments where only the best of multiple scores are counted. (Chinoy 2018) Students of sufficient financial means can afford to do that (and tutor up between tests). The Virginia research suggested that subsidizing some form of universal free testing would be money well spent by local, state and federal governments, as well as by philanthropic entities, to show their support for equitable academic opportunities. (Olsen-Phillips 2016)

Eric Hoover summarized the situation succinctly in a 2019 article in the *Chronicle of Higher Education*:

> Students from low-income backgrounds are greatly underrepresented at the nation's most-selective colleges. And standardized tests play a large role in that story: Applicants with affluent, college-educated parents tend to far outscore their disadvantaged peers, just as white and Asian-American students, on average, fare better on the exam than black and Hispanic students do. Some researchers believe that richer information about the opportunities available to such underrepresented students

would help admission officers better understand their achievements. (Hoover May 16, 2019)

Hoover also pointed to research by Michael N. Bastedo, director of the University of Michigan's Center for the Study of Higher Education, that found admissions officers were up to 28 percent more likely to admit a low-income applicant when they had detailed information about the applicant's high school. (Ibid.) The College Board, having finally admitted that coaching can influence SAT scores, has, to its credit, used Bastedo's approach and its own homework to propose a new "adversity score" for submission to admissions departments as a companion to SAT results. That score attempts to contextualize SAT test scores (and correlated values for ACT scores) with selected data about the quality of test takers' high schools as well as their socioeconomic status and neighborhoods.

Hoover reported that the adversity score, as part of an "Environmental Context Dashboard," was beta tested first with fifty college admissions departments and, more than a much broader set, including some of America's most elite schools. It does not present socioeconomic data or other particular information relating to any student's application materials. Instead, the score tool used publicly available federal statistics and the College Board's own data sources to show measures of disadvantage or privilege relative to the student. The local data was derived from census track records that can be more useful than just knowing the applicant's zip code, which has been the prevailing shorthand for economic advantage or disadvantage. The high school data also used census track information for all students at the school.

The *Wall Street Journal*'s front-page treatment of the adversity score on May 17, 2019, illustrated its potential on the admissions process and outcomes. The *Journal* disclosed that the score actually included three distinct measures of adversity. First of all, a family environment assessment focused on median income, single parenting, adult education and employment levels, and English as a second language among all the families at the applicant's school. These factors were coupled with a broader neighborhood score covering crime rate, poverty rate, home values and vacancy rates, as well as a high school environment rating that considered the school's degree of under-matching (students with better potential than the school can serve), overall curricular rigor, the share of students qualifying for free lunches and the opportunities at the school to take AP courses. (Belkin 2019)

The adversity score for each applicant would show up as a number between 1 and 100 on the Environmental Context Dashboard, accompanying a comparison of the applicant's SAT score with those of classmates. The adversity score is not sent directly to admissions departments with the applicant's test score itself, however. An adversity score of 50 would be considered the "average" or neutral benchmark; above 50 would indicate a relative level of adversity; below 50, a relative level of privilege. It was proposed that admissions departments would use the dashboard information as they saw fit. Some, like Yale, told the *Journal* that it had affected its view of all the applications they reviewed and helped increase the economic diversity of its incoming classes. Similar results were reported at Florida State University, although an official there told the *Journal* he expected pushback from parents and counselors: "'If I am going to make room for more of the [poor and minority students] we want to admit and I have a finite number of spaces, then someone has to suffer and that will be privileged kids on the bubble.'" (Ibid.)

That comment exposed a potential controversy that could arise if the adversity score or something like it were to be applied in a way analogous to racial affirmative action. Barely a week after the details of the adversity score concept was publicly circulated, Eric Hoover of the *Chronicle of Higher Education* began his follow-up article this way: "Alarm, Anger. Confusion. News of the College

Board's Environmental Context Dashboard has caused all of the above." (Hoover May 23, 2019) A *Wall Street Journal* opinion piece trashed the adversity score concept as a "patch to liberalism's great failure." (Henninger 2019) In the context of the litigation surrounding that topic at Harvard and elsewhere, it is understandable that the College Board chose to leave out race or ethnicity from any neighborhood or family data used in calculating its adversity index. But Elissa Salas, CEO of the nonprofit CollegeTracks, which works with first-generation and other low-income high school students, pointed out to *Time* that omitting race leaves an incomplete picture of the challenges certain students face.

Perhaps considering these potential controversies, the College Board first wrapped their adversity score calculations in a version of the admissions black box. Test takers are not made aware of their own adversity scores; nor does the board disclose to admissions departments how it calculates the score or the relative weighting it applies to each of the several factors it takes into consideration — a posture that admissions departments similarly assume with respect to their own admissions screening algorithms. (Greenspan 2019)

The thrust of the adversity score initiative was certainly a step forward from the College Board's previous efforts to contextualize test scores for socioeconomic disadvantage by creating a notional "expected" SAT score for each applicant based on such factors (an effort that collapsed two decades ago). Nevertheless, faced with so much immediate negative blowback, the College Board CEO David Coleman announced in late August 2019 that the adversity score as such was being shelved, primarily because reducing the context of an individual student's SAT performance to a single numerical "score" had proven to be both "wrong" and "confusing." (Feuerherd 2019) Note that the College Board *itself* has never been reluctant to reduce a students' SAT performance to a single numerical score!

The adversity score experiment is to be replaced by a revised tool called "Landscape" that will include neighborhood demographic information from governmental and College Board sources, as well as high school data points from the Environmental Context Dashboard. Applicants will get to see the information about their neighborhoods and schools, while admission officers will also see a range of test scores from each applicant's school. (Thompson 2019)

The *Chronicle* observed in a 2015 article titled "College Admissions Isn't Fair…Whatever That Means" that admissions officers "who weigh a poor applicant's record against his hardships work in a realm of contradictory criticisms: They're doing too little to help the have-nots, they're doing so much that it's hurting everyone else's chances." (Hoover and Supiano 2015) The greater problem today, however, is that the gap between haves and have-nots has continued to increase, and is being cemented by the pattern of elite college admissions practices and preferences.

Even Test-Optional Policies Can Work to Help Wealthy Applicants

Test-optional applications have been introduced at many elite colleges to counteract the socioeconomic correlation problem associated with standardized tests. The University of Chicago, a perennially top *US News* elite university in terms of selectivity, stunned many observers in 2018 when it was the first among its elite peers to adopt this policy going forward. As one former admissions dean and advocate of test optional policies put it, "This certainly feels like a big Antarctic ice shelf just fell into the ocean." (Hoover June 14, 2018) Chicago's admissions dean specifically addressed its intention, in making this change, to encourage an increase in diversity of economic and social experience in its entering classes going forward. Chicago also eliminated even the optional (and eminently coachable) applicant interviews in favor of allowing students to submit two-minute videos as a way to distinguish their personalities and achievements. Researchers at the University of Georgia, however, has concluded that selective liberal arts colleges that have adopted test-optional policies have not increased their enrollment of underrepresented minorities or Pell grant recipients. To its credit, the University of Chicago also backed up its test-optional policy intentions with a material expansion of its financial aid programs, offering free tuition to successful applicants whose families earn less than $125,000 per year, as well as special scholarships and internship guarantees for first-generation students. (Simon 2015)

Critics point out that the likely effect of eliminating the requirement to submit standardized tests by any elite college would be to increase the total number of applicants. That selectivity-boosting effect, however, has been documented in only about 50 percent of the schools where test optional policy was adopted. More significantly the policy can boost the averages of the test scores actually submitted, allowing the college to show a higher level of SAT and ACT achievement in its entering class in its *US News* rankings submissions, which also would increase their selectivity score. (Anderson June 14, 2018) Switching to a test-optional policy can result in raising average reported scores by twenty to thirty points. Moreover, only a handful of colleges with test-optional policies specifically disclose in their recruiting material that the figures they show for standardized test score ranges and averages are affected by those policies. Some don't even inform *US News*. Only four schools have reportedly taken the trouble to obtain the test scores of entering students who took advantage of the test-optional policy to use in their average score calculations. (O'Shaughnessy 2015, 83)

Upper-income families can ironically become the real, albeit unintended, beneficiaries of test-optional admissions because they can hire tutors to help their children ace the standardized tests at a level where it makes it advantageous to forgo the test-optional option. If paid professional tutoring does not do the trick for their offspring, wealthy families can instead provide enrichment experiences and campus visits to strengthen their children's applications. Students in high schools in less-wealthy zip codes, however, will likely have fewer opportunities to embellish their test-taking skills with private tutoring or raise their GPAs with advanced-level course offerings and high-quality extracurricular activities.

Officials of both the SAT and ACT billion-dollar testing services cast aspersions on test-optional policies, noting widespread concern about incomparability and inflation of the GPAs that colleges would be forced to rely on to evaluate academic ability without standardized testing. A *Wall Street Journal* article defended the value of the ACT and SAT in predicting college and post-college success based on research by two professors who, prior to the article, had received research grants from the SAT's provider, the College Board. The *Journal* article, nevertheless, acknowledged "a correlation between test scores and social class." The article also conceded that commercial test prep coaching "that is clearly expensive" will likely aid test performance. (Kuncel and Sackett 2018)

Although the College Board has partnered with Khan Academy to provide free test-prep services, the gold standard of test tutoring remains a very commercial matter. The single best strategy for improving standardized test scores is to take the test multiple times, particularly as most colleges allow for "superscoring" — that is, considering only the best scores from each test element regardless of how many times the particular test was taken. Of course, taking these tests multiple times can cost more money than the poorer families can afford. Subsidizing these costs would be a very effective benefit for lower-income applicants, and some school districts are doing so. Federal test-cost subsidies for students qualifying for free school lunches could be well funded by taxing the income of the College Board, which remains classified as a nonprofit organization owned by the elite colleges themselves. That form of subsidy would make "test optional" a real choice for high school students across all income groups.

It may seem that an easy response to the fact that standardized test criteria advantage the richest applicants in the admissions process would be for the richest colleges to lower the secret relative *weight* assigned to these tests in their decision algorithms. Yet that solution would put more focus and weight on the applicants' grade point averages, which are subject to the vagaries of grading standards between different schools and even within the same school. Admissions office representatives already point out that, because of such disparities, most applicants wind up competing primarily with applicants from their own high schools, which serves to increase the anxiety and pressures that can build up as senior year approaches and students are encouraged by the process to look for any way to differentiate their records from their nearest peers. Paid tutoring for wealthy kids helps with regular high school coursework as well as with ACT and SAT performance, especially in AP courses and AP tests served up by the College Board as another revenue stream to exploit the pressure on students to distinguish themselves. The College Board wins, whether a student is forced to compete in the SAT or the AP intramural competition or both.

The College Board has even upped the ante for accessing the AP tests by requiring applicants for spring testing to sign up (at a cost of over ninety dollars) by the prior November 15 or pay an additional late fee of forty dollars. This requirement can also be an obstacle especially to seniors, because they will be forced to register and pay for spring AP tests (which will be too late to count toward their admissions case) before they know whether the college they will attend will, in fact, give them credit for their AP test grade. (Strauss February 7, 2019) The same pay-to-play marketplace prevails in terms of establishing the record of extracurricular and volunteer activities that elite colleges demand for consideration for admission. The wealthy can afford to provide their children time off in the summer to take a community college version of the same AP course they will take in their next high school semester to better assure that the "A" grade the top colleges expect will materialize when the student takes the course over in the next high school term! The wealthy can also buy their children special community service opportunities on faraway continents, special unpaid internships offered by placement firms, and educational or athletic summer camps located on elite college campuses (but not necessarily operated or endorsed by them, although they are happy to pocket the building rentals for their otherwise seasonally vacant classrooms).

For Applicants Who Can Pay, Luxury-Level Test Tutoring and a Private Consulting Industry to Decode the Admissions Black Box

Town & Country magazine, a long-established chronicler of the upper-classes, published a colorful and extensive five-page survey of how to navigate cutthroat admissions, including a game-board mock-up of the cost of a full dose of "Birth to BA" college prep for the rich. Highlights start with $29,870 for music and art classes from six months to age three and moving on through preschool admissions coaching at $4,500; private schools from age three through high school ($558,990); private language, math, and STEM tutoring ($196,588); music lessons ($138,240); annual summer camps and volunteer experiences ($161,500); summer school during high school ($32,270); homework coaching from middle school onward ($64,000); college application consulting ($100,000);

and, if needed, a suitable gap-year immersion program ($55,000) — as well as the cost of college itself ($282,280) and the unpaid but nonetheless purchased summer internships provided by an emerging new internship finder industry ($6,200). The article did acknowledge that some of these real-life options on the game board "long since passed the point of ridiculousness." (Schwartz 2017)

Referring to the bull market in college counseling in 2017 (the year of a 25 percent stock market run-up), *T&C* profiled the fortunes and the fees of Kat Cohen, founder of IvyWise, "widely regarded as the Rolls-Royce" of the college admissions counseling industry. Their starting fee for junior counselors is $1,000 per hour, ranging up to $3,000 for Ms. Cohen herself. Quoting a past admission dean at an Ivy League university, however, the article did question the IvyWise approach that features a four-year program to "help students understand their passions." In the dean's words, "I can understand why parents might look to outsource their child's motivation to a private counselor…The trouble comes later, when such students come to feel they're fakes." (Ibid.)

In *Where You Go Is Not Who You'll Be*, Frank Bruni also profiled high-end admissions consultants like Michele Hernandez, who by 2014 was charging around $50,000 to families who signed their children up as early as the eighth or ninth grade for guidance on through high school: "which courses to take, which summer programs to enter, and how to prioritize or reconfigure their extracurricular activities." She also offers a lower-priced (in the mid-teen thousands of dollars) Application Boot Camp for students to work with professional editors on multiple drafts of their essay submissions — travel, food, and hotel bill not included in the price, while ensconced in a hotel. Bruni likened this expensive level of admissions consulting to the professional coaches who work with beauty pageant contestants. (Bruni 2015, 77)

Admission Matters referred to a platinum package including hiring a multi-year personal application trainer who will make elite admission the central focus of the teenage client's life, noting the complete *absence* of irony in the packager's pitch despite how it begins: "'Ironically, you want to look unpackaged and raw — someone like me can be behind the scenes and make someone look raw without over-packaging them.'" (Springer, Reider, and Morgan 2015, 57)

The author of *The College Solution,* Lynn O'Shaughnessy, also found it "ironic" that some elite college admissions officials complain about the artifice and gamesmanship associated with admissions consulting that severely test the mostly amateur forensic skills of overworked admissions staffs trying to work out what is genuine and what is not in the avalanche of oft-coached applications and related essays. O'Shaughnessy cited the comments of an Amherst College admissions dean that seemed to place the blame for admissions mania directly on applicants' parents and their ability to leverage their wealth for their own ends: "What is important to understand about families who make use of independent college counselors is that they are both highly competitive and used to controlling their own destinies. In their eyes the college-admissions process is reduced to little more than a contest...to be won (perhaps at all costs) and process that is to be tightly controlled." (O'Shaughnessy 2015, 210) The 2019 federal admissions bribery and fraud indictments strongly suggest that the dean was right about "at all costs." Ms. O'Shaughnessy, however, concluded that the elite colleges "are the ones responsible for most of the nation's admission hysteria...[T]he odds of being anointed by these admission gods keep declining as some of those elite schools insist on encouraging ever more student to apply so...[those schools] can generate even greater rejection rates...The only people who can really play this admissions game at the highest level are the wealthy." (Ibid.)

Wealth brought to bear in the admissions game has attracted a lot of suitors: the number of full-time independent admissions counselors quadruped to around 10,000 from 2005 to 2019, with another few thousand part-timers. But only about 2,500 of these professionals sign-on to professional groups like the Independent Educational Consultants Association, which requires that its members have a level of education and experience in counseling, not write essays for student clients, and refrain from guaranteeing admission placements or outcomes. (Golden September 12, 2019)

The vast majority of college admissions consultants don't charge such high prices as IvyWise and the like profiled by *T&C,* and offer their services well under the "platinum package" price level, with slimmer and trimmer versions of advice, test prep and essay editing, and application lists preparation (from reach to safety and every category in between), as well as more modest boot camps and weekend intensives. They certainly cannot be blamed for meeting the demand of applicant families that have learned from all the admissions guidebooks, not to mention the direct mail and online consultant marketing, that outside help can make a considerable difference in what has become an insider's game. Some consultants even offer their services on a pro bono basis through local college access programs. How else would college-worthy kids in school districts where a large majority of them qualify for free school lunches because of their families' economic hardship learn how to use their strong records to their best advantage in the elite admissions process? Their harried public school guidance counselors simply do not have the time to keep up with demand. Yet there are some consultants (like the indicted and confessed Rick Singer) who have blatantly played on admissions anxieties with enticing and personalized offers of free up-front advisory services along with extraordinary claims of success in raising applicants' test scores with their proprietary "formulas."

For example, here is an opening cold-call pitch addressed to the parents of a senior in a public high school:

> You and your student, [first name redacted], are scheduled to participate in an educational group presentation followed by a personal interview to help determine college admission and financial aid eligibility. Colleges are now identifying prospective students as early as the 9th grade for admission and financial aid assistance. Therefore you need to attend in order to receive assistance in making critical decisions that will arise in the next few months. [First name redacted]'s future is too important not to attend….Your reservation number is #####. Appointment times are limited…There is no cost for the educational instruction or the student interview. [First name redacted]'s unique educational needs will be addressed during the personal interview following the presentation. *Additional services will be made available for those needing additional assistance.*" (Emphasis added.)

Of course, there is no mention of fees or costs — yet. Anyone who has been to a "free" timeshare sales weekend knows this marketing model.

Or consider another letter addressed to parents of a high school junior:

> Tutoring for the fall PSAT, SAT, and ACT is starting soon…If you want to start preparing [first name redacted] for these exams and eliminate the stress of this dreaded process, I encourage you to consider carefully the prep program you choose…Ours is a straightforward formula that has worked for thousands of families, and the results prove it — students who completed our programs this past school year increased their scores as much as 470 points on the SAT and 8 points on the ACT…If your child completes our 30-hour SAT Program and doesn't

improve by at least 140 points from his or her actual PSAT score, we will provide you with an additional 18 hours of SAT tutoring for free.

And for those fretting about the authenticity and persuasive power of their children's admissions essays, there is always help available:

[Our] Essay Editing Program has been internationally recognized for providing the most comprehensive essay revisions by our hand-selected specialists from top universities. You can work with one of our essay specialists personally by signing up for our full program...[I]f you are looking for just a quick review of one essay, you can submit it to us online and receive a comprehensive edit within 1.5, 3, 6, 12 or 48 hours. All edits are personally made by our Elite Essay Specialists and include: Concept and Theme Review...Diction and Syntax Corrections...Spelling and Grammar Perfection...You are billed on the max word count of the [essay] prompt.

Do elite colleges somehow take pride in knowing that their graduates' first jobs after graduation might turn out to be editing the essays of the next round of applicants to those same colleges? We should not simply blame this aspect of the admissions mania on the consultants and the test tutors, however, who by and large are serious professionals meeting market demand (and charging what the market will bear) to help match up teenagers with the elite colleges' impossibly opaque criteria. Vague disclosures and mixed marketing messages about the relative weight of GPAs, test scores, AP classes, extracurricular achievements, recommendations, and interview outcomes serve to mask the specific algorithms many elite colleges use to peremptorily screen out most applicants via strict arithmetic cutoffs based on grades and test scores linked with ratings of their home high schools. We saw in chapter 3 how these algorithms and factor weightings are purposely kept secret, which helps trigger a flood of hopeless application that help elite colleges sustain their low admissions rates and exclusive reputations.

Secrecy also attracts sleuths, however, and the good sleuths tend to be well paid. For example, Wall Street stock analysts probe between the lines of mandated public company disclosures and question officials to gain sharper insights into how company business plans are trending, and then pass those insights on to their clientele. As seasoned stock market observers know, there is a big value difference between standard stock analysis and more well-informed viewpoints just on the legal side of "inside" information. The most powerful hedge funds on Wall Street have routinely engaged former insiders as consultants to decode corporate performance and likely courses of action on the basis of their informed experience only and not on any current access to material undisclosed data. (Cross over that line and they risk indictment.)

In the college admissions context, families that can afford it are likewise simply engaging highly skilled professionals to decode the admissions black box, to deliver the up-to-date inside information on where students would be best advantaged in terms of real admissions odds, based on their frequent private visits with admissions deans and staff. Some of this information does filter out through parent networks, especially in our wealthiest high school districts, but the private insights mostly stay with the parents who bought them. As a result, the children of affluent families are best equipped to compete for those admissions slots remaining even after the affluence-related admissions hooks are accounted for.

Elite college officials know full well that their admissions processes and practices, including their closely guarded black box approach to transparency about actual admissions standards, have spawned the $2 billion consulting industry that, in its most intensive and successful formats, caters primarily to the wealthy. Even modestly priced admissions counseling and tutoring add extra costs (and stress) to the total college tab for the shrinking middle class as well as families that struggle daily to make ends meet. Yet elite colleges that say they want more economic diversity in their entering classes persist with their secrecy regime. Is that because they are more than happy to outsource to consultants paid by parents the task of assuring themselves a steady flow of well-coached and notionally certifiable candidates from the upper class among the hordes of borderline-hopeless applicants they have essentially purchased and seduced in order to secure their all-important acceptance rate rankings?

Is the admissions playing field subtly tilted to the rich not simply a collateral effect of a competitive seller's market, but rather a design to meet elite colleges' own business and financial objectives, including enriching their endowments via an assured flow of grateful parents who can afford to be generous donors? Is the notion that admissions is a "game" not just a superficial analogy but an actual fact, designed to disguise the real business that is going on — amassing multibillion dollar endowments by clearing special paths to admission for the offspring of families of the top 10 percent — who are themselves complicit as they seek to build a moat around and "hoard" (in Richard Reeves's term) their families' ongoing economic privilege by assuring that their heirs carry forward an elite college degree to start their own economic lives?

Elite colleges exhibit no interest whatsoever in opening up their admission black boxes, except as necessary to enable (or tease) the paid decoders. Meanwhile admissions officers themselves consult with enrollment management professionals who employ state-of-the-art artificial intelligence capabilities to design predictive yield models, "trade secret" admissions practices and marketing programs, proprietary screening algorithms and wait-listing strategies.

Why has the college admissions process become so complex and opaque that students and their families need the equivalent of a federal income tax consulting service to work through it with a reasonable degree of confidence and competence? Why are the great minds in American college administration unable to come up with a simple, straightforward, and transparent way to apply for admission? Perhaps the most logical answer is that elite colleges simply don't want to: they prefer an admissions process where the rich have an inside track because it serves their own enrollment, ranking, and financial goals. The next chapter will consider the most direct and blatant ways elite colleges have instituted, aggressively defended, and cleverly disguised special admissions avenues for wealthy applicants.

CHAPTER 5

Need Blind, Increasingly — Wealth Blind, Not So Much! Special High-Affluence Lanes Pave the Way for Wealthy and Well-Connected Applicants

The previous chapter revealed how certain admissions practices and policies of elite colleges work indirectly (but effectively) to favor applicants who come from families in and above the top 20 percent income category. Most elite college admissions officials will admit the tilt-to-the-rich effects of these aspects of their setup but strongly defend them as solely intended to best assure that they will be able to assemble an enrollment population that features the talents and fit that constitute the college's branded character and provide the learning and social environment that will work best for all those enrolled. Any bias toward wealthy applicants is portrayed as merely an incidental consequence of those benign purposes. Should we not give these highly respected educational institutions the benefit of the doubt? One way to answer that question is to examine whether they also pursue admissions practices that deliberately and unquestionably favor the wealthiest applicants, as well as the degree to which those and other policies result in a persistent, majority wealth quota in the enrollment. If elite colleges are, in fact, creating special pathways to admit wealthy applicants resulting in a very substantial percentage of their enrollment being controlled by those with a lot of money and influence, it becomes more likely that admissions practices that provide more subtle and indirect advantages to the rich are not merely happenstance either, but rather intended and integral to the overall admissions business plan.

This chapter will examine four specific ways elite admissions practices more or less secretly discriminate against ordinary Americans and are set up directly to favor the wealthy and well connected: (1) early decision; (2) special consideration ("tips" in Harvard-ese) for legacy, faculty children, and children of donors; (3) "country club" athletics preferences; and (4) wealth-targeted merit aid. For example, it was revealed during the Harvard Asian discrimination litigation that recruited athletes, the children of alumni, the children of Harvard faculty and staff, and children on a special list of donors account for only 5 percent of the overall applicant pool but represent 29 percent of accepted students. Chapter 6 will then examine the broader consequences when the reality of admissions practices of elite colleges has produced an enrollment pattern that reflects the increasing income disparity in the United States, severely undermining American higher education's traditional role of fostering socioeconomic mobility.

Jerome Karabell, author of *The Chosen: The Hidden History of Admission and Exclusion at Harvard, Yale, and Princeton,* reflected on how the 2019 admissions bribery and fraud allegations exposed the role that secrecy has played in creating the circumstances where some parents "'transgress the boundaries of the permissible'" in attempting to use their wealth to exploit one or another of these four hooks — or overcome lack of them through a side door.

> The fact that the admissions process is opaque rather than transparent certainly provides more room for these kinds of abuses to occur, and I think it is one element of this scandal. But I think the underlying issue has to do with the

capacity of privileged people to use the admissions process in a way that enhances the privileges of already privileged people. Specifically, things we already take for granted as normal, such as donating a building or getting special consideration for your child or grandchild, could be considered corrupt and scandalous. But they are taken for granted as the way we do things in the United States. In other countries, that could be considered immoral or illegal. (Bartlett 2019)

To begin consideration of whether these four high-affluence admissions lanes should any longer be taken for granted (as well as considered perfectly legal) we will *not* start with the most obvious example of elite admissions departments' practices that blatantly discriminate in favor of children of the wealthy and powerful — the special back-door access for children of past or potential donors, celebrities, and politicians. Rather, it is more important to first consider two practices that show the greatest overall impact on enrollment composition. One of these practices is fairly new in terms of its impact, and one is deeply traditional. Both, however, create special lanes for admissions consideration for two types of applicants who are highly likely to be members of the economic upper classes: those who are able and willing to apply for, and abide by, an early decision on their applications, and those who constitute legacies at the college because their parents or other ancestors are graduates.

The Coercive Early Decision Conundrum

Elite colleges have worked to control the pace of the overall admissions cycle by their leadership in forging an agreement among all colleges on the framework of the admissions calendar through admissions offices' own trade association. Per agreement, the calendar starts with the official release of admissions requirements (for example, the text of this year's essay questions or any adjustment to either the Common App or the school's own application documents) for the following year's autumnal enrollment class, with a deadline of January of the next year for submissions, the end of March for notification, and the first of May for acceptance by the student via a deposit on tuition, plus a potential for wait list acceptance, usually running thorough to July if the applicant chooses to remain under consideration. This is the regular admissions cycle.

Elite colleges, however, have led the way in providing a separate calendar for advance consideration of an application with the so-called early decision option, which has been widely adopted under the admissions trade association norms as an exception from the regular admissions calendar pursuant to the following terms, which the schools have cooperated (not to yet say colluded) in enforcing. Application processes are not generally different from those required under the regular calendar, but the required documents (including the documents requesting financial aid including recent family tax returns) must be submitted on a faster schedule, by the first of November at the latest. The applicants' senior year mid-term grades might not yet be available, but full first semester grades are required to validate any early admission decision that may be announced, usually by mid-December or even sooner if the college announces such admissions on a rolling basis.

In submitting such an early decision application, however, the applicant *must agree in advance to enroll* in the college as a condition of even being considered under that cycle, and also must commit not to submit an early decision application to any other college. This rule distinguishes early decision from the early *action* option, which follows a similar submission and notification schedule but does not require a prior commitment to accept the offer and allows time for the successful applicant to compare its terms with regular cycle decisions. A variant of early action employed by a few top universities does restrict applicants to one such application, as in the case of early decision. Over 600 colleges and universities offer some form of early admission decision: some offer two or even three versions. (Springer, Reider, and Morgan 2013, 148)

The "early action" option tips the balance of market leverage more in the applicant's favor. The binding nature of the early decision option, on the other hand, provides a trifecta of "enrollment management" benefits — lower acceptance rates enhancing selectivity reputations; a level of guaranteed higher yield on offers; and more full-tuition paying customers. (Bernard 2019) But for most applicants, early decision means harder decisions, more pressure, and less bargaining power, and decidedly favors children of wealthy families that best can turn those circumstances to their advantage.

Early decision limits students to only one such application. That's a hard choice for any 17-year-old, and even harder if they lack the economic advantages enabling them to scope out the academic landscape, check them out in person, and convince colleges that their commitment is genuine as well as binding. As one college counselor put it to a reporter from the *Wall Street Journal*, many of his students apply early not because they are really strongly attached to one school, but because they fear missing the chance to at least get in somewhere! (Korn March 28, 2018)

Some elite colleges have made a practice of sharing among their peer groups (such as the Ivy League) identification of their early decision applicants as a way to enforce this one-app limitation. The Department of Justice, however, has initiated an investigation of whether colleges violate antitrust laws by exchanging information about applicants they have admitted through early decision. (Korn April 11, 2018) Normally, the Common App and financial aid submissions forms do not result in a college knowing where each of its applicants (early or regular cycle) has otherwise applied, unless the applicants themselves choose to disclose that data. Students who apply for early decision and are not admitted under that round may also be considered under the regular admissions cycle. They are free at the outset to apply to other colleges under the regular cycle, and while awaiting early decision results. But an early decision offer ends that exploration because of the required binding pre-commitment.

The applicant's early decision "first choice" of college essentially becomes the "only choice" under the early decision process. Anyone who earns this form of early admission, therefore, will have surrendered a good deal of "bargaining power" with respect to financial aid. A proposed aid package will accompany or follow shortly after an early admission offer, but it will be open for discussion, and some level of negotiation, with the applicant's family for usually no more than one month, and thus cannot be compared to any regular cycle admission offer, no matter how generous such a later package turns out to be in terms of tuition discounts or loans. Only if the final early decision aid terms are clearly inadequate in light of the applicant's financial need will there be any possibility of release from the advance commitment to accept. (Springer, Reider, and Morgan 2013, 150-51, 267-68)

The early decision admissions process has been a controversial matter off and on since the seminal critique by James Fallows ("The Early-Decision Racket") published in *The Atlantic* magazine at the beginning of the 2001-02 academic year. Fallows characterized early decision as "an arranged marriage" where "both parties gain security at the expense of freedom…But the loss is asymmetrical, constraining the student much more than the institution." (Fallows 2001) Nothing about this has changed in the nearly two decades since Fallows' article.

If an employer seeking to hire students through the career services or similar office on the campus of a college offering the early decision option were to require that any student seeking an interview had to agree in advance to take any resulting job on the employer's terms, on the spot, that employer would most likely these days be banned from interviewing on those campuses for violating its prohibitions on predatory recruiting practices, including so-called "exploding" or "bullet" offers where you only have a few minutes to decide. Why would our most elite colleges choose to protect their own graduating seniors who generally *know the score* when it comes to competitive job interviews from the most dog-eat-dog, coercive practices of the world of investment banking while themselves inflicting those same practices on much younger high school seniors who don't even know the *game*? Early decision admission offers are even more coercive than bankers' "exploding" or "bullet" entry-level offers. With the latter, at least you get to hear the offer before it "expires." Even in the investment banking business, it is not generally considered a proper recruiting practice to require — as elite colleges do in the early decision process — that just to get *considered*, you must agree in advance to not to pursue any similar opportunity.

Elite colleges have given themselves a pass on the very standards of decency and fairness enforced by their own career services offices, arguing that the early decision option is intended to address the pressures and anxiety suffered by admission applicants during the long admissions season (where everyone starts on the "wait" list). As admissions offices tell it, pursuing an early decision allows high school seniors to at least reduce the *duration* of application stress and enjoy a greater portion of their graduation year (*assuming* they get a favorable decision). All they have to do is use the demonstrated interest processes at their disposal to discern very early on their number-one college choice firmly enough to refrain from applying for early decision anywhere else — and (it more or less goes without saying, unfortunately) give up their option to bargain the early decision college's financial aid offer against any other. So, in an apparently very considerate way, colleges offer a kind of an admissions-anxiety sedative to alleviate student stress. But that pill comes with not only a "take-it-or-leave-it" proposition, but also with a "you-have-to-take-it" pre-condition!

Who would be prepared to accept such an obviously one-sided proposition? The answer is a person who can afford to do so, and who has likely been counseled by professional admissions advisers to know that, all other things being equal in terms of test scores, grades, and extracurricular activities, the odds are marginally better under early decision than in the regular cycle, despite what colleges sometimes say. In fact, many elite schools are giving up saying that the odds are equal lately because they just aren't. After factoring out athletes and legacies who sometimes get in through early decision, that option increases other applicants' chances of admission by as much as an extra 100 points on the SAT, according to a study initially published by Harvard University Press (Avery, Fairbanks and Zeckhauser 2004). The authors of *Admission Matters* also reported the overall admission rates run two to three times higher for early decision applicants. (Springer, Reider, and Morgan 2013, 150)

Later studies at the University of Southern California came to a similar conclusion, as did the Jack Kent Cooke Foundation in its 2017 "True Merit" report on the wealth bias in college admissions generally. (Levy 2017) Data in that report on the percent of early decision applicants at elite colleges who gain acceptance compared with those schools' acceptance rates for regular cycle applicants bears out this early decision advantage, with estimates that early applicants can enjoy a three to five times higher likelihood of admission. A 2019 student newspaper at the University of Virginia reported that, for their fall 2017 entering classes, the acceptance rates for early decision applicants compared to early action and regular cycle applicants combined were 26.9 versus 7.2 percent at Northwestern, 51.9 versus 36.7 percent at the College of William & Mary and 24 versus 9.2 percent at Vanderbilt. (Meyer 2019)

Why are the admissions odds so much better with early decision? Why do admissions offices set a lower bar for early applicants' test scores? It starts with the fact that elite college admissions departments know they can go a long way toward securing their all-important targeted admissions *yield* rate using early decision admissions. It's basically 100 percent for up to half the class or more. Such results, by the way, go a long way toward pleasing the colleges' bond rating agencies. They signify that the admissions process is running quite efficiently and not at risk of any serious downturn in enrollment (and tuition revenue) at the last minute. An undergraduate admissions director, noting that all colleges need to address the business of paying the bills, conceded that early decision "'is useful in securing revenues'" while adding: "'[I]s it a perfect or fair solution? No. Are there sometimes other motivations for having an ED process? Yes, of course. It can serve to lower admit rate, increase yield, and could have implications for some of the methodologies within US News rankings.'" (Barnard 2019)

A very high yield percentage among early decision applicants with strong academic records and high test scores does allow elite colleges to take some calculated risks with applicants they may want to accept as legacies or donors' relatives, who have lesser academic scores that could otherwise drag down test score medians and ranges below the targets they want hit in their *US News* submissions. The admissions offices know they can just jack up the test score and GPA targets for the other regular-cycle applicants to make up for the lower academic quality of some specially-preferred early decision admits. As one early critic of early decision pointed out in a 2003 *New Yorker* article, colleges can use early decision to adjust the benchmark of the low end for the range of its enrollees' test scores that they make public for ranking purposes. "There will be a bottom tier in every class, and early admissions is a way of hand-picking it, making sure of getting students who really want to attend, and who satisfy one or another institutional need as well," including admissions for legacies and athletes. (Menand 2003) The admissions offices will then know precisely how much higher to set their test score hurdle rates for the regular round, making up for the fact that some legacy and athletic admits will have marginal academic qualifications. This practice, of course, automatically moves the odds of admission further against regular round applicants.

Early decisions also help a college to achieve the lowest possible acceptance rate. Consider an elite college where generally 50 percent of all applicants accept an admission offer, and the goal is an entry class of 800. If the college receives 8,000 applications for those 800 spots, without providing an early decision option it would need to offer admission to at least 1600 of them, resulting in a 20 percent admission rate. But the college could make 400 offers via early decision and fill half the targeted yield, and accordingly make only 800 instead of 1200 more offers to all other applicants in order to meet its enrollment target, reducing its overall acceptance rate to 15 percent. As a result, the college could gain a higher place on the *US News* ladder ranking the 100 schools with the lowest acceptance rates and thus achieve an even higher reputation for exclusivity, which in turn will attract even more early applicants from wealthier families who can afford to forego financial aid bargaining power in exchange for an easier and faster path to a favorable outcome. Business professors would call this phenomenon a good example of self-reinforcing "strategic fit" in a successful business model.

The early decision option has indeed been working very well lately for the elite colleges' business enrollment and financial goals. Ivy League schools other than Harvard, Yale and Princeton now use it, despite previous resistance. Harvard and Princeton had scrapped their early decision program in 2008, with admissions and academic officials noting its overall adverse effects on financially disadvantaged applicants and the resulting absence of economic diversity in their entering classes. But only the University of Virginia among major elite colleges followed their lead, citing similar concerns. Nevertheless, citing other apparently more-important concerns about losing highly-coveted potential applicants to competitors offering some form of early consideration, Harvard, Princeton and Virginia adopted a somewhat more flexible form of "early action" known as "restricted" early action — where the applicant could make such an application to only one school, but need not commit in advance to accept, and could take more time to consider offers from any regular cycle admissions they obtain. Since that time, however, only Stanford and Yale among their elite peers have offered this restrictive but far less coercive early application option. (Lewin 2011)

Princeton dropped the restrictive early action option for the 2020-21 admission cycle due to considerations relating to the Covid-19 pandemic in favor of only one application deadline of January 1, 2021, which puts all applicants regardless of their high school learning situation in the same position, with more time to take standardized tests and submit senior first semester grades. (Rim 2020)

In 2019 the University of Virginia fully restored the "binding" early decision application as another option in order to deal with competitive recruiting pressures and facilitate earlier determination of the size of its entering class, but an admission official said it would hold applicants to the same standards in both early and regular cycle admissions consideration (unlike certain direct competitors. (Meyer ibid.) And many more elite colleges recently have been significantly increasing the percentage of their enrollment yield target that they are, in effect, allocating to the early decision process, with its guaranteed "100 percent" acceptance rate.

Until the past few years, the percentage of students accepted on an early decision basis had tended to be in the mid-teens, with few as high as the twenties or thirties. But recent data is showing that 40 to 50 percent or more of many elite colleges' enrollment has already been, and will going forward be, accounted for by early decision. The *Washington Post* reported that by 2015, 48 of *US News'* 60 highest-ranked colleges took at least one-third of their applicants via the early decision route. Roughly half of new freshmen at Northwestern, Emory, Tufts, Vanderbilt, Davidson, Bowdoin, Swarthmore and Claremont McKenna were early decision winners, among a total of 37 high-ranking colleges where early decision accounted for at least 40 percent of entry enrollment. (Anderson March 16, 2016) Frank Bruni reported in December that same year that early decision would account for 47 percent of the class of 2021 at Williams College, a perennial "number one" ranked *US News* liberal arts school. (Bruni December 25, 2016) In 2018, Northwestern disclosed that *over* 50 percent of its freshmen enrollment would come through early decision.

As a direct consequence of the shift toward higher and higher percentages of admissions captured by early decision candidates, those left in the regular application pile or turned down for early decision automatically find their odds of admission significantly reduced. Given the preference the most elite colleges are giving to early decision applicants, even the very low published odds of admission at those schools are ridiculously overstated. If an elite school with a strong yield record to begin with is now taking up to 50 percent or more of its enrollment on early decision, the published 5 to 10 percent selectivity number is more likely much closer to 2.5 to 5 percent for the regular cycle applicants (unless they are legacies or donors' children, who further reduce the chances of everybody else). In terms of the elite college business model, however, admissions directors can see that the early decision process works well for them and relieves their anxieties!

Another major — perhaps *the* major — benefit of the early decision process for elite schools is that the applicants best positioned to compete for early decision are likely to be from relatively wealthy families. They can afford to pursue the highest level of demonstrated interest (now a high-ranking admissions criterion at most elite colleges, as discussed in chapter 4) by visiting multiple campuses, attending summer programs, and meeting key admissions personnel via in-person, on-location interviews. They can afford private counseling and tutoring to boost their understanding of what their number-one preferred college requires to meet its early decision threshold.

Most importantly, applicants from wealthy families can take the risk of giving up most of their bargaining power when it comes to financial aid packages (for which they would not qualify anyway) Admissions deans likewise need not worry that rich early decision students will try to renege on their commitments to accept because their financial aid package did not meet their "need." (At most there might be some pressure for a "merit aid" grant.)   Frank Bruni pointed that early decision "significantly disadvantages students from low-income and middle-income families...already underrepresented" at elite colleges. "There's plenty of evidence that applying early improves odds of admission and that students who do so — largely to gain competitive advantage — come disproportionately from privileged backgrounds with parents and counselors who know how to game the system and can assemble the necessary tests scores and references by the November deadline." (Ibid.)

Applicants from lower-income and even middle-class families will also be far less able to afford the most direct forms of demonstrated interest like on-campus visits and interviews, which would help secure an early decision admission and also help them decide in advance on their fit with a one and only first-choice college. An online or virtual tour might help them show the level of interest necessary to even be considered for early admission, but will not convey the certain sense of personal fit that would justify putting all their admissions eggs in only one basket (from which they cannot escape if they do come in first in the early admissions race, but have second thoughts or are offered only third-rate financial aid). Moreover, in many school districts across the country affected by poverty, nearly a majority of children in high school lack computers in their home, if they have a home other than a car or a homeless shelter. Applicants in these circumstances will have to seek out online time at a public library or school computer facilities to virtually document their "demonstrate interest." Even if they were to somehow win early admission, they cannot risk being put in a "take-it-or-leave-it" situation when it comes to financial aid. But the wealthy can — because for them the risk of having to pay more is well worth it.

It is no surprise given the rising attractiveness of early decision in terms of scoring coveted elite college admissions that the sheer number of such applications has surged. The *Washington Post* reported that early decisions applications for fall 2019 entry accounted for over 60 percent of the total college applications for the entire year, and up 17 percent from the previous year. Early decision application were up 35 percent at the University of Rochester, 39 percent at Rice, 17 percent at Notre Dame, 42 percent at NYU, and 21 percent at Brown. (Anderson January 7, 2019). Research by the Jack Kent Cooke Foundation, a leading advocate for more broader access to elite colleges, has shown that early decision programs do little to encourage students from lower-income families to apply for early decision because the required advance acceptance discouraged them from doing so.

The Cooke Foundation's "True Merit" report found that only 16 percent of high-achieving students from families with annual incomes below $50,000 applied for early decision, compared to 29 percent of high-achieving students from families earning over $250,000. As the late Harold Levy, executive director of the Foundation observed, "That's just unfair in a profound way" (Bruni ibid.) In a 2017 article published in *Inside Higher Ed,* Levy quoted a study by researchers at the University of Southern California that concluded "early decision in particular works as a sort of class-based affirmative action that gives wealthier applicants a 'plus' factor: a higher likelihood of being admitted than if they applied under the regular-decision deadline." (Levy 2017) And we know from the data cited above that the test score hurdle rates are indeed lower, and the admission rates are higher, for the early decision pool at most elite colleges.

There have been some instances when successful early decision applicants have been released from their advance obligations to accept and enroll because of unresolved disputes over financial aid packages, which are more likely to occur at the middle-class income level, which is being squeezed severely by rising college costs, outpacing both consumer-related inflation and salary growth. Moreover, some applicants from poor families, who can count on a need-blind policy or generous free-tuition benchmarks of over $100,000 in family income like Stanford, would have little to lose in applying for early decision there. In general, however, admissions offices with fewer financial aid resources than Stanford know that with early decision admissions, they are in the driver's seat with respect to any financial aid offers, either on a need-blind or merit aid basis, because those applicants will have no other financial aid offers as yet on the table before the typical thirty-day negotiating period expires, along with the admissions offer. They could not apply for early decision elsewhere, foregoing early admission and deferring any decision to the regular round puts them at a statistical disadvantage in terms of admissions odds. Even the *US News* website has conceded that experts say early admissions decisions "could come at a price of receiving less financial aid."

The Department of Education has attempted to mitigate this problem somewhat by advancing the timeline for submission of the famous Free Application for Federal Student Financial Aid (FAFSA) detailed forms required to qualify for federal student loans and grants and allowing such submissions to be based on family income tax data that is up to two years old. These changes are helping all applicants, both early and regular cycle, make their best cases for federal assistance before either type of admissions decision is on offer. But this reform is not enough to level the playing field for applicants from families that cannot afford to send them on campus visits or to take the risk that financial aid offered with an early admission will turn out to be insufficient.

Elite colleges can count on most early decision applicants being able to pay close to or right in line with full sticker price without substantial discounting. This fact also creates room for them to be more creative with their merit aid budgets to support other enrollment management purposes (including helping other rich or well-connected applicants). The elite college early decision admissions game has become primarily an upper-class intramural sport, and a very serious competitive game at that. Given the very high percentage of admissions and enrollment at elite colleges that early decision increasingly accounts for, James Fallows' conclusion nearly two decades ago that the most "glaring defect" of the early decisions programs is "how much they are biased toward privileged students" is even more accurate and relevant today. (Fallows 2001)

Many colleges in the upper ranks (and others just trying to keep pace with them) have recently added a second cycle of early decision in the December to January period. This enables them to get some comfort factors from knowing how close they have already come to hitting their desired test score and GPA average targets in the first round. In the second round, they will also know the first semester senior year grades of the applicants, which would be unavailable for the first early decision round. The second early decision cycle is often used especially for certain types of applicants colleges already want to accept for reasons not driven fundamentally by demonstrated academic excellence, such as legacies, donors' kids, or their own faculties' kids, as well as athletes or artists needed to fill out non-scholarship sports teams or performing arts programs. (Anderson January 7, 2019)

Elite colleges, including the Ivy League and others with similar reputations for selectivity, have also employed what amounts to a virtual third round of early decision through the use of so-called "likely letters" during the closing days of the regular admissions cycle. Before the date when admissions decisions will be announced officially, they send a few selected applicants a letter (or perhaps now an email or text) that tells them that they are highly likely to be admitted — while stating formally that this statement should not be considered a formal offer of admission! The intent is to freeze the applicant from accepting an admission offer that may come from a lesser competitor on an earlier date and induce a quick, advance commitment to accept — sort of an "early decision" late! (Springer, Reider, and Morgan 2013, 157-58) In that sense, the highly likely admissions letter is actually a collegiate take on the Wall Street leveraged buyout technique, in which a consortium of prestigious lenders give support to a potential buyout bid for a company by producing a letter indicating that they are "highly confident" that financing will be available to support the bid, and thereby seal the deal with the sellers. In the academic world, the ""likely letter is essentially a way of interjecting the "offer-you-can't-refuse" dramatics of the early decision process into the regular decision calendar — as if the entire admissions process was not already stressful enough.

A recent, even more pernicious, play on the early decision option involves literally transposing the concept of early decision into the regular decision calendar, with offers of cash prizes, preferred dormitory reservations, and enhanced scholarships to students willing to accept a "regular" admissions offer even months before the traditional May 1 deadline. This particular high-pressure sales tactic is designed to "take the customer off the market asap." It emerged in 2019 right after the Department of Justice raised questions about the "anti-competitive" effects of several provisions of the voluntary admissions practices code promulgated by the National Association for College Admission Counseling. NACAC deleted sections of the code that might be construed to ban this new "early closing" practice, and suspended policing of the entire code for good measure! Although most colleges did not adopt exactly this route to entice "early-regular" acceptances, the crunch of competition in the face of enrollment declines especially at tuition-dependent colleges (more fully considered in chapter 6) led some admissions offices to push the recruiting envelope with even boulder enrollment incentive, which included literally poaching students after they had already made deposits accepting competing offers, and cold-calling *already-enrolled* students at other colleges who had not contacted them about transferring. (Hoover February 11, 2020)

Unfortunately, we can expect broader use of these high-pressured tactics in the wake of the COVID-19 pandemic as colleges endeavor to counter expected enrollment shortfalls.

For most high school students and their families, the "likely letters" as well as multiple rounds of quasi-early decision drama turn out to be just more examples of exploitation of student stress for the benefit of the colleges' rankings and revenues, rather than an easy way to escape the multi-month anxiety of the regular admissions calendar. A similar form of pressure has been introduced whereby the admissions offices of elite colleges invite selected students who have applied under the regular calendar to switch their apps to early decision status (with, of course, the required commitment to accept the offer if it comes).

The *Wall Street Journal* reported in early 2019 how selective colleges including Tufts, Tulane, and Colorado College, were hopping on what the Colorado school's vice president for enrollment called this "runaway train" admissions practice. But, at Tulane, for example, only 95 of the 625 who switched actually got in via early decision. One high school guidance counselor spoke for many when she told the *Journal* that the colleges, in "nudging" (the *Journal's* headline word) students to decide early in this way, were tapping into the students' vulnerabilities to benefit themselves with better acceptance rates and yields. (Belkin 2019)

Pushed to justify the pressures on students unique to the early decision process, elite college leaders fall back on the argument that it is an important way to enhance school spirit because it is the ,most effective way to isolate the applicants who really want to be there. But we have seen this is just another way of saying that early decision allows the college to make a large number (even over 50 percent of targeted enrollment) of zero-risk (to the college) admissions offers that produce a baseline 100 percent yield. Admissions officials know it takes a lot of money and resources for an applicant's family to be able to make such an important choice on a fully informed basis in advance of seeing all the cards on the admissions table. Early decision shamefully uses student anxiety about the lengthy, opaque, and unpredictable overall admissions process that elite colleges have taken the lead in designing as leverage to get wealthy applicants to do whatever it takes to gain an early decision and underwrite the colleges' yield targets and advance their rankings. Early decision, with few exceptions, turns out to be a win-win for the elite colleges and the most affluent, at the expense of everybody else. It defies all logic and experience to believe that result is mere happenstance.

All colleges have the option of providing a form of the alternative early action protocol and provide a decision — not binding on the applicant but binding on the college — in December, which would accomplish the stated (and worthy) goal of reducing student stress, while leaving applicants in the position to apply elsewhere and still have the flexibility to defer their decision on acceptance until May. Georgetown, certainly an elite university, forgoes offering early decision but does offer "early action" whereby the applicant can request and receive an offer by January but has until the end of the regular admissions cycle in early May to decide whether to accept. Under early action, the applicant also need not withdraw any other pending applications. Most schools do not limit early action applications to one school or any particular number. Georgetown and other colleges using early action approach have thus given themselves several extra months in which to inform and sell their early admits on the benefits of enrolling at their campuses, and to arrive at a mutually satisfactory, bargained-for financial aid arrangement. That seems like a more generally balanced win-win for students of all economic and social classes. It does not reflect the clear restraint-of-trade aspects of the early decision format r that that forbids a student from applying early elsewhere. Perhaps there should be a federal agency focused on the college admissions process and empowered to examine critically why colleges can get away with such market-fixing collusion to the clear detriment of most of their consumers.

What might a wise and powerful federal College Admissions Commission require to preserve the benefits of early decision for those who are genuinely able to make an early, informed and un-coerced decision, and also enable those students to exercise the bargaining power their capabilities should command? Indeed, federal trade remedies might well be considered because, in driving the current structure for and emphasis on early decision applications, the elite colleges are acting as an oligopolistic group that has conspired to impose an inherently coercive restraint of trade in the admissions market, which is also highly prejudicial to a broad sector of potential consumers.

What if early decision applications were not limited coercively to a one-to-a-customer opportunity that must be accepted in advance? Could elite colleges not live with a hybrid in which applicants would be permitted to select up to four colleges and would have to decide among them (or reject them all) within a one-month period following any offer or offers? This would leave time for campus visits perhaps during school breaks, quite possibly subsidized by the colleges that have offered early decision to the chosen applicants because they represent the college's "first choices." Compliance with such a limit could be monitored and enforced by a confidential and neutral technological means, which would not share the students' full list of choices with the colleges concerned. In that scenario, even students with limited resources could, with a reasonable amount of work, choose among up to four favorites in exchange for the privilege of early resolution of their admissions quest, and colleges would get some early indication of their yield prospects before they make regular cycle offers.

Perhaps applicants could even apply to four Ivies — they have highly-sophisticated admissions departments and could handle "early" competitive situations just as they do in the regular cycle. Or applicants for modified early decision might go with four very diverse campus types: one Ivy, one Little Ivy, one home-state school, and one "college that changes lives." The schools would be precluded from sharing information about who is applying for early decision because there would be no need for them to police cheating on a "one-and-only-one" early application limitation — technology would handle enforcement of the overall limit.

In such a system, it would be a safe bet that the colleges would each put their best financial aid offer on the table up front, and applicants could compare and reflect before making a final choice about where they "really, really" want to go. In a competitive market for the best students under such a modified early admissions, decisions by even the elite colleges might actually become more about merit than money. It would also be likely that the percentage that early decision winners constitute of total enrollment in their class will trend down, leaving more room for regular cycle applicants to compete successfully.

The alternative to such a hybrid process, and perhaps the only effective way to reform an early decision process so skewed to the interests of the colleges versus the students, would be to eliminate all its coercive elements. This would require an outright prohibition on the wealth-favoring requirement of an advance commitment to accept an early decision offer, and the related limitation of one such application per student. Essentially, this would mean that any early application process would be limited to a form of non-binding early action option, with a possible restriction on the number of such applications a student could submit in order to provide colleges with more flexibility in evaluating applications over a reasonable period of time and encourage students to give some indication of their priority interests without limiting them to just one choice. Schools would no longer be able to use the early application process to attract wealthy families that can pay the full tuition "sticker price," underwrite their yield targets, lower their reported admission rates and enhance their *US News* rankings. So what? A semblance of real balance would be established in the "market" for admissions between the elite colleges and high school students, especially in respect to applicants from disadvantaged backgrounds. And wealthier applicants could not complain of discrimination either, as all applications, no matter their timing on the cycle would be subject to the same standards with no preferences for those who can afford to make an early decision themselves before they know the terms of the offer.

Eliminating the wealth-biased preference for such early deciders, however, would not address other major and secretive admission preferences that favor the wealthy and well-connected — including the controversial legacy and donor-related admissions that, like early decision, materially reduce the odds of admission for everyone else not so "well-born."

Legacy Admissions: a Semi-Secret Golden Handshake for the Wealthy and Well-Connected

Legacy admissions preferences are a distinctly American practice among the developed world's prestigious universities. Oxford and Cambridge gave them up decades ago. (Reeves June 10, 2016) In both France and Germany, admission is exclusively by exam in public institution — only 1 percent of students in western Europe attend private colleges except in formerly Communist states, where a much larger percentage attend private schools that basically accept all applicants. No direct legacy preferences exist in Japan, although there is a university pipeline from affiliated high schools. (Golden, in Kahlenberg, ed, 2010, 84-85) And it would be illegal in Japan and France to try to buy a university admission with a donation. (Morrison 2019)

In the U.S., however, legacies remain a gift that keeps on giving to our elite higher education institutions, as well as to the families of their graduates who have done well — the chief defense ofegacy admissions has been that they are needed to meet college fundraising goals! Nearly all elite liberal arts colleges and three-quarters of selective research universities have practiced some degree of legacy favoritism. Writing for the Atlantic magazine, Richard D. Kahlenburg reported that the Century Foundation (where he is a senior fellow) had determined that about 75 percent of the *US News'* top 100 universities provide admission preferences for relatives of alumni. (Kahlenberg 2018) Daniel Golden's 2006 book, *The Price of Admission: How America's Ruling Class Buys Its Way into Elite College — and Who Gets Left Outside the Gates*, included an entire chapter on legacy preferences, and argued persuasively (but so far unsuccessfully) for their elimination because of their socio-economic effects. (Golden 2006, 118-44, 291-93)

Unfortunately, we do not know comprehensive numbers or the full impact of legacy admissions on elite college enrollment profiles for sure because admissions offices generally keep legacy admissions statistics confidential. There have been leaks and disclosures in litigation and media investigations, however, that have suggested the general pattern. Of the colleges and universities with the 25 largest endowments as of 2019, fewer than half provide public data on the proportion of legacies in their undergraduate enrollments. Available data has shown, for example, that religiously affiliated schools have long been at the forefront of legacy admissions. (Golden 2006, 75) Notre Dame tops a list of known legacy admissions leaders among universities with the twenty-five largest endowments tracked by *Bloomberg* in 2019, with 22 percent of its class of 2022 admitted as legacies. Some other religious colleges outside that leading endowment group admit even more legacies — for example, Baylor, with 35 percent. (Kochkodin 2019)

Writing in *Affirmative Action for the Rich*, Daniel Golden provided extensive research data on how legacies' chances for admission in the Ivy League and other top-ranked colleges was two to five times greater than for non-legacy applicants — with acceptance rates as high as 30 to 40 percent or more among Ivy League schools whose overall admission rates were in single digits or the teens. He also estimated that 10 to 25 percent of Ivy League enrollment was made up of children of alumni. (Golden, in Kahlenberg, ed. 2010, 73-76)

More recent research has shown that at Harvard, the percentage of the class of 2021 accounted for by legacies of any alumni relative was 29.3 percent, and of parents only was 18.3 percent. For 2022, children of alumni parents were 14 percent of the entering class and also accounted for 40 percent of freshmen with household incomes of $500,000 or more. For the class of 2022, in the *Bloomberg* data, Princeton's was 16 percent children of alumni, and Yale's was 11 percent legacy affiliation. Cornell's 2022 class included 22.1 percent children of parent or grandparent alumni, the University of North Carolina's included 18 percent children of alumni, and USC's 2022 class was 16 percent "scions." For its class of 2021, the University of Chicago's enrollment included 19.7 percent who are children of alumni family members. At the University of Virginia, legacies constitute 15 percent of the class of 2022 although they account for only 5 percent of all applications. The *Daily Cavalier* reported that 47 percent of legacy applicants received an offer for the class of 2022, compared to 25 percent of all other applicants. (Kochkodin ibid.)

Middlebury College is a rare example of an elite school that proudly discloses its legacy admissions rate, nearly 50 percent in recent years. Middlebury is also among those elite colleges found to have enrolled more students from the top 1 percent than the bottom 60. (McClay 2017) Bowdoin College, which has an overall admissions rate in the high teens similar to Middlebury's, also maintains an admissions *rate* for legacy applicants of around 40 percent. Princeton's entering class ran between 11 and 15 percent legacies for over a quarter century, according to its admissions dean, as reported in a *Town & Country* magazine interview in 2016. On the other hand, the admissions office at the University of Pennsylvania asserted to *T&C* that it would give advantage to only those legacy candidates who apply via early decisions, in order to validate in the clearest possible way their intent to enroll and not just collect another admissions ticket (in this case, based on their ancestry). *T&C* also reported that legacies had accounted for one in ten entering students at Georgetown, with legacy applicants admitted at a 30 percent rate there, compared to an overall rate of less than 20 percent. More broadly, *T&C* cited elite college practices to recruit children of alumni with special legacy luncheons, application workshops and early dorm move-in arrangements. (Golden November 21, 2016)

Some elite colleges have directly advertised a general preference for legacy applicants. On its alumni website, Duke University has asserted that "special consideration" will be given to legacy applicants, including a second round of review by the admissions staff and perhaps even the admissions dean before final decisions are made. And Columbia University has disclosed on its admissions website that legacies will have a "slight advantage" if they are "extremely competitive," while Harvard's site says applicants whose parents attended Harvard could get "an additional look…among similarly distinguished applicants." (Korn July 9, 2018)

As in the case of early decision applicants, elite colleges' preferences for legacy applicants provide them a leg up in dealing with those schools' criteria in terms of demonstrated academic prowess. Research by Thomas Epenshade of Princeton has estimated that the legacy preference delivers the equivalent of an additional 160 points on an SAT score. (O'Shaughnessy 2012, 108) Put another way, for a given SAT score range, being a legacy could increase the chances of admission by 20 to 45 percent. Legacy status can also provide a level of exemption from the secret algorithms that determine which applications will make it past the first direct screening cuts for review of such matters as recommendations, essays and extracurricular activities. The admissions director at Amherst, quoted in *The Price of Admission,* told an audience of alumni that the college had admitted 50 percent of alumni children over a fifteen-year period, compared to 20 percent of all applicants. In the case of students with a 2 rating (signifying a challenging high school course load and scoring in the 1400s on their SATs), Amherst admitted 100 percent of legacies but only 40 percent of such applicants overall. She also revealed that, despite the general Amherst policy not to interview applicants as part of their evaluation process, admissions officials would always be available for informal conversations with graduates' children. (Golden 2006, 288)

Michael Hurwitz of the College Board and the National Bureau of Economic Research found in his 2011 study of legacy impact on admissions at thirty selective colleges that legacies were roughly three times as likely to be admitted as non-legacy students with similar backgrounds, even if they had submitted scores at the lower end of what those colleges accept in terms of test scores. Hurwitz concluded that the consistent advantage of legacy applicants, regardless of their academic background, "strongly contradicts the widely held notion that legacy status [merely] serves as tip factor." (Jia 2918) He was certainly right in the case of Harvard, where legacy applicants from 2010 through 2015 were admitted at five times the rate of non-legacy applicants. (Korn July 9, 2018)

The Harvard admissions dean has asserted that the legacy preference comes down to an "ever so slight tip" toward the end of the process — a tip that the dean himself participates in triggering by reading personally every single legacy application each year. As a former Harvard official described the process in Daniel Golden's *The Price of Admissions*, "It comes down to the last day and you have twenty tickets still to give. You're tipping people in and out. It's not over till it's over." Golden concluded that it was more likely that a "hooked" applicant, such as a legacy, would likely get the nod. (Golden 2006, 35) Legacy status matters especially at the end of the admissions review process, when it comes down to a final choice between two applicants from the same high school or with otherwise similar qualifications, when the legacy may have a lower set of test scores but win admission.

A former Princeton admissions officer estimated in a letter published in the *New York Times* that, although all the legacies he saw were fully capable of succeeding at a demanding college, 5 to 10 percent of the admitted students were legacies who would not otherwise have been admitted. According to this official, the legacy pool has been and remains "overwhelmingly white" and will remain so "until the race and ethnicity of college graduates more accurately reflect those of the overall population." (Rawls 2017) But when the dean of Harvard College was asked by a lawyer for the plaintiffs in the discrimination lawsuit what is "'so special about wealthy people that Harvard needs to have them overrepresented by a factor of six,'" he replied that the question was missing the point and asserted his school is "'not trying to mirror the socioeconomic or income distribution of the United States.'" (Ryan 2018) But as seen in Raj Chetty's "Mobility Report Cards" cited in chapter 2, the extent of family income disparity among students at selective colleges often looks like what can be observed among households in an average America city!

The special "Z-list" at Harvard's admissions office referred to in previous chapters — kept close to the vest until exposed in the discrimination trial — serves as a last-chance option for legacies. It was so named by the admissions IT staff because it consists of the very last round of admits. All admissions on the Z-list are on a deferred basis. (Reeves 2017, 112-13; Zauzmer 2010) Harvard is not the only elite college to strategically award deferred admissions to a selected few, regardless of what the list of such admits is called. Although Harvard was forced to be concede that its Z-list exits existence, its response to inquiries about who exactly gets on it and why during the Asian-American discrimination litigation was evasive. One admissions official described it as just a bunch of names and said that a lot of work would be needed to unearth more data on the list's composition The dean of admissions initially called it a list relating to persons with greater dedication to Harvard. But over the years, the *Harvard Crimson* has revealed that the names on the Z-list are mostly white and legacy applicants who graduated from elite private high schools and whose families are too rich to qualify for financial aid. The *Crimson* characterized the Z-list as an important Harvard recruiting tool that one admissions consultant called an "early early admissions" list – but for the following academic year! (Brown 2014)

Document discovery during the Asian American discrimination lawsuit revealed that there were an estimated 50-60 names on the z-list from 2014 through 2019 that were mostly white legacies or also on special interest lists kept by the admissions department. (Hartocollis, Harmon and Smith 2018) A study released after the trial by a team of researchers including an expert witness for the Harvard case plaintiffs, Peter Arcidiacono, further disclosed that over six admissions cycles, 46.5 percent of z-list students were legacies, and 58.8 percent of those on that list were also on the separate "deans' interest list" that often contained the names of relatives of major past and potential donors. Also, 70 percent of the z-list admissions were white, and first generation students accounted for only 1.8 percent of the list. (Golden July 11, 2018)

There has been speculation that a good number of those who gain deferred admission via the z-list fall below Harvard's standard academic benchmarks and need a bit more maturing to handle the workload. (Golden ibid). Another theory is that the list serves as a way to handle sensitivities of important alumni parents who would otherwise have to bear the "shame" of their offspring not gaining admission and retaliate by halting donations — while the admission office quietly hopes that the applicant will accept immediate admission to another college rather than wait around a year or more. (Kester 2012, 80) The deferred legacy applicants who accept the wait, of course, take up places in the next year's entering class, creating a *legacy double-dip* that further reduces the number of seats for other current-year applicants. (Reeves 2017, 112)

Of course, not all legacy applicants at Harvard or other elite colleges are ultimately admitted even on a deferred basis despite their statistical advantage over what professional bettors would call "the field." Nor are all legacy applicants unqualified for admission to elite schools; many no doubt would be strong candidates for admission without such status. Having college-educated parents from any school is a documented asset in terms of a student's admissions chances, if only because of the likelihood of a more sophisticated vocabulary at home, more support for doing well in high school, and a parental commitment to do whatever it takes to attain a desired college admission. Legacies are also more likely to have the benefit of private high schools, tutors and professional test preparation courses that will result in higher ACT and SAT test scores. The enduring practice of special consideration for legacy applicants unquestionably places yet another barrier in the path of children who do not enjoy the advantage of a college-oriented upbringing. As Richard Kahlenburg, quoted by Eric Hoover of the *Chronicle of Higher Education*, put it: "'The system is rigged against disadvantaged students, and legacy preferences are the most blatant example.'" (Hoover August 7, 2017)

Preferential treatment of legacy applications clearly outweighs any general commitment to increasing diversity of enrollment. William Bowen, former president of Princeton, as quoted by in *The Price of Admissions*, concluded that legacies "serve to reproduce the high-income/high-educational/white profile that is characteristic" of elite colleges. (Golden 2006, 121) Moreover, applicants who would be first-generation collegians obviously have no chance whatsoever to take advantage of legacy preferences at any college. Sadly, the zeal (and efficacy) of admissions offices in catering to legacies is hardly matched by their often stated but usually unmet goals of attracting more enrollment from "first-generation" college applicants as well as from historically disadvantaged racial and economic groups.

The legacy privilege has deep roots in terms of discrimination against economic have-nots seeking upward social mobility in order to preserve the status of the incumbent elites. In private colleges in the U.S., an official, reserved pathway for legacy admissions began to take shape in the early part of the twentieth century. Before that, as chronicled by Peter Schmidt in *Affirmative Action for the Rich*, most private colleges were private, enrolled only one hundred or fewer students at a time, and served mostly local communities. They relied heavily on tuition, and thus rarely turned away any applicant with enough money who met their general admissions criteria, which were clearly spelled out publicly. (Wouldn't that be refreshing today?) Many private colleges had set up relationships with feeder high schools that "prepped" students for those admissions requirements. Sometimes those who performed poorly in high school were admitted conditionally, as long as they could keep up with the college coursework.

The working-class youth of the first half of the nineteenth century could neither afford private college tuition nor attend public high schools offering the courses required to qualify for admission to them. The need for a more educated populace as industrialization expanded from midcentury onward, however, led to creation of land-grant public colleges in many states. These new institutions took as many applicants as they could fit in, even those with minimal academic qualifications, training their charges in engineering and, of course, agriculture. These were not the usual occupations of the elite, who could afford to gravitate toward the convenience and social familiarity of the likes of Harvard, which saw its role as educating old-money offspring because, as its president put it, "'The country suffers when the rich are ignorant and unrefined.'" (Schmidt, in Kahlenberg, ed. 2010, 37)

Most of the wealthy students pursued their refinement at schools we would now recognize as the Ivy League or Little Ivies. Those schools' admission standards, however, were not nearly as tough as they are today. Growing demand in the economy for college graduates in the early twentieth century did not yet translate to more rigorous admissions. Schools like Princeton were proud to focus on developing character and providing their students a country club learning environment. In that social environment, a legacy admission at the turn of the century was more or less taken for granted at elite colleges -- no special procedures had to be implemented for what was a socially expected outcome.

Frustrated by the poor academic performance of students admitted under standards that were modest at best, however, elite colleges did begin (for the sake of their academic reputations) to adjust their admissions and academic performance standards in the early decades of the twentieth century. While de-emphasizing high school subject requirements like Greek and Latin, they started to apply more rigorous tests of aptitude before granting admissions. At the same time, however, immigrant families fleeing European oppression, disease, and conflict were migrating in large numbers to the United States. They brought with them a strong cultural attachment to the value of higher education, and intellectual qualities and determination to advance that served them well in gaining admission under the elite colleges' new, tighter standards. (Schmidt ibid., 38-43)

Many of these newly successful applicants were Jewish, however, and as their enrollments rose in elite schools, a wave of anti-Semitism fed alarm about these schools' ability to hold on to their upper-class enrollees. So many Jews, Catholics, and other immigrants were winning enrollment that lesser-qualified well-to-do students had to be turned away, including legacies. (Brittain and Bloom, in Kahlenberg, ed. 2010, 136-37) Dartmouth was the first of the Ivies to adopt an overall admissions strategy and policy that specifically codified a special preference for the sons of Dartmouth alumni and officers. Dartmouth's action was evidently not motivated by anti-Semitism, but similar practices in the rest of the Ivy League that followed suit almost certainly were. After the first World War, the practice of favoring legacy admissions at elite colleges changed from being a routine occurrence based merely on tradition from the Gilded Age to an intentionally designed form of specific discrimination against children from immigrant cultures, especially those from Jewish households. (Schmidt ibid., 40-42)

The overtly anti-Semitic spell associated with legacy admissions was broken for a time in a wave of revulsion against mistreatment of Jews after World War II. With the GI bill democratizing college affordability, the rise of standardized college entrance exams and the related increase in demand for expanded enrollments, pressures to keep alumni of elite colleges happy (and donating) led to a renewed focus on legacy preferences as a way to get the children of rich alumni in the door even if their test scores were not up to snuff. Heading into the 1970s, moreover, as prestigious all-male private colleges turned co-ed, the number of potential legacy admissions obviously increased in line with the female birth rate among their graduates. (Schmidt ibid., 40-53)

A focus on legacy preferences among public research universities, on the other hand, came much later in the twentieth century as a result of the gradual decline in taxpayer support for higher education that began in the 1970s, exacerbated by a series of recessions. Flagship state universities initiated huge fundraising efforts to keep tuition increases within some sort of bounds, focusing on large alumni donations deemed crucial to support institutional quality and reputation. In that connection, legacy preferences, as the University of Virginia's president stated, were initiated specifically to help assure continuing alumni financial and committee service support in light of "very deep budget cuts from the state." (Schmidt ibid., 56) Does this sound something like a *quid pro quo*? (More on this matter later under the heading of tax exemptions for admissions-related donations.)

The establishment of a specific *hereditary* privilege for access to a state college or university is troubling in view of the Founding Fathers' documented constitutional disdain for inherited status of any official kind. Yet America is distinctive in the developed and "democratic" world in its tolerance, and indirect subsidization by its tax policy, for legacy admissions preferences in state-funded higher education institutions.

America is also a distinctively litigious society, however, and legal arguments have been advanced that the hereditary aspect of legacy preferences (at least in state-funded colleges) runs afoul of the provisions of Article 1 of the Constitution that expressly forbids both the United States and any state from granting "any Title of Nobility." Some proponents of interpreting the "original-meaning" of the Constitution's language have argued that this provision should not be understood as applying merely to classic English-style titles of nobility. Carlton F. W. Larson, writing in *Affirmative Action for the Rich*, concluded based in his research into the contemporary meaning of the "nobility clause" that legacy preferences at elite public universities could constitute precisely the type of hereditary privileges that the Revolutionary War generation wanted to eliminate. Larson cited statements to this effect by George Washington, Thomas Jefferson, Samuel and John Adams, Thomas Paine, and others opposing state-sanctioned hereditary privileges of any kind, including even granting state legislative recognition to a *private* war veterans group (the Society of the Cincinnati) that passed down membership to their first-born sons. (Larson, in Kahlenberg, ed. 2010, 146-61) It has also been argued that legacy admissions violate the equal protection of the laws owed by states to all persons under the Fourteenth Amendment, as well as the Civil Rights Act of 1866. (Shadowen and Tulante, in Kahlenberg, ed. 2010, 173-98) No court ruling to date, however, has endorsed any of these Constitutional arguments against legacy admissions.

In the absence of any effective Constitutional or other legal challenges to the legacy privilege, Senator Edward Kennedy of Massachusetts introduced an amendment to the Higher Education Act in 2004 that would have required colleges to disclose annually what percentages of their entering classes were legacies, or had benefitted from early decision. He took this step in the context of Republican colleagues' interest in providing friend-of-the-court briefs in support of litigation seeking to invalidate affirmative action related to racial diversity in state-funded universities. Members of his staff wanted him to go much further and propose banning legacies, which a poll by the *Chronicle of Higher Education* found were opposed by 75 percent of Americans. (Golden 2006, 245-50; Selingo 2004)

Influential college and university leaders and associations, including the American Council on Education, lobbied vociferously against Kennedy's proposal, however, arguing that such action would seriously jeopardize higher education funding overall. Their intervention weakened support for Kennedy's proposal even among Democrats. Moreover, the 2003 Supreme Court decision in *Grutter v. Bollinger* affirming the constitutionality of very limited race-conscious admission policies at the University of Michigan's Law School had for the time being obviated the argument that if race-based admissions for minorities were held constitutionally illegitimate, legacy preferences should be also. (Schmidt, ibid., 65-66) In March 2006, the House of Representatives killed (by a 337 to 83 vote) a proposal to require colleges to disclose just the *number* of legacy admissions. (Golden 2006, 258)

As the issue of race-conscious admissions policy is coming under renewed scrutiny in cases like the Asian discrimination lawsuit against Harvard, and with a more solidly conservative Supreme Court pursuant to President Trump's successful nominations perhaps more hostile to affirmative action, it may be that legacy admissions will face renewed legal and political attack, and just not by progressives. Advocates for banning legacy admissions as being as constitutionally suspect as any ethnic- or race-based considerations might even be tempted to cite the dissent of Justice Clarence Thomas in *Grutter v. Bollinger*, where he suggested that the court majority had preserved racially focused affirmative action primarily to defend against attacks on legacies or other forms of admission not driven by merit. Thomas opined that such a possibility was "'not lost, I am certain, on the elites (both individual and institutional) supporting the Law School in this case.'" Thomas, however, made clear that he would "'not twist the Constitution'" in order to invalidate legacy preferences or otherwise impose his personal views of higher education admissions. (Schmidt ibid., 66; Golden ibid., 255)

Admissions officers and other elite college leaders sometimes argue that constitutionally-based property and freedom-of-association rights allow private schools to establish distinctive campus cultures and their own particular versions of diversity. Private colleges also assert that analogies to legacy privilege can be found in the practice of state universities that still admit primarily residents of their home states with material tuition discounts, compared to the admission rates for, and tuition paid by, out-of-state students. But this so-called analogy ignores the fundamental fact that in-state students get these breaks because their parents are *taxpayers* (and voters) in that state, not necessarily state college alumni or donors. Some advocates of legacy admissions have gone further by questioning the very idea that there should be an element of fairness or merit when it comes to college admissions outcomes. An official at Rice University argued in asserting the property rights rationale that "'objective merit and fairness are attractive concepts with no basis in reality,'" but Richard Reeves, in his recent book *Opportunity Hoarding*, responded that if fairness is merely an attractive concept, "anything goes." (Reeves 2017, 97) Rice also asserted that decisions about the potential of applicants are essentially an art, not a science — and that *fair* has "'no meaning in art...We should strive to describe our admissions processes as what they are; not fair, but rational.'" (Sachs, in Kahlenburg, ed. 2010, 217)

What is "rational" in relation to admissions policy, however, seems at bottom to be all about the money. As elite colleges have become big business enterprise — including billion-dollar TV sports and sports equipment contracts, lucrative commercialized research and rental income for summer programs, as well as billions in endowment capital. They have reframed the funding-dependence argument with respect to legacies in terms of the well-recognized corporate goal of good customer relationship management. They have been motivated to take this approach by their emphasis on strategic *enrollment* management, tuition pricing efficiency, and sustainable fundraising. These matters are among the concerns of private agencies that rate the relative quality and security of colleges' public debt securities. Their published ratings materially affect the schools' abilities to borrow money and the cost of doing so in the ordinary course of running their businesses: a poor (junk) rating has often threatened the viability of higher education institutions. As we shall see in chapter 6, this is becoming a much more frequent occurrence for colleges that have not achieved or maintained elite status. Rating agencies are equivalent in importance to the *US News* in elite college CFO offices and boardrooms.

With tuition reaching astronomical levels but nonetheless covering only a small fraction of the cost of running college, their leaders argue that finding enough funding to service debt and continue growth increasingly depends on the parents of the newly and gratefully enrolled, and on their graduates when they come into their own advantaged fortunes. Apart from government or private research contracts and non-educational (and therefore potentially taxed) income lines, colleges assert that their financial destinies depend also on attracting donors who are intent on leaving their mark on society (and earning valuable tax deductions in the process). Welcome to the world of the university "advancement" or "development" office -- and their close working relationships with the college admissions office. To such college fundraising officials, legacy (and donor-related) admissions are the low-hanging fruit.

College admissions, advancement and development offices are well aware that post-secondary degrees in the family are a significant economic differentiating factor — indeed, probably the most significant factor except for inherited family wealth in terms of realized lifetime income and wealth. Although all legacy candidates are not necessarily wealthy, the odds are clearly in favor of the colleges' bottom lines when they cultivate this category with special consideration for admission. Other factors they cite in defending legacy preferences, such as enhancement of school spirit and class social cohesion, are considered to have a positive effect on long-term endowment funding strategies, based on the perception that fond memories of campus life (which graduates want their children also to enjoy) will contribute to more giving to their *alma maters.*

Yet it is far from clear that legacy admissions have a material positive effect on giving levels even at the most elite colleges, despite their insistence that sustaining school funding is the main reason for legacy preferences. Several studies in recent years have found little evidence that there is such a connection. Chad Coffman and his co-authors "Empirical Analysis of the Impact of Legacy Preferences on Alumni Giving at Top Universities" in *Affirmative Action for the Rich,* found "no statistically significant evidence of a causal relationship" between such policies and total alumni giving to the top 100 universities as determined by *US News,* after controlling for various factors including a proxy for alumni wealth. However, they also found that, prior to controlling for wealth, schools with legacy preference policies experienced higher alumni giving, suggesting that legacy admissions preferences allow their admissions departments to "over-select from their own wealthy alumni" and thereby "discriminate based on socioeconomic status...rather than basing admissions on merit alone." (Coffman, O'Neil, and Starr, in Kahlenberg, ed. 2010, 101-02) Students at institutions that do not give special preferences to legacies qualified for 70 percent more government aid than those at colleges with legacy preferences. (Ibid., 111)

Coffman's research team surmised that the reason colleges with legacy preferences tend to admit wealthier students overall is that they admit legacies disproportionately from the wealthiest alumni families. They also found that there was no "short-term measurable reduction in alumni giving" at several schools that had abolished legacy preferences. (Ibid., 115-16) The absence of legacy admission preferences has not hurt MIT or Caltech. Noting this fact, one alumnus of Vanderbilt, in a 2019 opinion piece on the *Inside Higher Ed* website, pledged a symbolic $5,000 donation to his alma mater if it would *end* legacy admissions! (Singh 2019) The decision by Johns Hopkins University to abandon legacy preferences triggered a 10-year period during which it more than doubled the percentage of their freshmen that were first-generation college students (15.1 versus 7.1percent). In that time there was an over 200 percent increase in African American, Hispanic, Native American, Native Alaskan and Pacific Islanders. (Gluckman 2020)

Although the assertion by admissions officials that legacies are necessary and desirable to keep endowment funds growing lacks substantial empirical support, that argument itself confirms that the intended purpose of that particular admissions hook is to serve the economic interests of elite colleges themselves because it favors applicants from families understood to be both loyal and wealthy. No less an authority on wealth and the economy than William Dudley, former Wall Street executive and president of the Federal Reserve Bank of New York, took on legacy preferences in a speech on the importance of higher education for economic mobility. Decrying the adverse effects of legacy preferences, Dudley asserted that scrapping such policies would be a positive step. "I really don't see how our best universities can continue to justify this practice….[D]o we really want to encourage what is essentially a 'donate to admit' policy at our major universities? Such an approach only preserves the status quo and constrains economic mobility." (Dudley 2017; see also Berman 2017)

Admissions personnel have expressed similar conclusions based on their own experience. In a 2017 essay in the *Chronicle of Higher Education*, Jason England, a former assistant admissions dean, wrote: "My three years in the admissions process made it depressingly clear that it exists chiefly to replicate the elite, privileged class of society...I often felt that I was less an evaluator than a rubber stamper for the children of the wealthy." Legacies, he concluded, are "the tip of the insidious iceberg." (England 2017)

The question of whether legacy preferences are just a modest tip in the final admissions rounds or, in reality, the tip of an iceberg of bias toward families of wealth finds its answer in the parallel emphasis by elite college admissions offices on cultivating candidates who are the children of major donors, celebrities, and public officials. Special admissions considerations for these students are not as significant in terms of numbers or percentage of overall admissions as the early decision and legacy preferences, but they are clearly the most obvious cases of intentional bias in favor of the wealthy and well connected.

Admitting the Donor Class — With an Assist from the IRS

As with legacies, there are no comprehensive annual statistics of donor- and connections-related admissions because colleges are not required (and do not offer) to disclose them, even to *US News*. There is, nonetheless, clear evidence that these admissions take precedence over merit, also reducing the stated admissions odds of other, more qualified applicants who don't have the benefit of this golden hook, regardless of how "rational" the donor lane is in terms of the colleges' business models and financial objectives. The authors of *Admission Matters* cogently summarized this practice:

> Many selective colleges have a small number of so-called development admits each year — students who would be

unlikely to be admitted were it not for their potential to bring significant donations to the college. The children of alumni who are major donors to a college get a double hook when they apply: as legacies and as development cases....

The development office may or may not be actively involved in recruiting such students, but they are certainly gracious and welcoming to these families. Once they apply, development prospects are usually flagged for special admissions consideration. (Springer, Reider, and Morgan 2013, 38)

There is no specific price point for development admits. Amounts involved vary from school to school, and colleges usually do not advertise this type of admissions in any event because of the risk of adverse publicity, especially after the publication of Daniel Golden's 2006 book *The Price of Admission.* Along with attacking legacy admissions, his book revealed that leaders of various elite schools with sterling academic reputations like Emory, Stanford, NYU, and others have acknowledged that they have given some form of special, systematic consideration to parental wealth in their admissions decisions. In terms of directly recruiting the children of the rich, Golden cited the example of Duke University's explicit (and successful) strategy during a capital campaign during the late 1990s stock market bubble of relaxing its admissions standards to bring in over a hundred applicants annually recommended by Duke's development office who would not have been accepted otherwise. More than half of those so admitted enrolled at Duke, amounting to up to 5 percent of its entering classes, and many of those children's parents then joined the fundraising campaign, which helped place Duke first among all universities in donations from non-alumni parents. (Golden 2006, 54-57) During periods of stock market declines as well, elite colleges also have the incentive to adjust admissions criteria for development cases in order to make up for market losses in their endowments. Admissions officials have even defended development admissions by arguing that providing an elite education to young persons who will someday inherit very substantial wealth is a socially desirable objective! Supposedly, an elite education will teach them to spend their fortunes more wisely. (Presumably, this would include becoming grateful donors to their school.)

The election of President Donald Trump in 2016 has brought renewed attention to development admissions practices. Three of Trump's children were admitted and enrolled at the Wharton School or the University of Pennsylvania as legacies (as well as obvious development cases). And his daughter Ivanka's husband, Jared Kushner, was admitted to Harvard despite a relatively modest high school and standardized test record in the admissions cycle coinciding with his wealthy real estate developer father Charles Kushner's $2.5 million gift to the university. Young Kushner's parents were subsequently recognized with membership to Harvard's Committee on University Resources, its elite donor leadership group. (Golden 2016)

More recent and even broader concern about the role of money in obtaining elite college admissions has emerged from the explosive March 12, 2019, federal bribery indictments. The charges implicated fifty well-to-do parents, the CEO of The Key (an admissions consulting firm), admission test administrative staff, and athletic coaches at some of the nation's most prestigious universities who took bribes to provide admission tickets for applicants with falsified SAT scores and fictitious athletic resumes. Bribes were disguised as legitimate contributions in support of university sports, and ranged from $200,000 to $6 million. In addition, substantial sums were allegedly paid to doctors for false certifications that applicants needed special accommodations for taking tests due to (non-existent) learning disabilities. (Medina, Benner, and Taylor 2019)

A few years earlier, complaints from regents at the University of Texas-Austin against its president alleging he had helped well-connected applicants gain admissions despite poor academic credentials triggered an investigation by the forensic security firm Kroll Associates. Kroll's 2015 report took note that university officials frequently faced immense pressure to favor certain applicants in the admissions process, and that "money and influence are always significant factors." Kroll likened the result to "affirmative action for the advantaged." Kroll found no explicit "inappropriate promise" or "quid pro quo" deal for admissions (and the president served out his term). The study by Kroll, however, also brought focus to the university's practice of using admission "holds" that prevented certain applicants from being rejected without notifying a dean or the president's office, identifying seventy-three such students who gained admission over five years with GPAs below 2.9 and combined SAT scores below 1100 (neither of which would be considered to match up with even the low end of elite college admissions standards). There was also some document shredding involved. Kroll concluded that since the president is expected to raise large amounts of money, some university officials therefore believe "that a factor that advances the interests of the university is fair game and can be taken into consideration when conducting a holistic review of a particular applicant." (Root and Najmabadi 2019)

UT Austin subsequently established new guidelines for how and when its president can override other administrators to admit applicants "who might not otherwise be admitted through the normal process." Regent Wallace Hall, however, called the new rule a "'joke'" lacking in transparency. "'Maintaining the 'black box' approach where nobody gets to know how we let people in is ridiculous...[and] almost always corrupt. The focus should be on transparent and objective admissions.'" (Ibid.)

Examples of high-level official interventions to admit scions of the wealthy and well connected abound. The 2015 Survey of College and University Admissions Directors reported that a quarter of all respondents said they had experienced pressure, including from university trustees, to admit applicants who were well-connected politically or otherwise. A *Chronicle of Higher Education* investigation in 2019 of emails from 13 public universities revealed routine incidents of presidents and trustees personally inquiring about the fates of individual applicants, on behalf of wealthy and well-connected families. (Stripling and Hoover 2015) Although some elite colleges assert they maintain informational firewalls between their development or advancement departments on the one hand and their admissions offices on the other, *The Price of Admission* concluded that "[i]n reality, there is no such wall — not even a trench." Referring to the increasing number of billionaires among the *Forbes* magazine's annual listings of the four hundred richest families, Daniel Golden observed that, in common with other nonprofits, "colleges want a piece of that action — and the easiest way is to admit these moguls' children." (Golden 2006, 55)

As a professor of education at the University of San Francisco explained to *Town & Country*, that means "'there's probably more pressure on admissions offices around legacies and development admits.'" A Notre Dame admissions officer also told *T&C* that people think that "'if they give a couple hundred thousand or a million they're big donors. That's just no longer the case at major universities.'" To justify the admissions tip to a child of wealth, the same official pointed out that a gift of $15 million could fund up to fifteen scholarships in terms of the expected 5 per cent returned from that capital each year so awarding these kids "'some special interest'" in terms of admissions would be OK, "'assuming the children were quite good.'" (Golden 2016)

Brown University's hometown *Providence Journal* reported in early 2019 that the university does a particularly good job of supporting their wealthy undergraduates with "invitation-only" semi-annual on-campus network events specifically for the children of prominent politicians, Fortune 500 executives, and financial moguls. These dinners are funded by a wealthy donor and, until publicized, logistically supported by Brown's advancement office, which emailed the invitation to dine with the dinner's sponsor. As one attendee explained, "'You either personally know…[the donor] or you're there because your parents' names are in the news.'" (Larson, Rock, August. and Barber 2019)

This is not to say that donation-related admissions represent an *explicit* example of the art of the deal. Colleges take care to avoid any documented commitments or any tangible evidence of a "quid pro quo," primarily because of even the remote risk that such arrangements could be characterized by the Internal Revenue Service as something other than a disinterested charitable contribution and rather more an exchange of money for a "thing of value" to the donor's family. In a more strictly enforced federal tax system than we presently have, that finding would seriously jeopardize the tax deductibility of the donation. Under IRS regulations (see IRS Publication 526), when donors receive a substantial benefit as a result of their donation, the tax deduction should be disallowed to the extent of the value of that benefit. But Charles Kushner's millions to Harvard in advance of his son's admission, in common with other such gifts, was apparently never challenged by the federal tax authorities. The economist Richard Vedder estimated that the combination of the tax-exempt status of college endowment earnings (breached only to a very minor extent in the 2017 tax bill) and the deductibility of donations to higher education had cost the government $45,000 per student at an ultra-elite college. (Dreier and Kahlenberg 2012, citing Vedder)

In his chapter in *Affirmative Action for the Rich*, Peter Sachs challenged the whole notion that elite nonprofit educational institutions are unquestionably operating for the public benefit and are therefore entitled to the benefit of the doubt as charitable organizations not subject to income tax (except for clearly unrelated business activities). He cited an IRS ruling in 1983 that whether a donation "'is made with no expectation of obtaining a commensurate benefit depends upon whether a reasonable person, taking all the facts and circumstances into account, would conclude that enrollment in the school was in no manner contingent upon making the payment, that the payment was not made pursuant to a plan (whether expressed or implied) to convert nondeductible tuition into charitable contributions, and that receipt of the benefit was not otherwise dependent upon making the payment.'" (Sachs, in Kahlenberg, ed. 2010, 227)

As a reasonable person, you be the judge. As noted in chapter 2, a college education, especially at an elite institution, whether private or public, is clearly a "commensurate benefit" in terms of expectable lifetime income, reaching well into the millions of dollars for the individual student. If a positive admissions decision — or even just an improved chance of admission — is in fact in some way contingent upon a donation, it would seem on its face that the donation should not be tax deductible. A donation by a related person (whether pledged or cash) made in *proximity* to the college application by the donor's relative should at least be suspect. Game theory strongly suggests that there is a contingent relationship between the donation and any admissions preference. Consider the admission of a legacy or a major donor. Elite colleges of course do not let all legacies or donor's children in — they only offer (quietly) a preferential pathway with lesser standards. Peter Sachs asked why alumni parent donors would try to shorten the odds of admission for their children with a major donation if admission were already certain. He concluded they make major donations obviously to change what is a mere potentiality to a more likely reality. (Sachs ibid., 229-30) the college would be receiving "something of value," as they have openly asserted that legacy-related donations are critical to their fundraising goals.

Elite colleges have certainly found ways to communicate just what level of donations might impact admission considerations well into six- or even seven-figure territory. But why are any donations in contemplation of improved odds of admission *ever* considered tax deductible by the IRS? We know that colleges are intentionally using admissions decisions as leverage to raise funds beyond tuition, room, and board. A *New York Times* editorial touching on the subject of the tax deduction that is central to this "donation and admissions" arrangement called it a "well-rehearsed pas de deux." (Editorial Board, *New York Times*, March 12, 2017). Labeling this transaction with a neat French phrase, however, does not make it less of a *deal,* and a mutually beneficial, essentially commercial deal at that.

If "gifts" in contemplation of admissions benefits were not tax deductible, then might they also be construed as business income that might even be considered taxable in the case of a private college because it is fundamentally unrelated to its non-profit purpose? Why should selling admission preferences be considered any differently for income tax purposes than selling the spaghetti manufactured by the pasta company a donor once left to a prestigious university to support its educational mission? Selling admissions is distinctly different from charging tuition, room and board for the related services rendered. The fact that tuition does not cover the full cost of providing four to six years or more of academic content to each student is a matter between the college budgeting choices and the market forces that set those services' value. Colleges are certainly free, without a tax penalty, to supplement their revenue to meet their costs through genuine donations not contingent on admission preferences. Literally selling access to those preferences to wealthy families is not likely to be found as a stated public benefit purpose in elite college charters.

As the *New York Times* pointed out in the editorial cited above, colleges and their donors are obliged to execute together a kind of choreography to "comply with tax laws" so that the whole process is "made to appear as a voluntary exchange of gifts, not a binding deal." A development officer at Duke, quoted by Daniel Golden in *The Price of Admissions,* asserted that there is "'no quid pro quo, no bargains have been struck.'" But Golden concluded that there is "a mutual understanding that one good turn deserves another." (Golden 2006, 55) Such quietly coordinated camouflage itself suggests that a true *quid pro quo* exercise is in fact going on. Why the elaborate shadow dance if there's nothing to hide? And without that dance, the elite college business model (dependent as it is said to be on major tax-deductible donations) would fail to work, and the "donors" would likely have to pay higher income taxes. Donor-related admissions seems to be a case where for both sides of the matter, necessity is the mother of circumvention.

Elite colleges seemed to recognize the critical importance, however, of keeping up the *appearance* of no quid pro quo. This concern was clearly evident in their furious (and successful) efforts to thwart Senator Kennedy's proposal merely to require regular public disclosure of legacy and also donor-related admissions. Mandatory disclosure of anything leads ineluctably to record keeping, and it is precisely the *absence* of paper trails that allows the legacy and donor related admissions tax dance to work for both partners.

In the end, as in so many shady business practice cases, internal emails have revealed the truth about the relationship between advancement and admissions. Consider the online exchanges discovered in the Asian American discrimination lawsuit and published by the *Harvard Crimson.* In one 2013 email (headed "My Hero"), the former dean of the Harvard Kennedy School thanked the admissions dean for his help admitting certain applicants who were connected with major donors: "'Once again you have done wonders. I am simply thrilled about the folks you were able to admit. [Redacted] and [redacted] are all big wins. [Redacted] has already committed to a building.'" (Whether his "already" meant before or after the admission decision was known is not disclosed.) Another email showed how a development officer flagged to the admissions office an applicant whose family was a multi-million dollar donor in the past and has "'an art collection which conceivably could come our way.'" (Franklin and Zwickel 2018)

The existence of another "dean's list" at Harvard also came out in the trial. This previously secret "dean's interest list," does not signify any academic honor but rather an admission dean's special attention on individual applicants who are "high-priority" because they have close university connections with top donors and influential alumni. William Fitzsimmons, the dean of admissions and financial aid, gave guarded testimony on the make-up of his interest list, but did reveal that it involves special consideration for donor-related candidates. Asked to explain the purpose of his dean's interest list, the dean first said he used it to keep track of what might happen to a particular application, such as someone he personally met on a recruiting trip who he thought would be of interest to the admissions committee. Under further questioning, however, he acknowledged that it is "possible" that a Harvard donor's interest in an application might land that applicant on the list as well. He further explained that candidates on the list could then receive a separate rating in consultation with people connected to the alumni association and development office. Asked if he is rating the applicant, or are rating the level of interest that other people at Harvard have in the applicant's admission, Mr. Fitzsimmons replied, "'The latter.'" (Hartocollis, Harmon and Smith 2018) Harvard's own data showed that 10 percent of the class of 2019 was comprised of students from the admissions dean's interest list and a similar one compiled by the director of admissions. (Ibid.; Eustachewich and Brown 2018)

Together with legacy admission preferences also tied to fundraising goals, donor-related admissions seem to have been doing a great job for Harvard and many other elite colleges in terms of their bottom lines. They use tax-free donations to lead to more billions in tax-free income from massive endowments. An *American Scene* article several years ago concluded that Harvard "is really a $40 billion [FY 2007] tax-free hedge fund with a very large marketing and PR arm called Harvard University that has the job of raising investment capital and protecting the fund's preferential tax treatment." (Manzi 2008)

Beyond serious questions about tax-deductible donations in connection with admissions, there lurks an even greater tax-related issue for elite colleges as they continue to use wealth-related admission preferences to prioritize endowment maximization over enrollment equity. The new threat, moreover, comes from a political persuasion quite opposite from Senator Kennedy's. It is already clear that many supporters of President Trump and the Republican members of Congress have a dim view of higher education in America. A 2017 survey by the Pew Research Center found that 58 percent of Republicans and right-leaning independents hold the view that colleges have a negative impact on the nation (an increase from 32 percent just seven years earlier. Similar findings from Gallup and New American surveys, along with Pew's, illustrate that although Americans generally believe college degrees are more important than ever for individual economic progress, rising costs, a growing disconnect from ordinary lives and a perception of college admissions as a zero-sum game have fed the rise in negative sentiments about higher education's promise. (Selingo July 18, 2017)

This antipathy is warranted, especially with respect to the nation's most elite colleges and universities. When schools of this type routinely admit more from the top 1 percent of family wealth than the bottom 60 percent, there is bound to be resentment at the kind of class war top colleges seem to be waging on middle- and lower-income Americans. The six private colleges specifically caught up in the admissions bribery scandal enroll more students from the top 1 percent of family wealth than the bottom 40 percent. Joseph A. Soames, a sociology professor at Wake Forest (where the top 1 percent accounted for 22 percent of the fall 2017 entering class while the bottom 40 percent economically constituted only 8 percent), summed up his view of elite college admissions succinctly: "'The whole system is a pay-for-play system. But that's America.'" (Stripling April 17, 2019)

Republican stalwart and six-term Senator Charles Grassley of Iowa has been among those questioning that peculiarly American relationship of multi-billion-dollar endowments, elite admissions preferences for legacies and donors' children, and taxpayer subsidies to those donors and their favored schools. Back in 2006, he asserted that we "'need to think whether these reserved spaces at our top colleges is a public policy that should be subsidized by the tax code…and also whether it is in keeping with the requirement that as charities, colleges and universities operate in the public interest.'" (Sachs, in Kahlenberg, ed. 2010, 234) A decade later, a Republican-controlled Congress and a Republican president approved changes to the federal tax code as part of the 2017 Tax Cuts and Jobs Act that, along with a series of large-scale permanent corporate and more modest individual tax rate reductions, applied a new 1.4 percent annual tax on the net investment earnings of colleges with endowment assets amounting to $500 million per student or more, including the likes of Harvard and Stanford for example. Note that the average American nonprofit college holds $35,555 in net assets per student — and earns less than $150,000 in total net annual income from those assets.

The stated objective of the federal endowment tax was not

expressly to create an incentive to change admissions behavior but to open up a new source of revenue to reduce the deficit anticipated from the major tax cuts for upper income groups and corporations in the new law. Republican Representative Tom Reed of upstate New York, however, would have preferred that the tax proposal be framed specifically to "force schools with large endowments to spend more of them on tuition assistance" in the face of what he called the "runaway" tuition price issue. Ross Douthat, a conservative columnist for the *New York Times*, adopting the hedge-fund metaphor from a decade earlier, concluded that "as long as the best-endowed universities are running billion-dollar tax-free hedge funds while facilitating privilege, elite conformity and self-segregation, a small tax is entirely reasonable; a larger one would be just." (Douthat 2017)

Is it not fair to ask whether the taxpaying public really intends to subsidize, through forgone tax receipts, the incomes of a select group of rich individuals and elite colleges? This "hidden in plain sight" federal subsidy enables those schools to provide substantial admissions privileges for the children of those same wealthy individuals. And they do this with barely any consistent and transparent disclosure to taxpayers of the dimension of this intentional wealth bias in terms of access to elite higher education, which by definition discriminates against all other applicants merely because of their birth or family income status.

Another IRS Gift for Elite College Admissions: Preferences for Children of Faculty and Staff — The Ultimate Connection

Another tax-related question relating to equity of access to higher education arises from the common practice of elite colleges providing a special pathway to admissions for the children of their own faculty members, at zero or reduced cost — or even for the children of faculty members at other colleges (somewhat like the reciprocal privileges common among elite country clubs). Among a large number of similar examples, Columbia has waived full tuition for children of its own faculty and paid half the tuition of faculty children who enroll at other colleges. It faculty-related admits average lower test scores than the entry class as a whole, and have accounted for nearly 3 percent of enrollment in some years. (Golden 2006, 183-84)

Jon Reider, one of the authors of *Admission Matters* who also worked in the undergraduate admissions office at Stanford for fifteen years, was cited by the *Stanford Daily* as saying that if he could choose any hook to have as an applicant, he would want to be the child of a faculty member. According to Reider, that would mean that "you're already connected" enough to make it difficult for the admissions office to turn you down. The same article also included a quote from another former Stanford admissions office to a local media outlet that an influential professor "'can further leverage their influence'" to gain a child's admission "'by threatening to move valuable research funding to another university...that's something that is considered'" by the admissions office. The article also noted that faculty can use their direct access to the dean of admissions office to lobby on their children's admission cases. It also referenced a case described by Reider where a *nephew* of a dean of a grad school was admitted with middling high school grades because the admissions dean concluded that it would be "'probably good to have friends in the graduate schools.'" (Moore 2013)

Research by an expert witness in the Harvard Asian American discrimination lawsuit using data discovered in the trial calculated that over a six year period through 2019, Harvard accepted 46.7 percent of faculty children who applied — for a better boost in odds than offered to Hispanic and low-income students. (Golden July 11, 2019) Getting their children admitted under lesser standards than other special categories of applicants is not the only benefit enjoyed by faculty at elite universities. Under federal tax law, tuition waivers or discounts with respect to students who are children of faculty or staff are exempt from income tax (and not viewed as a form of indirect compensation), provided that there is no discrimination in terms of application of this benefit between higher- and lower-paid college employees. Elite colleges have acknowledged, however, that special admissions consideration for faculty children has been intentionally used to recruit highly desired additions to their faculties. It should be noted that housing costs in Columbia's and Stanford's locations in Manhattan and Palo Alto respectively are among the highest in the nation: a special pathway to lower college tuition would an attractive perk for prospective faculty and staff compared to more affordable college localities.

It is also evident that faculty children have been judged under lower admissions standards than apply not just to other preferential categories but also to the entire "unhooked" applicant pool (Moore, ibid.) Tufts University, an elite and highly competitive private school, has engaged in faculty and staff preferences over the years. As described in *The Price of Admission*, children of Tufts employees accounted at times for around 2 percent of entering enrollment. Tufts adjusted its previously more limited tuition discounts for children of lower-paid staff in order to assure compliance with the IRS rules requiring equivalent benefits to be offered for faculty and staff children across the board to justify the income tax exclusion for the tuition waivers. (Golden 2006, 191-94) In common with many colleges and universities, however, Tufts has seriously considered ways to cap the cost of the deep tuition discounts for these students, and also raise the academic standards for such admissions to the general norms. These efforts, however, were met with fierce faculty resistance. When a special admissions lane with substantial untaxed economic benefits becomes part of faculty and staff recruitment strategy, it is small wonder that, as a Tufts president conceded, "Expectations have been created among the faculty." (Ibid., 191)

The president of the Tufts chapter of the American Association of University Professors argued that faculty children should be exempt from the normal higher standards and comparative value judgments that are made as applications wax and wane from year to year against relatively fixed enrollment capacity. "It should be based on principles, such as 'has this faculty child met the minimum requirements'…rather than…based on the whims of demand." But ultimately a new president and admissions dean were able to bring admission standards for faculty children into line with the general norms, especially as Tufts successfully sought to enhance its academic and enrollment profile. (Ibid.)

Children of faculty at elite colleges are well-connected applicants. A faculty senate committee often is charged with some degree of oversight of admissions processes and outcomes, notwithstanding the professionalization and direct administrative reporting lines of the admissions office and dean. Faculties have done a very effective job in bending the tuition cost curve and defending related tax exemption, another trifecta of admissions-related preferences college folks effectively assign to themselves. Senator Jon Kyl of Arizona, a member of GOP leadership, tried in 2007 to eliminate the exemption from reported faculty income of the value of free or discounted tuition for their children. He argued that US taxpayers should not be subsidizing faculty recruiting and retention efforts at elite, well-endowed elite colleges. His amendment failed on a 50 to 42 vote. (Ibid., 302-02.) The GOP tax cuts of 2017 also left that benefit in place.

The number of faculty and staff children who gain the tax-exempt benefit of reduced cost elite college admission under lower academic standards is small. The tuition discounts involved, however, effectively reduces the amount of need-based financial aid the college itself can put on the table for more academically qualified but financially disadvantaged students. In effect, the tuition discounting for children of faculty and staff amounts to a *de facto* "merit aid" package based not on the applicant's merit but on the relative value of their parent or parents to a college's financial and reputational bottom lines. This is not the only way, however, that merit aid is weaponized in the battle among elite colleges to secure an entering class with a sufficient majority of wealthy and well-connected students to satisfy their own business models.

Not-So-Subtle Use of Merit Aid as a Discount for the Wealthy

Elite colleges are aware of continuing public concern about both the high cost of higher education and the evidence that their admissions practices tend to favor the rich. Many leading schools have accordingly turned to need-blind admissions policies that forgive, significantly reduce, or arrange loans and Federal grants for the tuition, room, and board expense for children whose families' income falls below a certain threshold, which can range to over $100,000. This practice does balance to some extent the impact on enrollment of high-affluence lanes for legacies, donors' children, and faculty offspring, as well as the increasing use of the wealth-friendly early decision process. Low-income applicants who are aware enough of the opportunity and confident enough in their first choice to apply to one school on an early decision basis can take advantage of such need-blind policies if they are selected on their own merits, provided that the schools have the resources to live up to such policies in good faith. Recent steps at several elite colleges to institute debt-free need-based financial aid packaging have been particularly helpful in this regard. The total number of colleges offering truly need-blind admissions, however, where no heed whatsoever is paid to any applicant's ability to pay, is about 100. "In other words, the vast majority of colleges and universities *do* consider income when reviewing applications, and this sometimes results in the shifting of scarce financial aid resources away from those most in need to non-need 'merit aid' programs." (Emphasis in original.) (Giancola and Kahlenburg 2016, 25)

Colleges that are not fully need blind but what is called "need aware" or "need sensitive" retain the flexibility to manage their admissions against the budget limits they have imposed on themselves in terms of need-based financial aid. In one example, 193 low-income candidates requiring more than $25,000 in grants each were removed from the accepted pool at Tufts University to avoid exceeding the university's aid budget. Because the majority of those whose admissions were pulled at the last minute ranked in the top tenth of their high school classes and nearly half attained test scores higher than Tufts' then-current SAT median, the result was an entering class that was wealthier, whiter, and academically weaker than it would have been under a true need-blind regime. (Golden 2006, 193)

The Tufts action shows that, under a need-aware approach, a college may accept a fairly large majority of the freshman class without regard one way or another to their families' income, but the limited financial circumstances of some applicants' families can come into play in a negative way for the final 20 percent or so of admissions. A *Wall Street Journal* reporter given access in 2020 to the inner workings of three selective colleges' admissions committees found that their final "shaping" of class is "when an applicant's background can push them over the line." "Legacies, children of faculty and staff, and applicants under the watchful eye of a college's president or fundraising office usually receive their biggest boost at this point." He also observed that this same point is when worthy applicants unable to pay tend to get cut. One of the committees reversed 200 admissions at the last minute because there was not enough aid to go around. (Selingo August 29-30, 2020).

Borderline judgments in the final batch of acceptances will tend to favor affluent applicants, with the usual explanation that somebody has to subsidize the aid for economically disadvantage students.

One college president of an elite university told this author that for every disadvantaged community where they recruit highly qualified minority students to meet diversity goals, they need to go to a rich zip code to recruit equally qualified wealthy applicants to fund their financial aid programs. This practice, however, does not mean that the rich students will pay full 'sticker price" — or even as much as the disadvantaged wind up paying counting the debt they incur. The *Chronicle of Higher Education* reported in 2017 that institutions that have opened their doors to large numbers of economically disadvantaged students have also routinely offered merit aid packages in order to enroll a sufficient number of students from the high end of the socioeconomic spectrum to help pay for aid to the disadvantaged. But as a result, "it is not at all uncommon for the lowest-income students to pay higher prices than those from families higher up the income scale." (Brown 2017)

Some leading colleges limit their financial aid packages to meeting demonstrated financial need only and offer no type of "merit" awards. (Selingo May 8, 2017) It is also common practice among elite schools, however, to budget funds for merit-based scholarships to admitted students they consider highly desirable in terms of their specific enrollment objectives. These goals can include increasing their reported median test scores and GPAs and selectivity rankings, filling out classes in selected major fields, and satisfying the needs of co-curricular activities such as theater and music with particularly talented and gifted artists. As a result, both private and public elite colleges and universities can find themselves in a merit aid bidding war for acceptances. (Bruni 2015, 98) They find themselves competing to win over students who likely have grown up with the benefit of sufficient wealth to provide professional SAT, ACT, and AP tutoring as well as elite artistic and athletic training. The winners in these affluence intramurals (both the colleges and the students) thus find they represent yet another way that the rich get richer at elite colleges.

These are not small number battles. Merit aid packages upward of $100,000 over four years are offered to applicants whose academic profiles would move those schools up in terms of test score selectivity rankings. In the state of Ohio, for example, public universities like Ohio State and Miami of Ohio have awarded merit grants to about 30 percent of their entering classes, and selective private schools in the same state such as Oberlin, Case Western Reserve, and Denison have provided no-need grants to 25 percent or more of their enrollees. (Anderson December 29, 2014) A coveted (and affluent) applicant awarded a six-figure merit aid offer by a safety school can shop the bid up the rankings chain to more selective elite colleges (with their own admissions consultants playing the investment banker role of scoping out the best deal for their client). A *Washington Post* study found that Duke University, provided merit aid averaging around $56,000 to a total of sixty-seven freshmen in the class of 2018 (not including athletic scholarships). This bargaining phenomenon can be even more intense and biased toward wealth and social standing when merit aid is used to assure that certain sports teams have the requisite number of scholar-athletes to field a competitive team, especially among the Ivy League and other elite colleges that do not offer athletic scholarships as such. (Ibid.)

The Jack Kent Cooke Foundation also reported in 2016 that the percentage of merit aid received by students in the wealthiest family income quartile (some of whom had relatively lower academic credentials) was rising, while merit aid targeted to the lowest quartile remained stagnant, characterizing this aspect of admissions as the "mediocre" student preference. (Giancola and Kahlenburg 2016, 25) The report also noted on how a considerable amount of merit aid was going to athletes recruited in certain sports mostly played by wealthy and white applicants, and that those recipients are often admitted despite having comparatively weak academic records, and then perform less well in college than their marginal high school records predicted. (Ibid., 23)

Recruiting the Wealthy for Aristocratic Sports — But Let's Not Sweat the Details

The college admissions guidebook *Admission Matters* cited a 2005 study of practices at thirteen selective colleges, including the entire Ivy League, by former Princeton president William Bowen. His report concluded that a recruited male athlete had four times the chance of being admitted than a male student with a comparable academic record who was not a recruited athlete and had no other admission hooks. *Admission Matters* advised prospective applicants that, aside from development admits, athletic talent "can be the biggest hook of all when it comes to admission at a selective college." (Springer, Reider, and Morgan 2013, 39-40, 199)

A former college track coach wrote shortly after the 2019 indictments for bribing non-revenue sports coaches to accept false athletic resumes that "most people don't realize that athletic departments are extensions of the admissions office, often lacking the same restrictions... Coaches have much more freedom in who they can recommend....Especially at small liberal arts institutions, coaches put 'butts in seats'...when general enrollment is down at a small college, the number of 'athletes' often goes up." (Perry 2019)

Some of the participants in the alleged admissions bribery scheme seem unaware of how to take advantage of the sports-related admissions pathway without resorting to outright payoffs. They could have just taken advantage of the easy-going cooperative relationship between athletic and admissions departments. Enrollment experts told the *Chronicle of Higher Education* in 2019 that admission officials don't know everything about each athlete who the coaches want. "It all gets a little fuzzy, especially in the minor sports," said one admissions dean at a prominent school, whose office sets aside a specific number of slots for athletes and as long as the coaches' choices are qualified, they get in. (Hoover March

13, 2019) The coaches indicted in the bribery scandal mostly worked in lower-profile Olympic sports, which often have coveted walk-on slots for admission under less scrutiny than major revenue sports. (Stripling May 29, 2019) An audit cited in the *San Francisco Chronicle* conducted after the indictments by the University of California found multiple specific weaknesses in recordkeeping and fraud prevention in its admissions processes, including repeated failures to generate or retain any documentation for "admissions by exception" such as athletes or others with reputedly "special" talents. (Asimov 2019)

The impact of the athletics preference is substantial, although the total numbers are kept close to the vest by most schools. The *Washington Post* asked 75 highly ranked research universities and liberal arts colleges about how many places they reserved for athletes in admissions decisions, or at least the actual number of athletes ultimately offered admission. Most of the schools declined to provide that data, but some disclosed the percentage of actual enrollment represented by varsity athletes, ranging from 13 to 36 percent among the 17 liberal art colleges that responded. Most of the top 50 research universities disclosed enrollment percentages for athletes in the single digits, although Ivy League schools and peers like MIT, Stanford and Cal Tech ranged in the mid-teens and up into the low 20 percent range. (Anderson and Svrluga 2019)

Preferential athletic admissions restrict access to college for students with no such hook even more acutely when linked to grants of merit aid. In athletics, merit is ordinarily assumed to be a matter of skill at the game: but in cases of merit grants to certain athletes, however, the real merit also includes the economic power of the athlete's family. Serious studies of the academic and financial corruption, and other moral and equity considerations, relating to big-time billion-dollar power conference budgets in football and basketball, could fill many bookshelves. This book's focus, however, is on the uses of merit aid and other preferential treatment for athletic admissions, particularly at elite colleges, that create advantages for applicants from wealthy families. This happens primarily through efforts to attract enough proficient athletes to field teams in so-called "non-revenue" or "aristocratic" sports, and the related interplay with those colleges' diversity goals. The potential for corruption in this segment of the admissions market was evident long before the bribery indictments exposed even more brazen ways the wealthy "pay to play."

Data collected on Harvard's admissions policies by the U.S. Department of Education during its investigation of potential discrimination against Asian Americans in the late 1980s showed that athletes (and legacies) who were accepted had lower SAT scores than the rest of their class, and had actually been rated as less attractive candidates by admissions officers. (Gerstein 2018) As Frank Bruni observed in *Where You Go Is Not Who You'll Be*: "[I]t's good to be a legacy. But it may be better still to be an athlete who is superior enough, or *plays a sport that's obscure enough*, to be of instant and sure use to a school." (Bruni 2015, 51) *The Price of Admission* brought attention to the role of the federal Title IX mandate to provide balanced athletic opportunities for male and female students in increasing the number of sports available to women and, in turn, a significant increase in all athletic recruitment activities at colleges generally. Some of the non-revenue, non-scholarship sports that have experienced recruiting growth after Title IX are often considered "aristocratic" or "country-club" sports commonly more popular in wealthier and whiter suburban high schools. (Golden 2006, 145-176)

Examples of those sort of sports abound, including crew, cross country, cycling, equestrian events, fencing, field hockey, golf, lacrosse, polo, rugby, sailing, skiing, squash, swimming and diving, soccer, volleyball and water polo. Sometimes at elite colleges, the rosters for those sports show total team members far in excess of the number needed to field a competitive team — for example, 125 for women's crew at USC. This phenomenon has provided a tremendous opportunity for wealthy families that can afford summer camps and other "sports tutoring" to their kids in these types of sports to exploit yet another high affluence pathway to preferential admissions consideration.

As an example, *The Price of Admission* compared the relative position of one public and one private high school in the Boston area — East Boston High and Phillips Academy at Andover — to illustrate how elite private high schools that traditionally send their graduates to the most elite colleges gain advantage from "the admissions power of aristocratic sports."

> East Boston High, with an enrollment of 1,435, is a typical urban public school; nearly three-quarters of the students are minorities, 68.4 percent are low income, and graduates rarely go to four-year colleges. Eastie offers football, basketball, baseball, softball, hockey (a boy's sport team shared with four other high schools), swimming, track, volleyball and soccer…and a city-wide cross-country team. Andover, enrollment 1,087, is a premier private school…has teams in all the sports that East Boston does, plus tennis, field hockey, golf, lacrosse, crew, squash, diving, water polo, girls' hockey, wrestling, cycling and skiing…Andover students can get into college as recruits in a dozen sports that Eastie students never had a chance to play in high school. (Golden 2006, 153)

When they choose athletes for the "obscure" — but not to the wealthy — sports that they sponsor in part to fulfill their federal Title IX obligations, elite colleges know in advance that they will be able to select from a pool that is largely upper class and Caucasian. Although large state universities dominate the high profile, "revenue" sports of football and basketball, recruited athletes actually comprise a far higher percentage of admissions in the Ivy league and elite colleges in general.

Some of these schools use a category called the "recruited walk-on" for applicants who are athletes but not assured a spot on a team. However, they are assured an admissions slot because they are on a list of five to twenty or so that a particular coach has been allocated under what *The Economist* has characterized as admissions offices' "lax standards…which help rich children." These allocations occur because coaches of the non-revenue sports are expected to be raising money to support their sports, and athletes' parents are their most reliable donors. Thus athletes from wealthy families can gain the advantage of a special admissions lane without careful scrutiny of their academic credentials, or even their athletic ability or intentions to play. Recruited walk-ons often do not show up for practice and the coaches don't care as long as the expected donations from their families hit the bank. (Thomason 2019) Rick Singer, the admissions consultant mastermind who pled guilty in the bribery indictments, systematically exploited what auditors would later term "material weakness" in ordinary recordkeeping in the elite college athletic-admissions complex. In almost every case in the bribery scandal where athletic credentials were forged yet admission was granted, the "athlete" appeared to be filling a "recruited walk-on" slot. (Pennington 2019) Some of the walk-ons (as at USC) never bothered actually to walk on.

Ivy League schools, which compete in the NCAA's Division I, offer up to thirty or more sports, double the average for all colleges and universities, but have chosen to offer no athletic scholarships as such. Colleges that field Division III teams also cannot offer athletic scholarships per their Division's rules. These schools are among the most selective liberal arts colleges that offer nearly the same number of sports as the Ivies. With total enrollments around two thousand or even fewer, admissions for athletes to those colleges are very significant, comprising 30 to 45 percent of the student body while their overall admissions rates are in the teens. (Ibid.)

A 2016 NPR editorial comparing the varsity sports at Harvard, Yale, and Princeton with the athletic programs in the public schools of Los Angeles, New York City, and Chicago made the same point. It quoted from the Bowen report research cited above that "many of these [recruited sports] slots…go to wealthy, suburban, white students." A study of Ivy league and elite liberal arts colleges cited in *The Price of Admission* found that only 6 percent of their sports recruits came from families in the bottom 25 percent of income, compared to 12 percent for all other students. In addition, the Bowen study found that elite college recruits in golf, fencing, crew, squash, and other upper class sports often find themselves in the bottom 50 percent of their class academically. (Kamenetz 2016)

The author of *The Price of Admission* asked directly why colleges "compromise their admissions standards for athletes in marginal sports that don't enhance racial or economic diversity and rarely generate revenue or media buzz." In the same book, the women's rowing coach at the elite public University of Virginia defended the practice even though it means some applicants get in despite marginal or worse academic credentials. "It's not just about having the best and brightest student…You should have academic diversity as well if you have kids who have to struggle, it brings a good mix. That kid may ask a more common-sense question." Daniel Golden suggested a more common-sense explanation for why elite colleges sometimes bend their academic standards to recruit and admit athletes — money. Performance in those aristocratic sports remains emotionally important to wealthy alumni donors who played them and enjoy watching them (especially if their team wins). They will put their dollars behind their sports passions. (Golden 2006, 155-57) Frank Bruni also noted that the feelings of alumni who played those sports about their alma mater's current performance could influence their donations: "Athletics, in other words, affect the business." (Bruni 2015, 59) And that "business" is to attract and sustain a mostly wealthy enrollment profile, even at it means sacrificing the goal of racial diversity.

The lead witness for the plaintiffs in the Asian American discrimination case, Peter Arcidiacono, working with data that Harvard was compelled to provide, concluded that recruited athletes got the biggest benefit of all in terms of admission: an 86 percent acceptance rate! They also accounted for 16.3 percent of all white students admitted to Harvard. (Golden 2018; see also Todd 2019)

Playing a Race Card in Admissions Poker — the Stakes are High

Some of the most revealing data about the elite colleges' purposeful admissions tilt toward the three *W*s' — wealthy, well connected, and white — has emerged in the lawsuit against Harvard by plaintiffs seeking to prove bias against Asian applicants. Harvard was required to disclose an internal study by its Office of Institutional Research showing that if admissions were based solely on grades and test scores, Asian Americans would comprise about 43 percent of the entering class rather than less than 19 percent, whereas whites would make up 38 percent rather than 43 percent, African Americans would account for less than 1 percent rather than 10 percent, and Hispanics a bit over 25 percent rather than just under 10 percent. Those bringing the lawsuit have been associated with negative sentiments about affirmative action with respect to black and Hispanic applicants. The United States Supreme Court, in closely divided decisions in three cases over recent decades, has essentially held that race may be taken into consideration as *one* (positive but not negative) factor in admissions decisions in view of compelling benefits in terms of diversity. Harvard has consistently argued that its "holistic" application review process is directly aligned with that objective and the Supreme Court's decisions. The trial court sided with Harvard, ruling that the university had not intentionally discriminated against applicants of Asian descent.

Yet other Harvard records revealed in pretrial discovery showing admissions officers categorizing Asian-American applicants as either lacking "compelling" or showing "typical" personal qualities suggest the admissions office has been using the holistic review of such subjective personality factors precisely in a *negative* way with respect to applicants with an Asian background. This sort of racial stereotyping would seem to violate the clear intent and limits of the Supreme Court's three holdings regarding consideration of race in admissions. It would have much the same racial exclusionary effect that Harvard's holistic admissions consideration of "personal character" in the 1920s and 1930s led to discrimination against Jewish applicants, who were surpassing the traditional Harvard applicant pool in grades and test scores, just as many Asian-American applicants have been doing at Harvard in our time.

Perhaps Harvard admissions officials have also come to believe that its wealthy, well-connected, and white prep school applicants would not be comfortable competing with more academically aggressive young men and women with "typically Asian" study habits. But combining two superficial forms of secret applicant stereotyping does not add up to one right way to go about achieving equity in admissions at Harvard. An opinion piece roughly contemporaneous with the Harvard trial in the *New York Times* by Natasha Warikoo, an associate professor at Harvard's Graduate School of Education and Nadirah Farah Foley, a former Penn admissions officer, asked "[w]ho deserves to get an elite education?" They framed the prevailing answer this way: "While standards of merit shift over time, prominent schools and even their critics usually take for granted admissions systems that uphold the privileges of elite groups. In the United States, 'elites' are mostly white people. That means Asian Americans and underrepresented minorities — Latinos, Native Americans and

African Americans — are pitted against one another for coveted spots at elite schools…in our highly unequal society, education systems have consistently found ways to favor elite, white applicants…." (Warikoo and Foley 2018)

For the NCCA's more than 400 Division III colleges, the available data shows that almost 80 percent of athletes were white. As noted above, colleges in Division III — and Ivy League schools — are precluded by their own rules from giving athletic scholarships, so they cannot give low-income sports stars a free ride. (Desai 2018) But as we have seen, they can and do use merit aid grants for the same purpose, if not the same level, of tuition relief for wealthy applicants. There is cause for hope for scholar-athletes from disadvantaged communities, however, in a recent initiative undertaken by leadership at Amherst. That excellent liberal arts college has in the past been lauded for its general effective commitment to diversity of enrollment but criticized for a jarring lack of diversity in its athletic teams.

The Amherst president, Biddy Martin, undertook a program to prove it could reshape its athletic rosters to include underrepresented racial, ethnic and socioeconomic groups. The core of the program was recognition that diversity recruiting could not be a passive, business-as-usual matter — that the economically and racially marginalized athletes were not going to just show up on their doorstep or happen to be discovered in the schools existing minority outreach efforts. Amherst concluded that real change would require a focused, sustained aggressive and tactical recruiting program, backed by realistic, dedicated budget dollars (tens of thousands, but not millions) — plus a commitment by athletic coaches to go to where the athletes actually live and play. This could mean nights at dimly lit urban fields rather than shiny suburban high school stadiums. The new recruiting program has shown signs of success. Over a period of three years, the percentage of athletes of color increased from 23 percent to 33 percent. Other colleges, even with lesser resources than the well-endowed Amherst, are following its lead. A coach of an inner-city soccer club remarked that what Amherst is doing can be replicated if "university presidents put their support behind it." (Pennington November 7, 2019) The former college track coach cited earlier in this chapter concluded his comments on the admissions bribery indictments with the observation that those caught in the FBI probe "are as wrong as the day is long." "But as long as universities don't make economic and racial diversity an essential goal of admissions, a so-called merit-based system will always create perverse incentives for rich people to cheat." (Perry 2019) That is especially true where the "system" does its business in a black box.

Putting It All Together…

In this chapter, we have seen the ways elite colleges directly use various admission processes to favor certain applicants, who predictably are from among the wealthiest economic income groups: the top quintile for sure, the top ten percent commonly, and the top 1 percent frequently. Of course, predictions aren't guarantees, and correlation is not causation. But the black box admissions model does somehow keep generating enrollment that routinely favors the most economically and racially privileged groups in American society. The available data suggests that we can no longer assume that this result is a mere accident of a "holistic" approach to admissions decisions — especially because the prevalence of the secretive black box model itself tells us elite colleges have some things they want to hide. The early decision model, popular at most elite colleges, is widely disclosed and theoretically made available to all applicants ostensibly as a means to reduce stress and anxiety for students and their families. But its deeper purposes in terms of providing substantial benefits to the college — assuring a lower admissions rate, a higher yield rate, and a higher revenue stream in both tuition and donations. But these intended goals are hidden in the black box that also obscures the fact that the early decision pool generally is three times as white as the regular decision pool. (Dannenburg 2018, citing Kahlenberg, Richard D. "The Legacy Packet: The Problem with College Admission Preferences for Children of Alumni." The Century Foundation. 2010)

We know the black box also hides the secret grade and test score algorithms that screen out thousands of applications before more qualitative evidence like essays and recommendations is ever reviewed by admissions officers. Yet these applications, which will surely fail the early screening algorithms, will nonetheless inflate the denominator of a college's admissions ratio and thus lead to a favorable ranking in terms of that aspect of selectivity by US News. The black box also contains the exact weightings the college will apply to various forms of applicants' demonstrated interest in the school, as well as the details of the private prep school pipeline that funnels admission advantages to the wealthiest applicants. Also hidden are the timing tricks the admissions trade has used to massage reporting of test scores of enrollees to create a public perception of extreme academic selectivity.

We know that elite colleges have endeavored to keep secret the details as to size, scope and criteria for the special "high affluence" admissions preference lanes they have created for legacies, donors' relatives, and faculty and staff children, and well as recruited and walk-on athletes in non-revenue sports. The *existence* of these preferences is now pretty much "out of the box" — not because the colleges suddenly turned transparent about admissions, but thanks to discoveries in litigation, federal investigations and good old fashion reporting (including by many student-run campus news media). The critical quantitative details, however, have only come out in limited and anecdotal ways through partially redacted discovery in a few lawsuits and admissions bribery prosecutions.

No one has done a better job of succinctly pulling together the facts about elite college admissions than Michael Dannenburg in a memo he circulated in June 2018 to "Interested Parties" on behalf of Education Reform Now: "Because schools are reluctant to disclose the extent or impact of alumni child preferences, there are limits to legacy research. But examination of groups of schools and individual institutions suggest that, like early decision, the legacy preference also significantly undermines racial and economic diversity as well as achievement-based admissions. Individual elements of the admission system that have disparate racial or class impact combine to have a cumulative effect that limits access to the most prestigious institutions of higher education. Wealthy high school students are disproportionately likely to take commercial test-prep courses…. to apply to early decision….to receive legacy preferences." (Dannenburg 2018)

In *The Price of Admission*, Daniel Golden recounted how a Notre Dame official told him, given that so many spaces at elite universities are reserved for well-connected students, "'the poor schmuck who has to get in on his own has to walk on water'" (Golden 2006, 14) Golden himself updated the metaphor in a later *Pro Publica* article — "The poor schmucks have to walk on water — during a tsunami." (Golden 2016)

Our peek inside the black box has confirmed not only a wealth and connections bias in these closely-guarded admission preferences, but also a related tilt favoring white applicants — some of whom, but for the wealth that gets them special consideration, would have had trouble getting in on their high school records alone. According to the model used by Peter Arcidiacono's team with the Harvard trial data, roughly 75 percent of white admits to that school over a six cycle period ending in 2019 were comprised of recruited athletes, legacies, children of faculty and staff and those on the dean's interest (which included many donor-related applicants who otherwise would have been rejected). (Todd 2019)

Those same categories represented only 5 percent of the total applicant pool but accounted for 29 percent of total admissions. (Hoover October 30, 2018) In other words, the special high-affluence admissions lanes reserved for only 7,000 applicants out of 150,0000 over six admission cycles wound up with nearly one-third of the coveted seats. (Gluckman October 25, 2018) This means that Harvard's published "admissions rate" of about 5.5 percent was really only a bit over 3.75 percent net of the reserved seats!

Disclosures in the Harvard trial of the effects of hidden admissions, as well as related media exposure of similar preferences at other elite campuses, essentially show that eliminating the wealth bias inherent in such practices must start with a transformative increase in transparency: namely, the end of the black box admission model. Commercial-in-confidence secrecy hides what is rotten in the elite college admissions business model: namely, that the wealth-biased outcomes of the black box process are *designed-in*. As the next chapter will show, elite colleges must be forced and not just coaxed to subordinate secrecy to the higher value of disclosure. Otherwise the American dream of socioeconomic mobility by dint of true merit will, ironically, die at the gates of exclusive higher education institutions that were originally chartered precisely to fulfill that dream. And along the way, a number of fine colleges that cannot replicate the black box model will eventually cease to exist as well. The dying has already started.

CHAPTER 6

Elite College Admission Outcomes Tracking Income Disparity Are Freezing Social Mobility and Squeezing the Economics of Other Colleges: Self-Reform Has Been Mostly Lip Service, But the Bribery Scandals and Covid-19 Could Force Change

When the dots from all the major decision points in the elite college admission practices are connected and weighted according to their effect on enrollment outcomes, it is increasingly obvious that they follow a pattern where applicants who are wealthy or, well-connected (and white) have a clear advantage even if they sometimes lack a competitive level of scholastic aptitude. The sheer magnitude of the admissions advantages directly provided to those applicants shows that even the indirect benefits enjoyed by the rich and famous are part of an overall admissions scheme designed to achieve annual entry enrollment featuring majority representation of the highest earners in American society. This outcome serves to preserve upper class wealth and privilege while sustaining the reputations of elite colleges as the chosen few schools that select the next generation's chosen few students.

That elite college admissions scheme must be kept secret to the maximum extent possible, however, lest its bias toward the already elite provoke too much public outcry in the land of opportunity. So the scheme is purposely obscured through the black box admissions process that only the elite themselves can best decipher. The data from chapter 2 regarding who gets in through black box admissions makes clear that the resulting enrollment profiles closely mirrors America's increasing income disparity, with clear advantage to the already rich. The evidence in chapters 3, 4, and 5 makes clear that this result is no accident, but rather reflects the successful execution of the most elite colleges' business models.

The triumph of their plans, however, has come with an overwhelming cost in two related dimensions: (1) the resulting social stratification, income stagnation, and wealth disparity that amounts to de fact socioeconomic segregation of America; and (2) an intense financial squeeze on less-selective, tuition-dependent colleges trying to keep pace in the elite admissions game. Ironically, many such "lesser" colleges are doing at least as well as, if not an even better job than, the higher-ranked colleges in fostering the social mobility!

The Big Squeeze in Elite Admissions Is Linked Directly to the Big Freeze in Socioeconomic Mobility

Income distribution has recently increased decisively in favor of the top 1 to 10 percent of family incomes, making the issue of selective access to four-year college degrees even more acute. Over the first four years after the Great Recession, the real incomes of the top 1 percent of incomes rose by 31 percent while everyone else saw their incomes rise by less than half a percent. Much of that appreciation in assets, of course, was derived from the remarkable post-recession rise in the stock market. Over 80 percent of total stock market value, as reported by PBS on August 23, 2018, had accrued to families in America's top 10 percent of income, which kicked in then at about $120,000 per year. According to Federal Reserve Board data, the richest 1 percent of Americans (with minimum net worth of $10 million) held nearly as much wealth as the entire middle and upper-class in the second quarter of 2019:

$35.4 compared to 36.9 held by those in the 50th to 90th percentiles of wealth. By way of comparison, in the same period, the bottom 50 percent held 6.1 percent of all assets on their balance sheets but also have 35.7 percent of liabilities. (Tanzi and Sasso 2019)

It is highly likely that the liabilities of the lower 50 percent of households in terms of net worth comprise a large share of the $1.6 trillion and counting total student loan debt outstanding. They have been driven into a very painful and dangerous bargain by the college admissions/government loan system. Based on balance sheet debt already in place, their student loans would probably not pass muster under ordinary lending standards. At the very least, they should be categorized as analogous to the famous "subprime" mortgages that brought down the housing market and almost did the same to our financial system in 2007-09. This would be true even in the case of loans included in "need blind" financial aid packages. Given that student loan debt cannot be discharged in bankruptcy, the only option for those financially swamped with this kind of debt would be to default. This would especially be the case among the 40 percent who start but never finish college, or the same percentage of those who don't even have $400 in the bank for emergencies.

The current college admissions/loan system actually tends to move more folks down the wealth ladder than up. But elite colleges that have no skin in the game in terms of responsibility for loan defaults continue to have their increasing tuition levels subsidized by federal loan flow at no charge or risk. Yet the most selective of all elite colleges admit very few applicants from families in the bottom quintile of the income scale, while giving preference to admissions from the highest quintile. As we shall see in this chapter, our very best colleges do give those in the bottom 20 percent of family income a good chance to reach the very top income level during their lifetimes — but those students comprise a share of enrollment in the low single digits — not enough to make a difference in the growing wealth disparity in this country.

Accelerating wealth concentration at the top end of American households is part of a global trend: OXFAM reported just before the Davos Conference of January 2019 that the fortunes of all the world's billionaires increased by 12 percent in 2018 ($2.3 billion per day) while the world's poorest 3.8 billion people experienced a wealth drop of $650 billion per day. The same report found that India's top 1 percent of fortunes rose 39 percent while the bottom half of that country's population only grew its wealth 3 percent. It is the United States, however, that has become both the richest and the most unequal country among the two hundred nations surveyed in the Credit Suisse Research Institute's Global Wealth Report, measured in terms of the income gap, top to bottom.

Data from the research of Emmanuel Saez and Thomas Piketty for the 1979 though 2013 period reveals an overwhelming 86 percent increase in the share of pretax income being amassed by the top 1 percent of Americans (defined as the 1.4 million taxpayers with adjusted gross incomes of at least $480,930), compared to an 8 percent decline for the bottom 90 percent of all tax filers. Some economists, including members of the U.S. Treasury and Congress's Joint Committee on Taxation staffs, have challenged the methodology and assumptions in deriving these figures. These researchers concluded that, after adjusting the share of the 1 percent for taxes and transfer payments, it had barely moved since the 1960s. They also shifted statistical focus from households to individuals, thereby adjusting for the decline in marriages among poorer Americans that makes single-person households at the low end of scale look poorer compared to the pooled marital incomes of households at upper income levels. They also ignored capital gains, however, which flow disproportionately to higher income households, and instead simply distributed corporate retained earnings in proportion to individual shareholdings, including through tax- advantaged retirement accounts. (*Economist* 2019) But poorer workers are not taking those unrealized gains as current income, while sophisticated upper-income investors can use synthetic securities, derivatives and other timing devices to control how they harvest their gains.

Economists are known to disagree, of course, usually based on conflicting methodologies. But as the pros say on the basketball court: "Ball don't lie!" We can see clear evidence of increasing economic disadvantage and disparity with the naked eye, as well as in official data. The Census Bureau reported in 2016 that the top 20 percent earned over 50 percent of total income, and the top 1 percent alone took home 20 percent. By 2020, the top 20 percent also owned 80 percent of the stock market's value.

Professor Saez's research was cited by Matthew Stewart in his *Atlantic* article "The Birth of a New American Aristocracy" to show that the top *one-tenth of 1 percent* households are the really big winners in terms of wealth concentration. This group of roughly 122,000 households had amassed 22 percent of America's collective wealth by 2012. Stewart went on to point out that the remaining 9.9 percent of the top 10 percent was also part of a new aristocracy of wealth, with net worth of $10 million at the top end to $2.4 million at the median and $1.23 million at the entry point of this grouping. The top 10 percent group is overwhelmingly white, with only 1.9 percent African American, 2.4 percent Hispanic, and 8.8 percent Asian or mixed race. Stewart contended that the top 10 percent have "left the 90 percent in the dust" and are "quietly tossing down roadblocks…to make sure that they never catch up." An American household in the middle of the nation's wealth distribution would need to increase its wealth by a factor of twenty-five to make it to the median of the top 9.9 percent cohort. Meanwhile, "9.9 percenters live in safer neighborhoods, *go to better schools*, have shorter commutes, receive higher quality health care, and, when circumstances require, serve time in better prisons." (Stewart 2018) (Emphasis added.)

Leaving aside the huge gap between the top 0.1 to 10 percent and everybody else, however, the broader upper middle class, measured nationally as the *top quintile* of incomes, has also been relentlessly pulling away from the lower 80 percent. For several decades, the top professional/managerial class (the focus of Richard Reeves's book *Dream Hoarders*) has dominated in terms of aggregate growth in income, while the bottom 80 percent has lagged further behind as a whole, while also experiencing significant disparities in income within its ranks. (Reeves 2017, 23-24) Reeves emphasizes that the upper middle class has also learned from their most wealthy betters the most effective strategies for hoarding economic opportunities. To best capture the benefits of an elite college education for their children, effective hoarding first means settling their families in well-schooled (either private or public) communities, and keeping them so by restrictive zoning laws limiting development to single-family housing and thus preserving their neighborhoods as high-income zip codes where the best colleges recruits. (Ibid., 102-06)

The top 20 percent group is also politically savvy enough to secure and rich enough to exploit the special so-called "529" college savings plans, a federal program that creates a trifecta of tax favors for student' parents and grandparents. Using an IRA-type structure, 529 accounts allow (1) annual gift-tax-free contributions up to fixed amounts to (2) build investments and accumulate related gains free of capital gains tax to (3) deploy as tax-free withdrawals to fund tuition, room, textbooks, and personal computers for their college-bound children, and now also to fund portion of private high school tuition and even pay off student loans. The benefits of 529 investment accounts accrue primarily to families that can afford to set a fair amount of money aside to grow while their children age into their mid and late teens. (Ibid., 136-37)

In addition to upper class political opportunity hoarding, however, there are other factors that directly impact intergenerational socioeconomic mobility — most basically, the income level of one's parents, and its effect on college admissions. The economic research of Raj Chetty and his Harvard and Berkeley colleagues published in 2014 ("Where Is the Land of Opportunity: The Geography of Intergenerational Mobility in the United States") demonstrated that the chances of children entering college directly after high school are strongly correlated with their parents' income: the higher the incomes, the better the chances of college admission. (Chetty et al. 2014) The follow-up 2017 "Mobility Report Cards" on college admissions (cited in chapter 2) by another economic research team headed by Chetty concluded that getting a college education dramatically increased the likelihood that students' adult income would exceed that of their parents. (Chetty et al. 2017) But note that such a result depends on getting reasonable access to college admissions, which in turn depends on their parents' income!

Six out of ten twenty-five-year-olds hold a bachelor's degree among the top 20 percent of family incomes, compared to just one-third in the middle 40 percent and only one in ten in the bottom 40 percent. (Chetty et al. 2017) The Mobility Report Card's conclusions regarding the effects on economic mobility were meticulously documented, and far-reaching. As Jenny Anderson's report in *Quartz* bluntly headlined: "America's top colleges are not the engines of social mobility they say they are." The "Ivy-plus" schools perform well on one particular metric — lifting those from the poorest 20 percent of incomes into the top 1 percent. But less than 4 percent of undergraduate enrollment at the most selective schools are from the lowest income quintile. Anderson's quote from Paul Tough, author of *The Years That Matter Most: How College Makes or Breaks Us*, neatly sums up a major truth from Chetty's research: "'Elite college campuses are almost entirely populated by the students who benefit the least from the education they receive there: the ones who were already wealthy when they arrived on campus.'" (Anderson, Jenny 2019)

Chetty's 2017 report measured social mobility for all students between 1999 and 2013 in terms of graduates' earnings at age 34 compared to their parents' income levels when those students entered college, focusing particularly on success measured by moves up from the bottom 20 percent to the top 20 percent. For each college, the research team calculated a college's "mobility rate" by multiplying the percentage of their students who make the top-to-bottom quintile leap by the percent of their students with parents in the bottom quintile. The team gave the following example: "51% of students from the bottom fifth reach the top fifth at SUNY Stony Brook. Because 16% of students at Stony Brook are from the bottom fifth compared with 4% at the Ivy-Plus colleges, Stony Brook has a bottom-to-top-fifth mobility rate of 8.4%, substantially higher than the 2.2% rate on average at Ivy-Plus colleges." (Chetty et al. 2017, Executive Summary)

Given that many mid-tier public colleges tend to have these higher mobility rates than elite colleges, Chetty's report suggested that policymakers should study them as potentially more scalable "engines of upward mobility" because of their lower instructional costs. But Chetty's team also found that access for poor students to those mid-tier colleges had been dropping significantly over the prior 15 years, most likely because of major cuts in public funding for state campuses by policymakers. (Ibid.) Yet "working-class colleges" funded by the public have sustained their commitment to upward mobility. For example, City College of New York helped 76 percent of its students whose parents were in the bottom quintile of income ultimately move at least into the top 60 percent. (Leonhardt 2017)

This book has also documented in chapter 5 how flagship state schools have responded to severe budget cuts by enrolling more upper-income (full-tuition-paying) applicants through aggressive out-of-state and international recruiting! By the way, the "high-tail" mobility success (bottom 20 percent to top 1 percent) that Chetty found was occurring among the very few low-income students that elite private colleges enroll, means those schools would likely suffer no loss of reputation if they significantly increased their admissions of low-income applicants!

In a "Social Mobility Memo" published by *Brookings*, Richard Reeves and Eleanor Krause summarized the Chetty team's findings succinctly: "In theory, college education is the great equalizer; in practice it is the great stratifier." (Reeves and Krause 2018) Matthew Stewarts's 2018 *Atlantic* article cited above put it more broadly: The "single best predictor" whether children will "get married, stay married, pursue advanced education, live in a good neighborhood, have an extensive social network, and experience good health is the performance of his or her parents on those same metrics." (Stewart ibid.) Access to higher education is at the heart of both Stewart's and Reeves' observations about America's gridlocked socioeconomic disparities. Elite colleges have quietly hoarded a high percentage of admissions lanes for those *already* wealthy or well-connected, thus cementing Chetty's basic finding that the "apple does not fall not far from the tree" for both the upper and lower ends of America's income and wealth spectrum.

Bloomberg Businessweek magazine, citing the "Great Gatsby Curve" introduced by the late Princeton economist Lawrence Kreuger, concluded that America is moving closer to the high-inequality, high-immobility pattern of some other advanced economies. The Gatsby Curve measures the relative degree to which children are likely to remain in the same income levels as their parents, a pattern that the International Monetary Fund has labeled intergenerational economic "stickiness." This phenomenon is more likely to occur (at both ends of the income scale and in between) in countries with higher income inequality than those with a more egalitarian wealth distribution. For example, Nordic counties, where earnings are more evenly spread among the populace than then in America, are good examples of where children's lifetime incomes are more in their own hands than in their ancestry. The IMF's economist Shekhar Alyar told *Bloomberg* that such intergenerational income stickiness also leads to "'talent misallocation...[w]hen high aptitude people are shunted to the margins of society...not only is it unfair, it's also bad for growth.'" (Smialek 2019)

Further research has indeed established that nations with increasing income inequality paired with low mobility will also experience lesser economic progress. According to the World Bank, countries where parental education level is less likely to predict or limit the level of their children's education enjoy more robust social mobility and related growth stimulus. A United Nations report also concluded that unequal societies grow more slowly and are less successful in maintaining economic progress. (Ingraham 2020)

Historically in America, the best pathway available to promote economic mobility has been higher education, but first-generation college applicants and those from lower- and even middle-income families now face monumental obstacles in terms of navigating the black box process and surmounting the odds tipped to wealthier applicants. Poorer students who do well on the standardized tests are so discouraged that a clear majority simply don't even try to get into elite colleges according research by economists Caroline M. Hoxby and Christopher Avery. They found that those students typically reside in districts too small to support selective pubic high schools and rarely come across teachers, counselors or older schools mates who have gone on to highly selective colleges. (Hoxby and Avery 2012) Their research strongly suggests there is no shortage of low-income, high-potential high school seniors, including those living in rural areas, but they are not being effectively courted by admissions departments of elite schools and informed that they could receive substantial financial aid. Those schools spend too much time looking for them primarily in the nation's most high-performing high school districts, instead of actively seeking them out where they actually live. (Jaschik 2012)

Ironically, the admissions bribery scandal could wind up discouraging or even preventing talented but disadvantaged students from even applying. Applicants with genuine disabilities may run up against higher administrative burdens of proof to qualify for extra SAT test-taking time, or their own fear of being wrongly accused of trying to game the system. Some wealthy parents have transferred legal guardianships of their children to less-well-off relatives in order to score admissions and financial aid awards under special criteria for applicants from economically deprived circumstances. This kind of subterfuge, of course, works against the interests of truly disadvantaged applicants. They are often literally homeless or otherwise legitimately living away from their parents under non-parental guardianships or foster care because of danger to them from their own families. Unfortunately, some politicians will be tempted to use the disclosure of fraudulent conduct in admissions practices by wealthy parents to justify cuts in programs like Pell grants under the guise of eliminating the usual suspects of "waste, fraud and abuse" of taxpayer subsidies for the poor. (Goldstein 2019)

Meanwhile, according to the 2017 Chetty research, the Ivy League and other ultra-elite colleges focus most of their Pell grants away from the bottom quintile of family income: 15 percent of their students hold Pell grants, but only 4.7 percent are from the lowest quintile. Other highly selective schools do little better in this regard, with Pell recipients at 18 percent of enrollment but only 3.8 percent from the bottom group. Non-selective colleges are doing the "heavy lifting" in terms of lifting up the prospects of students from the lowest income families. (Ezeugo and McCann 2017) According to Chetty's work, the *American* dream of social mobility at its most aspirational — moving from the bottom 20 percent to the top three quintiles percent — is two times more likely to occur in Canada than in the United States. (Remnick 2018)

To locate and recruit more highly qualified but lower-income students, college admissions offices could redirect more of their visits away from affluent suburbs to poorer, nontraditional recruitment areas. In evaluating applications, they should do more to neutralize the advantages of wealth, such as by giving less weight to experiences like unpaid internships that are more accessible to well-to-do applicants. In making financial aid offers, they could lessen or eliminate the debt burden on the neediest students. They could reduce or eliminate the preference they give to legacies without significantly reducing donations. Why lineage or donations should have anything to do with college admission — unless we accept that admission decisions should be intentionally used as leverage for college revenue-raising strategies extending well-beyond tuition, room, and board?

Chapters 3, 4, and 5 have presented clear and convincing evidence of a *de facto* rejection by the leading elite colleges of the traditional view of higher education as an engine of advancing social and economic progress. The proof is their systematic adoption of admissions practices that are inherently self-interested in financial terms and tilted toward favoring the wealthiest applicants. A University of Chicago doctoral student, Nikhil Goyal, concluded from his research that one need look no further than the present admissions system to design one that would give rich white children the best chances of getting into elite colleges. He found that ending legacy admissions and making standardized tests optional would boost both economic class diversity and racial diversity in America's colleges and universities. (Stauffer 2019) Poor and even middle-class students today, however, are still preemptively deprived of reasonable and fair access to college admission by the high-affluence lanes reserved for legacies, early decision applicants, faculty children and the children of donors and well-connected and socially influential parents. Even the newly expanded benefits of federal and state tax-advantaged section 529 investment programs for covering college expenses accrue largely to upper-income families.

In addition, the standard metrics for "demonstrated interest" favor families that can afford college road-trips and state-of-the-art home and mobile broadband access to enable their children's constant check-the-box check-ins with the college websites and chat rooms. Admissions preferences for athletes in nonrevenue sports with mostly white upper-class players at the high school level are commonly secured with separate front-of-the-line application reviews and lower-scored screening algorithms tracked by athletic departments, just as development apps are bird-dogged by advancement departments. These carve-outs from the publicly disclosed process for reviewing applications reduce the actual odds for applicants without special hooks to levels even lower than the elite schools' publicly disclosed (and celebrated) low admission rates.

We saw in chapter 5 how elite colleges also make use of their racial and global diversity programs by focusing on minority students from the upper-middle class on up, as well as multi-ethnic international applicants from wealthy families that can easily afford full tuition and travel costs. Even merit aid programs are increasingly used to win benefit bake-offs among very promising applicants who have scored multiple admissions and by lower-ranked colleges to entice very talented admits who considered them safeties or matches, even if these students do not qualify for financial aid.

Most applicants of modest means must pay with their time, money, stress loads, and long-term indebtedness merely to participate in a system designed primarily to tend to the needs of wealthy families and wealthy colleges. The elite admissions practices offer no participation trophies, and favor applicants from the wealthiest families from the get-go. Standardized test scoring issues and school-versus-school disparities in GPA metrics also mean that most domestic applicants compete for admission at the best colleges first and foremost with their own high school friends and peers, making admissions anxiety even more intense and personal.

Stressed-out applicants are driven to take more advanced placement courses and push themselves into multiple extracurricular and service activities in order to differentiate themselves from classmates in the brief time (sometimes just a few moments) available to application readers — whether human or machine. High school children now mimic their own cell phone apps, primed to respond on demand to texts, emails and Instagrams from elite admissions offices to earn a favorable score in the schools' demonstrated interest screening algorithms just to be competitive — but without knowing their real odds of success. The psychological impacts of admissions mania are yielding campus environments where upward of 25 percent of those who do get in are on anxiety medication and making frequent contact with campus wellness counseling centers due to stress. None of this is good for America.

Applicants have also been driven to take a maximum number of AP courses not only by college marketing reps, but also by their desire to get a head start on the now-elusive goal of finishing their education in the no-longer-normal four years. Six years to finish is now the standard measure for degree completion among those who track those statistics. To some degree, this is due to the huge marketing costs foisted on them by the practices and dominance of the most exclusive colleges, meaning that far less money goes to funding course availability at many state-funded and other tuition-dependent institutions that must compete with recruiting efforts funded by the earnings from multi-billion dollar endowments.

The notion that America's best-funded power colleges are seriously trying to reduce the intense stress of the application process or otherwise serving the public good as distinctive accelerators of social and economic mobility is at best quaint, and at worst a falsehood. Their business models now amount to a barrier to entry into the American dream for the vast majority of the college-age population. Instead of lighting a fire under American growth prospects by helping a broad economic and social spectrum of the population advance into the college-educated workforce of the future, these schools have built what the legendary investor Warren Buffett would call a "moat" around their endowments, their reputations for exclusivity, and the families who can buy their way into admission, one way or another. Buffett probably would also like the fact that elite colleges do not, like all his for profit businesses, have to treat the IRS as their silent partner at tax time.

The Success of Elite Colleges' Admissions Business Plans Threatens the Financial Models of State Schools and Jeopardizes the Viability of Tuition-Dependent Colleges

Competing with ultra-elite colleges' strong preferences for the wealthy applicants and their equally intense marketing efforts to capture them, a large number of more tuition-dependent colleges are feeling an intensifying financial squeeze. The market power of the most elite institutions forces other higher education institutions to play the admissions game by the elites' very expensive rules while they also seek out rich applicants, not to pad their endowments but just to sustain their financial viability. As the previous chapter has shown, this competitive squeeze has led relatively undercapitalized private colleges to increase rather than decrease sticker-price tuition rates, and even allocate most of their limited supply of traditional merit aid higher up the applicant income scale, in order to at least capture somewhat more net tuition revenue from a high-income family rather than see them enroll their child at a roughly equivalent college with a better offer .

At the same time, these schools have been forced into deep and widespread discounting of their stated tuition prices for a broad spectrum of admitted students, including especially those who have also been accepted by more elite colleges. Nearly one-fifth of private colleges discounted their first-year tuition by at least 60 percent for the 2018-19 academic year, significantly more than prior years. (Pettit 2018) The annual tuition discounting studies produced by the National Association of College and University Business Officers (NACUBO) recently have shown that students are being offered discounts at record rates, averaging 52.2 percent for first-time freshmen and 46.3 percent for all undergraduates for 2018-19. While published tuition rates increased by 47 percent over the ten years prior to the 2018-19 academic year, the average discount also increased by 91 percent, and nearly 90 percent of freshmen benefitted. This obviously led to a general decline in net tuition revenue, the source of about one-third of most private colleges' operating budgets. (Johnson May 10, 2019)

Some colleges have opted to skip the "discounting" step altogether, and have simply slashed their sticker price directly. St. John's College in Maryland, for example, joined many other schools that have cut their sticker prices, in its case from $52,734 to $35,000 for 2018-19. Sweet Briar College in Virginia made a similar move after nearly closing its doors in 2015 while also radically reducing its enrollment and reframing its faculty and curriculum. Elizabethtown College in Kentucky announced a 32 percent tuition cut for the 2019-20 academic year. (Anderson January 20, 2019; Biemiller 2018)

Although posted tuition reductions are accompanied in the most drastic cases by enrollment cuts or marketed as efforts to attract more 'middle class' enrollment by demonstrating "affordability," non-elite colleges in other cases are clearly attempting to attract more stable enrollment, period! By the middle of the past decade, 40 percent of private colleges were reporting flat or declining enrollment according to an annual survey of over 1000 colleges conducted by the *Chronicle of Higher Education*. (Hoover and Lipka 2016) Coupled with steep tuition discounting, smaller entering classes were already threatening to destabilize the business models of small, tuition-dependent private colleges that were losing the war for enrollment to the elites. (Douglas-Gabriel 2017) Commenting on the trend, Ken Rudd, director of research at NACUBO, opined to the *Wall Street Journal* that the "'path they're on may not be sustainable for very much longer.'" (Korn May 7, 2017) Things have not gotten better since, and they look to be getting worse. A *Chronicle of Higher Education's* survey found that about 60 percent of 292 responding colleges missed their enrollment goals for the 2019 entering class, 67 percent missed their net-revenue target for the year, and 52 percent missed both goals. (Carlson 2020) As data later in this chapter will show, the effects of the COVID-19 pandemic have added even greater risks to normal enrollment goals in terms of both new students and existing student retention.

The enrollment war has been increasingly one of attrition in any event, as the overall number of potential enrollees has been shrinking due to demographic factors including past declines in birth rates leading to fewer high school graduates as we approach the third decade of the twenty-first century. That pattern will become even more prominent in the latter half of the 2020s, as the sharp decline in births associated with the Great Recession of 2007-08 kicks in. (Hoover December 14, 2017; see also Conley 2019) Several private colleges in the Northeastern and mid-Atlantic states failed to achieve their enrollment targets for fall 2019. Even some prominent elite schools were feeling the competitive pinch in terms. For example, Bucknell University projected a 2 percent decline in freshmen entering in fall 2019 due to inadequate spending on student aid (i.e., tuition discounting) compared with its peer competitors according to William T. Conley, Bucknell's VP for enrollment management. (Kelderman 2019; Conley 2019) George Washington University — at the margin of elite school status with a 34 percent admission rate — adjusted its sales pitch to emphasize "better not bigger," shrinking its entering enrollment target by 20 percent for the five years beginning with 2020. GWU, at 60 percent of total revenue, is more tuition dependent than many elite private colleges. (Johnson July 17, 2019)

For colleges even more dramatically dependent on tuition revenue and without elite status, business model adjustments have proven far more drastic. *Chronicle of Higher Education* concluded that "in some cases, the business model has broken down entirely, with multiple colleges going out of business altogether or closing down multiple programs to make ends meet at least for the moment." (Kelderman ibid.)

Facing insurmountable pressures in recent years, many colleges across the country have opted to consolidate, merge, shut down their undergraduate programs or close permanently. Mills College in California declared a financial emergency allowing for faculty terminations while reframing its curriculum to create a "signature experience" for undergraduates. Agnes Scott College, Emory & Henry College and Simmons College also have pursued major redesigns of their curriculum. (Biemiller 2017 and 2018) The University of Vermont, McDaniel College in Maryland, and Carroll College in Montana announced major program cuts. Hampshire College, struggling to survive, radically pared down its freshman class for 2019-20 to include only its early decision selections and those who took a gap year from the previous year's admitted group. (Berrett 2019)

Ithaca College recently announced it would enroll 175 fewer freshmen (and collect $4.6 million less net tuition revenue) than it had initially planned. The University of Akron offered buyouts in 2019 to 47 percent of its faculty in an effort to balance its budget.

We have seen how the new president of Mt. St. Mary's tried to deal with its financial stress by suggesting that struggling freshmen should be forced out early in the first term, fired faculty who disagreed with him, and then lost his own job. (Selingo February 9, 2019) From 2016 to 2019, an average of 554 colleges facing the risk of not meeting their enrollment and revenue targets announced they would consider post-deadline applications — a 27 percent increase from the prior three years. (Conley ibid.) To carry their teaching loads, colleges facing the competitive cost squeeze and shrinking enrollment also have become more dependent on adjuncts rather than the career/tenure track professoriate, potentially jeopardizing their academic reputations and their tuition pricing power even more.

Data on potential and actual college closures varies according to the source, methodology, definition of terms and whether both public, private non-profit or for-profit schools are considered in the mix. For example, the *Chronicle of Higher Education* used federal data to show that 1,230 colleges shut down over five years through 2019 displacing a half a million students, mostly comprised of minorities and those on Pell grants. But 88 percent of these closures were for-profit colleges, which do not generally operate within the competitive framework of the non-profit private and state college calendar and admissions system. Leaving for-profit institutions aside, that would still mean that 12 percent or nearly 150 private and state colleges had closed during that period. (Vasquez and Bauman 2019)

A 2016 report produced by an affiliate of the accounting firm Ernst & Young concluded that 800 non-profit and state college campuses were facing "critical" challenges that put them in jeopardy of ultimately closing. Their vulnerability was correlated to several factors, including enrollments under 1,000, the absence of online programs, stated tuition increases greater than 8 percent coupled with discounts of more than 35 percent, dependence of tuition for over 85 percent of their revenue and high debt levels incurred due to increases in spending on campus amenity improvements (a weapon we have noted in the war for enrollment — and rankings). (Selingo September 7, 2016) The *Wall Street Journal* reported that a poll of private non-profit college finance executives in 2017 found that only 51 percent agreed or strongly agreed that their institutions would be financially stable for five years — down from 65 percent the prior year. (Korn September 1, 2017) A "Market Stress Test Score" created by the *Chronicle of Higher Education* to measure the financial health of higher education institutions based on enrollment, revenue streams and expenditures based on 2007-2016 data, while not forecasting as many closures as other studies have suggested, still concluded that 40 percent of colleges were destined to struggle financially. (Baldridge, Shaman, and Zemsky 2020).

Education Dive, in an online November 2019 update, listed 23 recent closures and consolidations among private liberal arts college, closures, including such regionally and nationally recognizable institutions as Burlington College, College of St. Joseph, Green Mountain College, Marlboro College and Southern Vermont College, all in Vermont; College of New Rochelle and Dowling College in New York; Concordia College in Alabama; Grace University in Nebraska; John Wesley College in North Carolina; Marygrove College in Michigan; Marylhurst College in Oregon; Mount Ida College and Newbury College in Massachusetts; St. Joseph's College in Indiana; Shimer College in Illinois; St. Catherine's College in Kentucky; St. Gregory's University in Oklahoma and Trinity Lutheran College in Washington. (*Education Dive* Staff 2019) A similar listing of private non-profit college closures have also been published by *Inside HigherEd.* (Jaschik 2019)

The pace of campus closures and consolidations in the wake of admissions mania has even created a new micro-business opportunity: namely, "going-out-of-business" sales of campus facilities and equipment. In a *Chronicle of Higher Education* article entitled "'Everything Must Go!' A Rash of College Closures Keeps This Liquidation Firm Busy," one academic liquidation specialist described the atmosphere as follows: "'For colleges, we have desks, chairs, computers, book cases, file cabinets, everything you would think of in a regular office...or a call center or operations center....We had a ton of people coming in just to buy the Mac computers, which we sold out in two days.'" (Ellis 2019)

State universities have also been seriously affected by the competitive pressures from the dominant elite college student recruiting practices and resources. Unfortunately, they have taken measures to assure their financial stability that have consequences that wind up favoring wealthier applicants. The financial pressure on public universities has been aggravated by baby-boomer taxpayers' multi-decade effort to cut higher education subsidies (now that they and their children have been well served by them). Middle-class and poorer students from ethnic and racial minorities face ever-increasing tuition on their own without sufficient resources to avoid huge indebtedness. (Fischer and Stripling 2014)

A senior university researcher asserted in a 2016 report published by the *Chronicle* of *Higher Education* that "[w]hite people my age are not going to vote to educate Hispanic kids or black kids...All the great advances in education [like the Morrill Act and the GI Bill] have come when there was a strong white majority." (Fischer et al. 2016) Researchers at Michigan State University found that in states where the Republican Party controlled both the legislative and executive branch, appropriations to higher education were on average about $220 less per student than in other states. That differential was less where white students were overrepresented in state college enrollment compared to the overall population. The Michigan State study, however, does not show that GOP officials actively chose to spend even less on more diverse college populations. (Kelderman 2020)

Confronting local taxpayer resistance, state universities have frequently also chosen to turn their recruiting attention not simply to rich in-state high school graduates but increasingly to out-of-state students whose families can afford full-sticker-price tuition, room, and board, plus the cost of long-distance transportation. (Mangan March 26, 2019) Flagship state college recruiters also noticed (and began to copy) how enrollment of full-tuition-paying non-US students in America had been surging in America's private colleges. In the Ivy League, for example, freshman enrollment grew only 5 percent in the decade through 2014, while the number of incoming foreign students rose 46 percent. (Anderson December 21, 2016) Foreign students are not eligible for federal financial aid: accordingly most of them come from families that can afford the high cost of elite college enrollment. (Leonhardt 2017)

The emphasis in state colleges on recruiting high-paying foreign and domestic out-of-state applicants has been squeezing out home-state children of middle- and lower-class taxpayers. These colleges, however, were intended to serve a primarily local population, going back to the Morrill Act of 1862, which created the first public land-grant colleges across the United States. This situation has been a major public issue in California and many other states in recent years. The total number of applicants to flagship campuses of the UC system like UCLA and Berkeley has soared, pushing both schools into the upper ranks of selectivity but disappointing many thousands of applicants who have met the stringent academic qualifications for these prestigious campuses but simply can't get in due to limits on class size, public funding cuts, and the general increase in admissions allocations to full-tuition out-of-state and international students. (Saul 2016)

The Trump Administration's more stringent review and more frequent rejections of student visas has somewhat diminished the overseas flow to elite private as well as state-sponsored colleges and universities. (Fischer 2017) In any event, the state schools' general tilt to the wealthy — whether from out of state or beyond our national borders — has not been sufficient to ward off budgetary stress. Nor has it immunized state colleges and universities from the recent trend among private schools toward more campus cutbacks, consolidations and closures. The Wisconsin University System has undertaken a major consolidation of two-year colleges into seven four-year institutions, and both the Georgia and Alabama systems have also been consolidating campuses to reduce operating costs. Nearly half the 40 college mergers from 2010 to 2017 involved state institutions. Through 2019, a total of 33 such closures or consolidations had been announced. (*Education Dive* Staff 2019) The Connecticut System announced a consolidation plan that was rejected by the system's accreditors in 2018, but its chief executive warned of possible future closures as a result. (Kelderman 2018)

Massachusetts officials are considering various emergency measures, including a requirement that at-risk colleges in that state's system notify students if the school may not be able to operate for a full 18 months going forward. (Camera 2019) Alaska's state legislature voted in mid-2019 at the governor's urging to severely cut the Alaska University System's budget by 41 percent (including scholarships for historically disadvantaged but academically qualified students), in order to fund as a higher priority the state's $3000 per year payment to its citizens as a "dividend" from the state's oil revenues in the midst of a global decrease in oil prices. (Brown 2019) This drastic reduction, however, was later significantly reduced due to public pressure.

The financial stresses and threats to the viability of so many private and state colleges and universities have raised serious concerns at Moody's, a major college bond rating agency. In 2016, budget battles in Illinois led the agency to downgrade the credit rating of three of that state's public universities. (Douglas-Gabriel 2016) In 2017, Moody's changed its credit outlook for higher education generally from stable to negative and reiterated that view in 2018 with a downbeat long-term economic outlook particularly for private colleges. Moody's pointed to low and declining revenue, increasing labor-intensive expenses and resulting financial stress that could lead to program reductions, mergers, and even closures in the coming years. (Crowe 2018)

Moody's focused on the fact that nearly a fifth of 174 colleges in its survey reported tuition discount rates of at least 60 percent — some more than 70 percent — although the agency had expected the median discount rate across all private colleges to rise no more than 40 percent for that period. Susan Fitzgerald, a Moody's associate management director and analyst, told the *Chronicle of Higher Education* that private colleges face "'a very complex environment on a number of fronts'" in the competitive pressure to attract students, particularly as the number of high school graduates has flattened out nationally and even decreased in the prime private college locales in the Northeast and Midwest. She noted that, given the opaque nature of the admissions process, some students are applying to up to dozens of schools and paying attention to the extent of financial aid offered. She concluded that private colleges "'are trying to figure out the model that's sustainable.'" As the *Chronicle* noted, rising discount rates will continue to stifle private colleges' pricing flexibility because, as the Moody's official said, "'once a certain discount rate is promised to incoming freshmen, it's really difficult to tell them the following year that they're getting less of a break.'" (Pettit 2018)

Moody's concerns about financial risk have even spread to some prestigious universities under pressure to invest to keep up with even more elite colleges spending. This concern was enough to trigger a reduction in Northwestern University's top-level Aaa credit rating by one notch. Moody's made a similar move with respect to Washington University of St. Louis's rating in 2017, and about Boston University's rating in 2019. (Bauman 2019)

Moody's is not the only interested observer of the state of competition among colleges for a steady flow of revenue as it affects their long-term viability. Those closest to the situation sometimes express the deepest misgivings about the future of higher education institutions in the United States. Professor Clayton Christianson of the Harvard Business School and author of *The Innovative University* has predicted that as many as half of America's colleges and universities will close or go bankrupt by 2030. (Camera ibid.) Andrew S. Rosen, former chairman and CEO of for-profit Kaplan University was cited in the *Chronicle of Higher Education's* 2018 report, "Sustaining the College Business Model," as predicting that the total number of colleges and universities in America (over 5000 currently counting the for-profit schools) would be reduced to 600 in the coming decades. The *Chronicle* noted that Kaplan was acquired by Purdue University after its own profit downturn.

Poor Students Face Another Barrier to College Success: Hunger — While Some Colleges Exploit Their Students with Excessive Fees

Colleges and universities, big and small, have been tempted onto the slippery slope of scamming the very same students they fight to enroll. Mandatory athletic fees (that don't provide actual seats at games as at the University of Michigan) and meal plan charges that conceal kickbacks to the schools from for-profit outsourced dining hall operators (common in many college dining halls) to help keep these schools' budgets in the black. Yet on some prestigious campuses that engage in those scams, the poor students who have been admitted with Pell grants simply don't get enough to eat in those dining halls, including even recruited scholarship athletes in high-revenue sports. A *New York Times* report in May 2019 was headlined: "Tuition or Dinner? Nearly Half of College Students

Surveyed in a New Report Are Going Hungry." The *Times* cited a study by Temple University's Hope Center for Colleges, Community, and Justice that found multiple examples among higher education institutions where over 45 percent of students reported "food insecurity" — the state of having limited or uncertain access to food — during a 30-day period while pursuing their academic programs. (Laterman 2019) The same study also concluded that 36 percent of all students were struggling with basic needs like food and housing, and that 40 percent of four-year college student were unable to pay for balanced meals. (Hess 2018) Although food insecurity is generally associated with students at community college, students at elite flagships like Cal Berkeley and private elite schools like Northwestern are not immune from experiencing periods of hunger. One in four college students today have a child, and those without must work 20-hours a week to qualify for food stamps. (Goldrick-Rab 2018) The Urban Institute found that, in 2015, 13 percent of students at two-year colleges and 11 percent at four-year colleges did not have enough to eat. (Thomas 2018)

The student hunger situation has given rise to a "college food pantry" movement. Over seven hundred members of the College and University Food Bank Alliance distribute leftover food from catered events and dining halls to food-needy students and help them obtain food stamps. (Laterman ibid.) The *Lexington Herald Leader* reported on a student hunger strike staged at the University of Kentucky to protest the lack of central resources to help students who cannot afford to fund their meals that ended with the University's president agreeing to a series of steps to give minority students more input in selection of university deans and high-level administrators, and to provide additional resources dedicated to a new Basic Needs Center addressing student food and housing insecurity. (Blackford 2019)

Finding and funding sufficient daily food is not the only problem for poor students, even on elite campuses. Brown University, which chapter 5 revealed had facilitated special "exposure lunches" for wealthy and well-connected students, was forced to confront the inability of low-income students to fund purchases of textbooks needed for their classes. To its credit, Brown responded with a program to cover free cafeteria meals for students with university financial aid scholarships whose parents' required contributions to their child's college costs was rated at zero dollars by the aid office. (Supiano April 11, 2019) At the other end of the campus wealth spectrum, community colleges in California have been looking at opening up their parking lots overnight to accommodate commuter students living in their cars to be able to afford even the low tuition rates these schools generally charge.

Another *New York Times* headline summed up the situation at one prestigious school caught up in the 2019 admissions bribery scandals this way: "Student Life at USC? It All Varies, by Income." The *Times* also found the problem is broader than just one elite college. "We know when low-income students get to these elite schools, they have a large problem with fit," said Jessica Thompson, the director of policy and planning at the Institute for College Planning and Success. "'These schools have built reputations in the world that they are operating to erase class lines, but they are actually sort of hardening the types of inequity they claim to eliminate.'" (Medina 2019)

Unaffordable student food, housing and textbook costs are symptoms of a broader lack of understanding, effort and targeted support for the experience of economically disadvantaged students enrolled at elite colleges. Even their diversity agendas are often bent toward minorities in the upper economic class, because that works better for college economics in terms of the need for extra support of low-income students. The Jack Kent Cooke Foundation Report, "True Merit: Ensuring Our Brightest Students Have Access to Our Best Colleges and Universities," prominently recommended that our most elite colleges should cease reliance on wealth biased SAT and ACT test results, and also create a "poverty preference" to match the multiple preferences afforded to the wealthy and well-connected. (Giancola and Kahlenburg 2016, 29; Hoover January 11, 2016) But as this chapter shows, even if they were to do so, much more would need to be done to help those economically disadvantaged but unquestionably bright students to physically and emotionally survive in those schools' socially sophisticated and judgmental cultures. As Jennifer Morton has pointed out in an essay ("The False Promise of Elite Education") in the *Chronicle of Higher Education*:

> It is important to recognize the extent to which social norms at elite colleges strongly discourage "outsider" students from revealing themselves as such. One recent graduate I interviewed admitted that she has joined one of Princeton's eating clubs as an undergraduate because she believed that not doing so would damage her prospects on the job market. She had been told that prospective employers would automatically presume that anyone who had not joined must have been unable to afford it. At elite universities, there is an incentive to conceal anything that could expose one as not really belonging. (Morton 2019)

In a July 2, 2019 headline, the *Chronicle* asked: "Why Don't Colleges Do More to Help Students in Need? Money, Attitudes and More." As a specific example of the priority some colleges place on their own financial well being, the article cited the profits they can reap pricing their on-campus meal plans to reflect the fact that some students won't be using all the meals they pay for. This profit priority in turn has led college administrators to actively resist the "Swipe Out Hunger" movement emerging on some campuses that would allow students to donate their unused meal plan card "swipes" to economically disadvantaged peers. (Blumenstyk July 12, 2019) Students at Spelman College in Atlanta petitioned to a "Swipe" program on campus and also staged a hunger strike, which ended with agreement on the part of Aramark, a $9 billion food services contractor, and the College to provide 7000 dining hall meals to students living off-campus.

Can we really expect a serious reform agenda addressing disadvantaged students' basic campus living and social needs to emerge from elite college managements that scam for extra dollars off dining hall bills or impose stadium fees for seats most students can never access? They take measures like these, that don't pass the smell test, because they are driven by their business models to increase operating income to fund marketing programs focused on higher income groups. Although they bring a few low-income students to campus, they fail to fully appreciate that those students, on arrival and throughout a four or more year path to a degree, will not have enough money for sufficient food or required textbooks .

Tuition-dependent campuses caught in the admissions marketing competitive cost squeeze may simply not have the resources to provide all the support relief necessary, although some are working valiantly. Non-elite and many state colleges, moreover, have been shown to do an equal or even better job of helping low-income students persist to graduation and progress toward strong careers compared to what most elite colleges do for the relatively small numbers they enroll from the lowest income rungs. (See the annual *US News* list of "Top Performers on Social Mobility" — a truly informative and useful ranking.) Ultra-elite Ivy League schools, however, actually do an excellent job for their most disadvantaged students, according to Raj Chetty's research group in its "Mobility Report Cards." Post-college, their graduates earn more than three-quarters of all Americans, and their low-income grads do almost as well in this regard as other, wealthier graduates. (Chetty et al. 2017)

The problem, however, is that low-income students typically make up only a low single digit percentage of their enrollment, nowhere near the share of the upper class, especially the 1 percent, who fill as many seats as the bottom 50 percent. (Kvaal 2017) The pattern of ultra-elite colleges instinctively focusing their educational mission largely on preserving the opportunities and privileges of the economic elite while leaving their poorer students to fend for themselves in a wealth-dominated environment remains all too common. It is also inexcusable, given their demonstrated capacity to do such a good job of enhancing social mobility for those disadvantaged students they manage to admit.

The book *Paying for the Party*, which was researched in a dormitory at an unnamed Midwest state's flagship university revealed that (as *New York Times* columnist Ross Douthat put it in his review) "the American way of college rewards those who come not just academically but socially prepared, while treating working class students more cruelly, and often leaving them adrift." (Douthat 2014) The party scene on such flagship campuses serves as the dominant pathway through the university years for many students of the top 1 percent, and even some from less affluent upper-middle-class families whose economic and social futures are nonetheless relatively secure. The party path rests on, as the authors put it, an implicit bargain between the university and the wealthy students to require little of each other apart from tuition, room and board payment on the one hand, and on the other, the assurance that those students' social associations with peers who are similarly situated financially will be facilitated. The social "wannabees" and students from families who must borrow their way into college, however, can get sucked into a scene that can wreck their more practical goal of graduating, getting a good job and moving up economically. (Armstrong and Hamilton 2013) Meanwhile, as Douthat observed, the impact of the party pathway described in the book demonstrates how inherited capital can reproduce and ratify privilege, even in an institution founded to foster democratic values and the common good. (Douthat ibid.)

This pattern could be reversed if leadership at the top — including presidents and boards — were willing to embrace fully the public purposes of higher education that justify their own tax-exempt money-raising privileges. Some board members, however, may themselves be more interested in preserving and extending high-affluence admission lanes for the benefit of their own relatives, friends and colleagues. Yet there are examples of private, well-regarded colleges that have been attempting to stand against the prevailing admissions culture by genuinely prioritizing enrollment and support for high-achieving low-income students in ways that do not disadvantage those schools' finances or reputations.

Daniel Porterfield, former president of Franklin & Marshall and president of the Aspen Institute, asserted that "there is an abundance of talent in every zip code in the country," and that the work his college did to attract more Pell grant recipients found they outperform the student body as a whole in terms of graduation rate, and statistically outperformed other graduates in terms of *magna* and *summa cum laude* honors. New students' SAT scores at Franklin and Marshall also trended up after it introduced a focus on attracting talent from all quarters. President Porterfield urged colleges to focus "on the needs of our country and its future…If we don't fight for educational excellence and equity, we're ultimately not serving our society and our democracy." He identified the College Advisory Corps, the Posse Foundation, the Schusterman Foundation, College Track and College Match in California, and Sponsors for Educational Opportunity in New York City as being among those organizations and programs that have partnered with efforts to expand college access to include all those with the talent to succeed regardless of family income. (Gardner 2018)

Some elite colleges and their donors have been aggressively setting an example of what it takes to help students from low-income families gain entry to their ranks. An effort backed by Bloomberg Philanthropies called the American Talent Initiative has persuaded scores of selective colleges to join an effort to increase low-income high-achieving student enrollment by 50,000 at the 270 schools with the best graduation rates by 2025 to reverse the nationwide trend of declining low-income enrollment. This initiative is paired with Bloomberg Philanthropies' CollegePoint program, which uses virtual advising to guide low- and moderate-income applicants through the admissions process. Through 2019, 120 colleges and universities including the Ivy League, elite liberal arts colleges and state flagship schools had signed up and enrolled nearly 7,300 additional lower-income students. (2019 Annual Report, *Bloomberg Philanthropies*)

Many individual elite colleges have also started programs to help less-affluent students gain entry to their ranks. Fordham and Georgetown, for example, have pledged to expand course credit agreements with community colleges to facilitate transfer. Stanford has stopped counting home equity as part of financial aid assessment for some degree programs.

Most elite colleges, however, seem to need a push to reconnect more fully with their public purpose when it comes to their admissions practices. Some are seeing the light, however, at least in terms of the broader national economic interests. The president of a top twenty-five elite university recently observed succinctly that higher education is underperforming the US economy (but if so, it is also overcharging). His words are on point in terms of producing the number of well-educated graduates we need for the workforce of the future, and even in recent years before the pandemic, when upwards of six million jobs in America went unfilled month after month because of a lack of workers with the requisite education and skills. This situation will only get worse with demographic trends showing more baby boomers retiring and insufficient numbers of graduates to replace them. Our most elite colleges today seem strategically comfortable performing the same role as when they were founded — in some cases, centuries ago: namely, educating the children of the elite upper economic class, and thereby reproducing and reinforcing not only those privileged classes, but also the colleges' own considerable, untaxed wealth.

The Rich Do Get Richer — Including Elite Colleges (Subject to Pandemics)

The law of large numbers sometimes catches up with massive private university endowments during times of financial market volatility like the Great Recession. The size of developments staffs at those institutions nevertheless kept growing as the schools sensed the opportunity to cultivate more rich donors, including especially their own graduates who were moving up the income ladder more quickly than in the past. This phenomenon was spurred by the success of new technology and social media firms where the millennial generation talent found a welcoming and wealth-producing opportunity in the Great Recession's aftermath prior to 2020.

Earnings of households in the top rungs of income distribution have continued to swell while incomes for almost everyone else stagnated, yielding a special dividend for elite colleges: the rise in donations spawned by the new affluence of younger graduates. In a perfect illustration of the enigmatic Matthew Effect (the tendency for the rich to get richer, so named by the sociologist Robert Merton with reference to a New Testament parable), these new donations have gravitated to institutions that are already well endowed. Indeed, inequality among college endowments has been fairly described as stunning in its reflection of America's broader divide between haves and have-nots. Ironically, a significant consequence of the country's unequal distribution of wealth — a phenomenon loudly decried by many university scholars — has been to boost the ability of rich donors to give large gifts (sometimes in the form of faculty "chairs") to the colleges that employ those same scholars.

Universities that have built the largest endowments also saw them grow the fastest. Research by Thomas Piketty found that, from 1980 to 2010, the universities with the largest endowments enjoyed higher average returns than those with small ones. Endowments greater than $1 billion earned an average of 8.8 percent a year after inflation, while those endowments with less than $100 million earned just 6.2 percent. In addition, a big share of the largest philanthropic gifts have been going to universities, and ultra-elite elite schools have been major beneficiaries since the ten year stock market boom took off early in the 2010-19 decade. "A significant consequence of the country's unequal distribution of wealth, a phenomenon loudly decried by scholars, has been to boost the ability of rich donors to give large gifts to the colleges that employ those scholars." (Clotfelter 2017)

The largest endowments have significant investments in riskier assets with higher average yields, such as stocks and real estate. In recent decades, the wealthiest universities have also significantly increased the proportion of their portfolios in private equity, hedge funds, venture capital, as well as investments in off-campus-based real estate, natural resources, and distressed debt. During the ten-year bull market following the Great Recession, many of these "alternative" investments have performed exceptionally well. If elite colleges truly want to reduce the degree of economic stratification that exists in society (and is reflected in their own enrollment), they clearly have the financial wherewithal to redouble their efforts to increase access for those less well off. Ironically, the fact that many endowment assets of elite colleges have been tied up in the forms of alternative investments that did well during the post-Recession financial markets has worked to their disadvantage during the financial aftershocks of the COVID-19 outbreak. The relative illiquidity of private equity and similar investments during this time triggered significant asset depreciation, which devalued their endowments sharply and reduced their financial flexibility just as their expected annual revenue flow from tuition and fees was taking an even more immediate cash hit. This happened again during the COVID-19 pandemic. As noted in chapter 2, the pandemic-related rating agency downgrades of collegiate creditworthiness further magnified the pandemic's impact on their ability to borrow to meet increasing financial expenses in terms of the sudden need for radical changes in their instructional and research operations.

Well before COVID-19 hit, the 2017 *Inside Higher Ed* Survey of College and University Admissions Directors revealed that clear majorities among admissions offices of private colleges planned to increase their recruiting focus on full-tuition-paying applicants, including those from outside the United States. Among state institutions, the survey found continued focus on international and out-of-state applicants who will pay a higher tuition rate than those from the home state. The admissions offices of 70 percent of private colleges also had planned to increase their focus on the use of merit aid (as distinct from support for students from the lowest income levels). As described more fully in the previous chapter, most colleges until recently used merit aid mainly to maintain a presence of middle-class students not eligible for Pell grants and for students from lower-income families without having to discount general tuition rates for all those enrolling. As the dominant elite colleges have led tuition pricing inexorably higher to satisfy their own business and financial agendas, more tuition-dependent, less well-endowed schools have been forced to increasingly offer merit aid to the upper middle class and beyond to capture at least something closer to full tuition income from wealthier families.

Another funding issue arises because of the *US News* rankings criteria, which awards points for increasing level spending per student on university resources.. Besides discouraging more enrollment against a static funding base, this metric encourages ambitious colleges to increase tuition, reduce discounting, ration financial aid, and spend more on faculty. All these moves push schools to admit more of the wealthiest applicants because they need less financial aid and can pay closer to sticker price. Colleges can also score ranking points generally if more faculty hiring would reduce average class sizes. This is a prime example of "strategic fit" planning advanced by enrollment consultants for the purpose of increasing an elite college's aura of exclusivity and reputation for "merit-based" admissions, which in turn attracts the interest of the wealthiest families As Leon Botstein has argued, measures of "meritocracy" such as standardized test scores, college rankings, grades *and income* (which we know are the key performance indicators in terms of elite admission departments' self-assessments) are "blunt and discriminatory instruments of comparison that trivialize merit by confusing wealth with excellence and reinforcing the power of money and privilege." (Botstein 2019)

Thousands of dedicated admissions leaders and staff, however, do collaborate on best practices through their professional associations and strive to make the admissions process more humane. Yet on the whole it shamefully remains a maniacal maze that the wealthy have the most favorable chance of finding their way through successfully. As noted in the introduction to this book, many other distinguished authors have, in recent decades, exposed the inherent biases and unfairness of the elite college admissions process, but shaming and naming alone has not changed the game. In addition, cooperation among even our best colleges on admissions reform has been actively discouraged by federal efforts to use antitrust law as a weapon to preserve an unregulated market allegedly for the benefit of its student consumers.

Cementing Wealth Disparity with Secretive Elite Admissions Preferences Is Contrary to Our Long-Term National Interest and Not Excusable as a Mere Accident of an Otherwise Benign Process

The net result of the triumph of the elite college admissions model has been to reinforce the status quo of wealth disparity in America, and to drive a stake through the heart of social and economic mobility in the nation. It turns the traditional public purpose of higher education — to facilitate upward mobility — literally upside down, to become merely an instrument for private gain for the already privileged. The *Chronicle Review* headlined what has happened: "How the Rich Universities Get Richer...and leave everyone else behind" --

> Over the last 40 years, no one has proposed that the guiding purpose of higher education should be to aggravate inequality. Indeed, policy makers and college leaders have declared the opposite aspiration. They have spoken of colleges as meritocratic engines of opportunity. Yet the historical record tells a contrary story, one of widening disparities in the college market. The richest colleges have become richer, gathering an increasing share of the most in-demand students and exposing them to the most sought-after faculty and the highest-quality facilities and campus resources. In short, the leaders of rich colleges have presided over a remarkable increase in inequality. (Clotfelder 2017.)

Most commentators on this result, however, including the *Chronicle*, tend to view this outcome as an *unintended* consequence of otherwise well-meaning and understandable admissions traditions and practices, noting that, under America's own traditions and constitutional freedoms of association, the choice of who gets into universities is best left to the schools themselves. As the *Chronicle Review's* author continued: "This matters precisely because increasing inequality is *not* the intent of policy makers or college leaders. Federal aid, state subsidies, and need-blind admissions all aim to make college open and affordable to qualified students regardless of economic circumstance. But other policies and practices used by colleges to attract students, including state-sponsored merit scholarships, tuition discounting, and admission preferences for children of alumni, often have the opposite effect — they exacerbate inequality." (Ibid.)

Even the Cooke Foundation's 2017 "True Merit" report — although highly critical of elite college admissions practices — concluded that the results of those practices were "presumably" inadvertent. To assert, however, that admission and enrollment preferences and outcomes decidedly beneficial to the most elite colleges' bottom lines are merely an unavoidable and unintended result of a basically decent process strains credulity. Chapters 3, 4, and 5 show that those colleges have adopted their own version of the seductive mantra of "shareholder value above all else" that has led generations of for-profit business leaders to deny the existence or relevance of any form of accountability to the public at large for their companies' actions — despite the fact that the public has granted their shareholders the privilege of limited liability!

All corporations, both public and nonprofit, however, literally begin their existence as beneficiaries of the unique legal privilege, granted by the public, to operate with limited personal financial liability for such actions for their shareholders and officers, except in very limited circumstances that are specified by law. The basic premise and purpose of this limit on liability for business enterprises has always been to facilitate the efficient aggregation of capital to support industrial and economic growth. But that aim does not mean that the public has granted this privilege as a license to disregard the public interest with utter impunity in pursuit of profit. This same understanding of public purpose surely applies with even more force to higher education institutions that also enjoy the benefits of nonprofit, tax-exempt status.

Elite Colleges Have Failed to Effectively Address Other Egregious Campus Practices and Offer Lip Service Even to Admission Reforms They Have Endorsed, But Some Leaders are Speaking Out

If we rely on the chance for self-regulation and voluntary reform of college admissions practices, we will be disappointed. Colleges generally have been unable for decades to clean up the money pit of big-time collegiate revenue sports: note the recent multiyear scandal at the University of North Carolina regarding phony courses and grades for football and basketball players, a fun-house mirror image of the phony athletic resumes for admitting children from wealthy families discovered by the Justice Department. The University of Southern California has been caught up in numerous scandals involving NCAA recruiting violations relating to illegal gifts to athletes and cover-ups of sexual and drug abuse.

The *Chronicle of Higher Education* complained in 2016 that the NCAA sports conferences had dragged their feet for 15 years in implementing the reforms proposed by the Knight Commission on Intercollegiate Athletics, particularly in terms of the "glacial pace of change" in how big-time sports dollars were distributed. (Kirwan and Duncan 2016) The *New York Times* characterized big-time college basketball for "unscrupulously competing for top talent to earn more from the immense pot of profit from television" and complained that the problem was "too often relegated to self-regulation by the universities and the NCAA". (Editorial Board, *New York Times*. September 28, 2017) The paper traced the (untaxed) financial windfall to colleges that comes from the annual "March Madness" basketball tournament — again, demonstrating the financial incentives that stand in the way of reform at powerful higher education institutions. (Bauman and Davis 2018)

Leading colleges also have had to be forced by the Department of

Education under Title IX to implement and frequently revise their standards for investigating sexual misconduct on their campuses. Misconduct in terms of Greek life hazing, racial intolerance, hate-filled protests, and free versus safe speech controversies have defied self-policing by current college administrative structures and protocols, with no end in sight. Elite college admissions systems would seem to be the least of the concerns of those schools' administrators and boards, although they should be at the top of their to-do lists.

A prominent and apparently well-intentioned 2016 report by the Harvard Graduate School of Education ("Turning the Tide: Inspiring Concern for Others and the Common Good Through College Admissions") made a powerful case for changes in admissions practices in the direction of a more equitable and public-serving approach. The report was endorsed by scores of deans of admission and other senior officials of elite colleges and prep schools. It suggested refocusing admissions decisions on applicants' "meaningful ethical and intellectual engagements" rather than primarily on evidence of extraordinary individual achievement, de-emphasizing extensive but shallow extracurricular engagements and multiple AP submissions. The report directly called out the secrecy around how much standardized test scores count or correlate with achievement at a particular college and decried the rampant over-coaching of applicants. The stated headline goals of the report's recommendations captured parts of the problem: — "Reducing Undue Achievement Pressure, Redefining Achievement, and Leveling the Playing Field for Economically Diverse Students"— but it fell short in terms of directly addressing the matter of the bias toward the wealthy inherent in the admissions system. (Weissbourd, Thacker et al. 2016; Heffernan and Wallace 2016)

The authors of the report suggested that admissions officers should "remind parents and students that authenticity, confidence and honesty are best reflected in the student's own voice" and invite them to "reflect on the ethical challenges they faced during the application process" but did not offer similar advice to admissions officers to reflect on the authenticity, honesty, and ethical challenges involved in their conduct of the admissions process. The report did offer a lament that "too few administrators and faculty see their role as ethical stewards" and acknowledged that we cannot "bring about a sea change in the messages our culture sends to young people unless educational institutions at every level elevate and embody a healthier set of values." (Weissbourd, Thacker et al. ibid.)

The report, however, did not include any timetable or set of benchmarks to measure the extent to which its recommendations would be adopted by the subscribing admissions departments. No such measures are currently available, although some major colleges have vowed to follow up. The report also prominently advised *applicants* to change their approach and behavior — even in the face of what they hear from college admission departments about what they consider an acceptable application. It urged high school students to focus on the quality of extracurricular activities, not the quantity; to do service that inspires real ethical awareness; and to avoid taking multiple AP courses at the cost of sustained achievement in one area. But why should applicants be even further stressed and burdened by being assigned the task of somehow forcing change in elite colleges' self-interested admissions criteria and decision processes?

In the absence of any accountability mechanisms for tracking the adoption of the report's proposals, college admissions officers' recruiting pitches, even by those whose officials signed on to the report, still urge applicants to take all the APs they can (and be sure to get As in them). No appreciable change in the content of recruiting pitches to reflect the Harvard report recommendations has been noted. With money on the line, we unfortunately must watch what admissions officials do and say, not just what they sign.

Catherine Bond Hill, former president of Vassar College, has called attention also to the trade-offs standing in the way of redirecting admissions practices toward more openness to economically disadvantaged applicants, in part due to rising income disparity in America. In a 2019 *Wall Street Journal* commentary supporting the proposition that all college admissions should be need-blind, she nonetheless pointed to conflicts between the financial needs of selective schools and those of the students they select. If they go need-blind but don't meet need in full, however, that could encourage their families to borrow excessively to attend. If colleges adopt less expansive "need aware" policies and then rely on admitting enough wealthy students to subsidize the applicants from economically disadvantaged families, then there will be a focus of competing for those wealthy students with attractive physical amenities and even wealth-directed merit aid.

Hill went on, however, to make the case for a significant shift in spending and admission priorities to benefit talented but lower-income applicants, even though it would mean the wealthy would lose out — but only because current policies are biased in their favor. The colleges, of course, would also suffer some loss of full-tuition payments and potential future donations from grateful wealthy graduates and their families.

> But if we are going to restore society's trust in higher education as contributor to the public good, a student's ability to pay shouldn't be one of the conditions…[of admission]….Factoring ability to pay into the admissions equation favors affluent students over equally-qualified low- and middle-income students, a regressive policy that works against equal opportunity and economic growth….Why is that a problem? After all, low and middle-income consumers are priced out of other markets: high-end cars, restaurants, homes. The difference is that

taxpayers subsidize higher education...under the premise that it benefits society as a whole. These subsidies are significantly higher at selective institutions, which reap the benefits of preferential tax treatment on endowment earnings and charitable giving. As a result, wealthy students receive more of these subsidies than their lower-income peers, a situation few would argue is ideal. (Ibid.)

In a separate essay published earlier by the American Council on Education in the "Money Issue" of its journal *The Presidency,* President Hill had presciently noted the irony that while higher education is not supporting equal opportunity and social mobility as much as it should, the "trade-offs involved in admitting a low-income student rather than a high-income one have increased as a result of increasing income inequality." They know that the lack of access to a college degree itself locks lower-income students into their economic status, such that that the wealth building effects of access to higher education is increasingly concentrated among the wealthy families they need to prioritize in recruiting! Hill likened elite colleges to car dealers who respond to "incentives in the market in which they compete." As a consequence, they tend to focus their resource on further developing the skills and attributes of the children of the rich because "they can pay," as opposed to low-income children who "have had to work rather than play violin or lacrosse, and need more financial aid." (Hill 2015)

The radical honesty of both of President Hill's observations is refreshing and daunting: it strongly suggests that some elite colleges truly want to find a way to do the right thing, but also that they lack the competitive flexibility under the current admissions system to do so. Essentially, this means that effective reform, even where it must be forced from the outside, must include supportive incentives as well as mandates for transparency and changes in current decision-making norms. As we saw in chapter 5 in the context of legacy admissions, William Dudley, former President of the Federal Reserve Bank of New York, has argued that such reforms are badly needed to assure the intergenerational economic mobility needed to support America's economic competitiveness and growth, as President Hill also noted in the *Journal* essay.

Dudley cited statistics showing that the percentage of American children who earn more than their parents has fallen from 90 percent to 50 percent over the past 50 years, and only 37 percent of parents believe their children will fare better financially. "While college graduations rates in the U.S. have stagnated, those in many other OECD countries have continued to rise. As a result, only one-quarter of those in the 25-to-34 age bracket in the United States have more education than their parents, compared with an OECD average of one-third. This represents a dramatic decline in college education's influence as an engine of upward mobility." Dudley blamed this negative economic trend not only on soaring college costs and student debt liabilities, and public underestimation of the value of college degrees, but also on inadequate preparation of students in K-12 for the rigors of college. He particularly focused on Raj Chetty's findings that access to the best universities is very closely related to parental income. Dudley specifically called for an end to the "patently unfair" practice of legacy admissions and also targeted "donate-to-admit" practices. (Dudley 2017)

In terms of the ongoing detrimental societal impact of special admission lanes like legacies favoring the wealthy, the dean of the College at Harvard perhaps inadvertently exposed the prevailing attitude in elite college circles. In his testimony in the Asian discrimination trial, he was quoted in the *Chronicle of Higher Education* as asserting that Harvard is "'not trying to mirror the socioeconomic or income distribution of the United States.'" (Gluckman November 2, 2018) But that is *precisely* what Harvard and other elite colleges are, in fact, doing — literally replicating the prevailing privileged status of the wealthy and white to very nearly the same degree that the latest socioeconomic statistics reveal: the already wealthy upper-classes get the lion's share of the golden ultra selective admission tickets, just as they get the largest share of national income.

The dean was most probably intending to refer to a hypothetical percentage distribution of first year enrollment correlating with the America's income distribution cohorts, so that the applicants from the top 20 percent of families' wealth would wind up with 20 percent of enrollment, and so on down the line. Harvard is neither intending to admit nor admitting 50 percent of its freshman class from the bottom 50 percent of family incomes. Nor should such an outcome — or, for example, allocation of admissions by equal shares for each income quintile — be a part of any true reform agenda. In terms of the *percentage* of admissions effectively reserved by Harvard and like institutions for wealthier candidates, however, Harvard is indeed tracking America's existing "winner take most" wealth concentration. The elite admissions winners are the early decision applicants who can afford to show maximum demonstrated interest and pay full sticker-price tuition, legacies, donors' and faculty and staff members' children, sons and daughters of the well-connected, and athletes in aristocratic sports. In addition, a major share of even regular-way admissions go to those who have enjoyed the benefit of substantial performance-enhancing dollars' worth of demonstrated interest, as well as coaching for tests, GPAs, APs, and essays. The outcome is not merely mirroring America's increasing wealth disparity: it is setting it in ivy-covered stone.

Elite colleges enjoy the benefits of a unique kind of seller's market that has also attracted its own elite class of buyers. These schools have for too long exploited this market situation, as well as the severe anxiety it creates among its consumers and the financial stress it causes its competitors, for the colleges' own financial and reputational benefit. The fact that these admissions practices, driven by the model at elite colleges, have served to reinforce rather than cut against income disparity in America is beyond serious dispute. Karin Fischer, writing in the *Chronicle of Higher Education* in December 2016 answered her article's headline question — "Are Colleges Engines of Inequality?' — with the following quotes from leading analysts of American higher education:

> Here's how Thomas G. Mortenson, an analyst who crunched the data, puts it: "The rich are getting richer because of higher education," says Mr. Mortenson, a senior scholar at the Pell Institute for the Study of Opportunity in Higher Education, "the poor are getting poorer because of it"….[H]igher education "takes the inequality given to it and magnifies it," says Anthony P. Carnevale, director of the Center on Education and the Workplace at Georgetown University. "It's an inequality machine." (Fischer et al 2016)

James V. Koch, professor of economics and president emeritus of Old Dominion University has come to similar conclusions in his 2019 book, *The Impoverishment of the American College Student*, which is based on his sense that the United States is near a crisis situation in terms of social mobility, and that higher education is a big reason why. Citing the work of Raj Chetty about the declining ability to move from the lowest to the highest income quintiles, he told the *Chronicle of Higher Education* that some elite institutions that think they are good at fostering mobility "'really aren't very good at it….Institutions can do better if they wanted to, but for a variety of reasons, they don't. Who wants to be the president who presides over a decline in the *US News & World Reports'* annual rankings?'" (Patel 2019)

The business models adopted by any institution, including the most elite colleges, are very deliberate choices and reflect purposive strategic plans, which are very hard to change for reasons of "mere" social responsibility — especially when they have been consistently financially successful! These models tend to get changed only if they are not working — and admissions mania is working well for our most highly ranked institutions of higher learning. We might as well call them institutions of higher income. The elite college admissions black box generates a replica of our society as it is. The statement of the Wake Forest sociologist cited in chapter 5 bears repeating: "'The whole system is a pay-for-play system. But that's America.'" (Stripling April 17, 2019)

Speaking of pay-for-play, the recently announced indictments of parents, admissions consultants, athletic coaches, and standardized test administrators in a scheme to use bribes disguised (and deducted) as charitable contributions to (successfully) gain admission for children to elite colleges across the country has revealed that these illegal actions are simply a side door to admissions with the same end result as entering via the back door of million-dollar donations. In remarks in the *Chronicle of Higher Education* ("It's an Aristocracy: What the Admissions-Bribery Scandal Has Exposed About Class on Campus"), Anthony Carnevale, of Georgetown further observed the "thing people are getting mad about is that meritocracy looks like it's locked in, so it's an aristocracy."

The *Chronicle* summed up his perspective on the prevailing admissions system this way: "But for the most selective institutions, the business model demands a steady stream of high-achieving, high-income students…Admitting those students, and rejecting a lot of others, drives up national rankings and creates a product that wealthy families are willing to pay for through tuition dollars, test preparation, and high-priced consulting…[here quoting Carnevale]: 'The business model is to climb or die.'" (Stripling ibid.)

The Bribery Scandals and the Impact of the Coronavirus Pandemic May Finally Move Public Opinion to Force Admissions Reform

Along with the admissions bribery scandal, perhaps the 2020 COVID-19 torpedo strike on most colleges' business models will at least (and at last) force serious rethinking about the admissions game at the highest institutional levels. This examination should engage the attention of top admissions offices but also the presidents and governing boards of colleges, as well as all three branches of the federal government. Its focus should be on the effects the current admissions system has on America's society and economy. Even the top quintile of elite colleges has suffered enormous financial losses of revenue and endowment value, undercutting their ability to expand educational opportunity. Their assets and secure reputations, however, will protect them from any sort of collapse even as they lose some number of full tuition paying international and out of state students. Some flagship state universities will also weather the storm but with reduced capacity to admit and fund the needs of students from poor residents. The pandemic impact will be even worse at the hundreds of private tuition-dependent and most state-supported institutions that, as data in this chapter shows, already do the heavy lifting when it comes to college access and completion for students from historically underserved minority and lower income families.

A March 2020 survey of 285 presidents and chancellors whose schools are members of the Association of American Colleges and Universities revealed that over half were already expecting at least 10 percent decreases in revenue as well as similar drops in enrollment. That expectation, however, reflected the fact that most of them also believed that the pandemic would resolve itself by the summer of 2020, and that campuses would be open for in-person classes and customary on-campus activities as usual for the 2020 fall term! Perhaps just to be on the safe side, 94 percent of the college executives surveyed were nonetheless planning to re-engineer operations that would include significant expansion of virtual learning capabilities. (Friga April 3, 2020) That precaution, of course, turned out to be prescient.

It became clear that the financial hits to university budgets were going to total into the billions of dollars overall. For example, the University of Michigan projected at least a $400 million loss for the calendar year. George Washington University likewise estimated its losses would amount to hundreds of millions of dollars. Stanford University predicted a $300 million budget shortfall. (Furstenberg 2020) By mid-spring 2020, various scenarios then under discussion for the fall 2020 resumption of classes envisioned major additional costs for facilitating safe social distancing on campus at odds with ordinary dormitory configurations, dining facility arrangements and extracurricular activities, in addition to radically altered physical arrangements of lecture halls, classrooms and labs. Those expenses proved necessary even if campuses opened only partially in combination with online teaching. (Gardner April 17, 2020) The additional costs to convert classes to optional or necessary online forms, combined with the expenses of preparing campuses for social distancing and quarantining infectious students were already pushing many colleges close to the financial breaking point, as all their normal external funding sources were being jeopardized at once by the COVID-19 impact. (Korn, Belkin, and Chung 2020)

By April 2020, published estimates predicted that American higher education would suffer a total annual revenue decrease of $146 billion in terms of state support, philanthropy and endowment returns (versus $584 billion in estimated overall expenditures). And that figure took no account of decreases in revenue due to enrollment declines, where estimates of shortfalls had quickly increased to at least 15 percent annually, including a 25 percent drop in international student enrollments. The prospect of continued reliance on distance learning modes was reducing projected enrollment at all colleges by full-tuition-paying foreign students. International enrollment income, of course, was already being radically curtailed by newly imposed international travel bans. Prior to the pandemic, students from China had accounted for an estimated $30 billion each year in terms of global university tuition. (Gross 2020)

University of Chicago students organized a spring 2020 tuition strike and Northwestern University student government called for major reductions in tuition rates due to the switch to the perceived lesser quality of streaming learning. (Cherney 2020) These calls were replicated at campuses across the country, with additional emphasis on the fact that students were being denied the value the in-person educational and networking experiences they had signed up and paid for. Similar demands emerged even at elite colleges from their students and families for significant tuition refunds and discounts due to the switch to virtual classes. (Friga ibid.)

Although some but by no means all colleges agreed to refund or credit room and board fees relating to the periods when most students were not allowed access to their campus, the schools also strongly resisted tuition refunds because the virtual courses were still credited toward degree requirements even if they did not deliver the full value of in-person learning. Some schools did announce tuition reductions for online summer session classes to attract at least some supplemental revenue, however, while insisting that those discounts would not constitute a precedent for courses during the regular academic calendar. (Anderson April 16, 2020)

Discounts on tuition were only one of the features of a mad scramble for fall 2020 enrollment that ensued in the wake of COVID-19. Deposit deadlines were delayed from the traditional May 1 date or even waived altogether; wait lists were sprung open well beyond prior year levels; tuition payment deadlines were extended in some cases up to a full academic year; financial aid packages were revised upward where funds could be found; in-state tuition rates were offered to out-of-state residents. Liberated by the official abandonment of the long-standing recruiting code of ethics as descried in chapter 5 in connection with the spread of early decision offers, one admissions office on the West Coast considered contacting applicants who had rejected admission offers the prior year about reconsidering and transferring. Elite colleges, meanwhile, faced resistance to their normal acceptance and billing procedures that played havoc with their own enrollment projections. Relatively wealthy families who could afford to do so hedged their enrollment bets by paying deposits on multiple acceptances for their children with a view to enrolling them at the one with the fewest online course and best financial terms, and just writing off their deposit losses. (Gardner May 18, 2020)

Moody's bond rating agency summed up the COVID-19 fiscal infection afflicting American colleges in spring 2020 by downgraded its outlook on the entire public and private non-profit higher education sector (not including community colleges) from stable to negative. (Friga April 22, 2020) For many domestic college students, the outlook on their educational experience also was turning sour. New reliance on remote forms of learning "magnified existing socioeconomic disparities" in terms of access to broadband connectivity and digital devices according to the Axios news service, which pointed out that that over 21 million Americans lacked high speed internet. (Hart and Snyder 2020). Children from lower income and other underserved communities, both rural and urban, often do not have a computer in their home. CBS radio reported in April 2020 that even in technology-rich California, 42 percent of households comprised of persons of color lacked a computer or fast broadband connectivity. Lack of high-speed online access also severely impacted the ability of students in those households to engage with proposed online versions of SAT, ACT and Advanced Placement tests when COVID-19 and social distancing norms threatened to make such tests impossible to administer at their usual physical venues. (Hoover April 24 and 29, 2020, and May 15, 2020)

The disparity in students' broadband access, sharply exposed anew by the consequences of the pandemic, also prompted reconsideration of admissions offices' substantial reliance on standardized tests in making admission decisions. The University of California system quickly chose to make SAT and ACT tests optional at least for the first post-COVID-19 admissions cycle, as did elite private colleges including Cornell, Haverford and Amherst. (Korn, Belkin, and Chung ibid.)

Other influential elite institutions, including Harvard, Yale and Purdue, just as quickly announced continuing commitments to their standardized test requirements. By mid-spring 2020, however, over 70 schools had adopted new test-optional policies to some degree, either as one-year exceptions, as pilot projects to evaluate a longer-term change, or as long-considered permanent policy. (Boeckenstedt 2020). Before the summer of 2020, the UC system Board of Regents went much further, by extending its test-optional policy for all California applicants for a second academic year, then discontinuing reference to SAT and ACT results in admission decisions for all California applicants for the following two years, and finally eliminating such consideration for out-of-state applicants as well beginning in 2025. Meanwhile, the 300,000-student system said it would work on developing its own assessment alternative, and applicants can continue to submit standardized test results for scholarship consideration and post-enrollment course placement. (Hubler 2020)

The UC Regents were facing a lawsuit claiming that the SAT and ACT discriminated against low-income black and Hispanic applicants in terms of their chances of admission, whereas the UC system's Faculty Senate presented the Regents with a study that concluded those tests helped some of those students gain admission despite having GPAs that were problematic. (Ibid.) The actual experiences during the COVID-19 outbreak of the large number of disadvantaged students in California and elsewhere who lacked effective broadband access to online admissions testing as well as virtual online classes may have tipped the scales in terms of Regent's decision to step away decisively from the SAT and ACT.

One distinguished academician, H. Holden Thorp (former chancellor of the University of North Carolina at Chapel Hill and former provost at Washington University St. Louis) suggested suspending both the *US News* rankings and the use of standardized tests. He viewed the rankings as putting too great a premium on reputations for low admission rates and on-time graduation rates, both of which could lead to further harm low-income students during the pandemic's continuance. Regarding the SAT and ACT, he cited the fact that test scores are highly correlated with family income. (Diep 2020) With 40 percent of families with annual income below $40,000 experiencing pandemic-related unemployment in 2020 just through April according to the Federal Reserve Board data, the income-related test performance inequity in admissions would likely become even more devastating.

A broader shift to application policies that ignore standardized test results or make their submission optional, however, will not become the new normal without a fight. Three giant "stakeholders" in the admissions world – the College Board (for its SAT), the ACT organization and *US News* view any such change as an existential threat to their own business models. The two main test sponsors have consistently asserted that their tests are essential in view of high school grade inflation which prevents comparability of GPA scores in evaluating applicants. (Ibid.)

In a test-optional world, the test sponsors would lose more than just their test administration fees: namely, the contact details for the potential applicants that they sell to admissions offices. As described in chapter 3, that data in turn enables elite colleges to inflate their application totals using well-funded and designed campaigns in order to improve their *US News* selectivity rankings (lowest being the top). *US News* would also struggle to find a replacement for the standardized test scores of entering students, the critical measure of a college's academic "selectivity" in their annual rankings. These potential costs to non-profit admissions stakeholders due to widespread adoption of test-optional policies, however, would not seem to outweigh the educational equities advanced by a decisive move away from overreliance on both the *US News* rankings and the SAT and ACT tests in the application and admissions process.

COVID-19's impact on large gatherings and travel generally could discourage at least temporarily the now-common joint recruiting visits to college fairs mainly in upscale high school zip codes by elite college admission staff. It could encourage reassessing the practice of rewarding extra credit toward admission (especially for early decision applicants) for forms of demonstrated interest that only financially secure applicants can routinely afford. These would include travel for on-campus personal visits and interviews, as well as the online forms of constant applicant "engagement" strongly encouraged in admission office marketing pitches, despite the fact that so many rural and inner-city students lack access to the necessary broadband technology.

After COVID-19, it should also be harder to warehouse donor-related admissions (bribed or not) on phony "walk-on" rosters for non-revenue aristocratic sports, especially if there is financial and Title IX pressure to discontinue some of these sports at least until the stadiums for big-time football and basketball programs are open and full enough to fund a full and balanced slate of both men's and women's teams.

Aside from the immediately devastating COVID-19 effects on

collegiate budgets, however, the most profound challenge to the elite college business model was the broadly negative reaction of enrolled undergraduates to the forms of virtual learning introduced on the fly by academic administrators who rightly emptied their campuses around the 2020 spring break as the pandemic hit full-force. (Friga April 22, 2020)

Students manifested quite negative opinions of the initial forms of "distance learning" that were often merely streamed classroom and lecture hall presentations by the instructor with cumbersome interactive dialog, accompanied by often non-existent online office hours. Most of the streamed classes were delivered "synchronously" (i.e., at the same as the scheduled class time), which proved difficult for many students scattered around the country or abroad to regularly participate. (Supiano 2020).

One survey by a Toronto-based online learning platform found that nearly 70 percent of 3,089 students in North American felt that the online instruction they received during the pandemic was inferior to in-person classes, and that about a quarter were reassessing their return for fall classes due to uncertainty about how those schools would reopen classes. (Red Hat 2020) A similar survey by niche.com of 14,000 undergraduate and graduate student showed that 67 percent also did not find the online experience classes as effective as the traditional classroom experience. A survey of 1,300 students by an online exam-prep firm found that 75 percent did not consider the early forms of distant collegiate learning amounted to a quality educational experience. Only 10 percent of students planning to enroll in fall 2020 would ordinarily consider taking a college class online. (Marcus 2020)

The fact is that the early forms of "remote instruction" in COVID-19 risks were simply not at the level of true "online learning" based on a well-developed professional research and best practices. (Supiano ibid.) Elite colleges were perhaps also at a disadvantage in terms of student reactions to the emerging virtual modes of teaching because they have long invested in and marketed the value of luxurious in-person campus amenities, easy student-faculty connections and a multitude of relationship-building clubs, events and activities. In a virtual campus world, all these benefits become devalued currency. Fully one-third of students in one survey said they would consider not going back to their college if courses were not conducted in-person on campus.

Understandably, few colleges were prepared in the spring of 2020 to switch most classes to the far more sophisticated platforms for "asynchronous" (students log-in on their own schedules) online learning pioneered by for-profit colleges. Slowly but surely, these more dynamic and interactive forms of online instruction were further professionalized and adopted by many well-established public and private non-profit undergraduate universities for their bachelor's degree programs. Many of these schools had already successfully introduced fully online and "hybrid" graduate degree programs, including MBA and doctorate level.

Schools like Arizona State and the University of Southern New Hampshire have demonstrated that asynchronous online and hybrid offerings (mixing in-person and online sessions) at the undergraduate level could radically expand access to higher education across a broader income spectrum to include otherwise underserved student populations, including working mothers and those who need to work while pursuing bachelor's degrees.

> Conceiving, planning, designing and developing a genuine online course or program can consume as much as a year of faculty training and collaboration with instructional designers, and often requires student orientation and support and a complex technological infrastructure. (Marcus ibid.)

A national effort to both realize the real potential of asynchronous, professionally designed online learning as a vital part of college learning delivery and simultaneously address socioeconomic broadband access disparities would need multi-billion dollar investments, requiring new federal stimulus funding. A commitment to such a game-changing undertaking would be a much-needed silver lining in the COVID-19 cloud. It also presents an opportunity to innovate that some academic and political leaders (including former Senator and college president Bob Kerrey) urged colleges to quickly seize, as a way to shift to more student-centered instruction. It would also immediately open more virtual admission doors to applicants from middle- and lower-income families. (Friga ibid.; Mazur and Kerrey 2020)

Angel B. Perez, named chief executive of the National Association for College Admission Counseling during the COVID-19 crisis, announced he would lead a push "to reinvent enrollment and college access in America." (Hoover May 4, 2020) Perez grew up in a poor family himself and as vice president for enrollment at Trinity College in Hartford championed efforts to help low-income and first-generation students. In a spring 2020 interview with the *Chronicle of Higher Education*, he offered encouraging words for advocates of wholesale admission reform:

> The fact that many colleges in this country are three months away from going bankrupt is an embarrassment to the nation….This is a huge opportunity to reimagine the process as more student-centered, to rethink what they actually have to submit in order to prove they're college-ready…. On the college side, the entire enrollment model is broken. On the high-school side, counselors don't know how to counsel the next class. There's going to be some sort of reinvention. The question is, what does it look like? (Friga, ibid., quoting Perez)

We can help answer that question. Having experienced a period when our usual way of life, including in higher education, seemed to be stuck on "pause," we can seize the opportunity to reflect on the more systematic ways equitable access to college opportunity has been denied in the "normal" course of the college admission process. And if we don't like what we *see* in that reflection, we owe it to the pandemic generation and those that will follow to *say* something — and do something — about it.

The admissions process operates at the juncture and under the influence of the three manifestly destructive "great disparities" that define core aspects of social and economic life in America: the vast differences among our households in terms of (1) income accumulation, (2) educational access, and (3) broadband connectivity. In short, "social distancing," writ large. The existing (and only) pathways to acceptance into each academic year's aggregate freshman class systematically reflects and reinforces these disparities.

In addition to the bribery scandals and COVID-19 effects on admission practices, this book has also highlighted the *gridlock* in social and economic mobility, made clearly visible in both academic research and the daily news, and directly connected to the three disparities in income, education and broadband. The most elite colleges, however, have used the admissions processes they designed and fostered to make only marginal efforts to foster socioeconomic mobility, while setting admission priorities that accommodated and even accentuated the three disparities.

For the sake of advancing their own business models and financial goals, they have allocated low-single-digit percentages of access and upside opportunity to the bottom income quintile of applicant families, focused their Pell grants toward the highest levels of eligible family income, and otherwise successfully skewed their big-league prospect scouting and digital marketing resources to what our Australian friends would call the "top end of town." Their priorities have even involved exploiting the constant stress and anxiety enveloping the admissions game (or *mania*) and its many participants, especially our children.

Here's how the *Chronicle of Higher Education* summarized college admissions reality as the 2020s approached: "To casual readers of news of the last six months, the college-admissions process must come across as an easily exploitable system that favors those who already have a head start." Even a test-prep company executive quoted in the *Chronicle's* article lamented: "'The American education system is death by a thousand cuts for low-income and underrepresented students.'" (Gluckman August 2, 2019)

The crisis of public confidence in both the *value* and the *values* of American higher education must not be allowed to go to waste in the public square. "Business as usual" in college admissions is unsustainable. This book, accordingly, is suggesting specific federal legislation as the only sure way to impose the necessary transparency, equity and fairness that would transform the college admissions process into something we can be proud of rather than make excuses for.

The tyranny of the rigged elite colleges admissions black box must no long be what America simply settles for. There is a choice available, even if elite colleges use the COVID-19 impact to extend and excuse their emphasis on favoring legacies and donors to preserve their "brands" and refresh their endowments. Shortly after the bribery indictments, President Brian Rosenberg of Macalester College told citizens to bear in mind the warning of Supreme Court Justice Louis Brandeis: "'We may have democracy, or we may have wealth concentrated in the hands of a few, but we can't have both.'" (Rosenberg 2019) That choice is now posed to the American public at the front, side and back doors of our most elite colleges, and a threatened democracy must respond.

Part III

How to Blow Up the Elite College Admissions Black Box and Reopen the Front Door to Social and Economic Mobility

CHAPTER 7

We Know What It Takes to Fix Big-Money Markets Rigged for Insiders: Public Disgust, Plus Federal Power and Financial Leverage

Social equity in higher education must start with replacing the black box culture of secrecy, special privileges, and double-talk surrounding elite college admissions with a completely new regime of full transparency, open access, and basic fairness. As this book reveals, some admissions officials have been quick to dismiss the idea that considerations of equity should play any part in their decisions. According to polling data reported by the Associated Press, Americans are about equally divided on whether college admissions practices are fair. The poll by affiliates of the National Opinion Research Center was conducted shortly after the bribery indictments were announced in 2019, and found that 38 percent of adult respondents considered college admissions practices very or somewhat fair, while 36 percent said they were very or somewhat unfair.

As to legacies, nearly 40 percent said that colleges give significant weight to that status, but only 11 percent think that legacies should get special consideration. Similarly, 50 percent believed donations make a positive difference in admission decisions, but only 13 percent thought that was right. And 46 percent held the view that that colleges tend to favor applicants whose families can pay full, undiscounted tuition, but only 23 percent thought that capacity should be a factor in admission decision. Three-quarters of those over fifty years of age believed SAT and ACT results are important admission factors, but only about 50 percent of those under thirty agreed. (Davorken and Grigonas 2019; Binkley 2019)

Some have suggested that admission offices should emulate dating sites like Match.com and let artificial intelligence sort out the applications and pick their optimal entry classes. Others have proposed turning the whole process over to specialized assessment centers that would evaluate applicants on the basis of in-person or even video interviews, observing their social and creative skills: a process many collegians routinely navigate in applying for internships and post-graduation jobs. In addition to the "Turning the Tide" admissions reform proposals from the Harvard Graduate School of Education discussed in chapter 6 — which had many elite college signatories but has produced little change in admission practices to date — plenty of ideas have been advanced by credible sources on how to reshape college admissions processes to be more fair, less stressful on students, more predictable, and less biased toward the upper income classes.

In his seminal article on the early decision "racket," James Fallows urged colleges to abandon buying mailing lists of high school sophomores from the Educational Testing Services, to offer equivalent financial aid offers to those it admits under the regular cycle and the early decision round, and to publish specific acceptance rates for each cycle. He also suggested they should suspend early decision programs indefinitely (which, as we have seen, was tried by some Ivy League schools but abandoned under competitive pressure). (Fallows 2001)

Daniel Golden's 2006 book proposed abolishing legacy preferences, and also establishing an information firewall between fundraising and admissions departments, developing conflict-of-interest policies for admissions staff regarding social relationships with applicants' families, and eliminating preferences for athletes and faculty children. (Golden 2006, 291-95) The Brookings Institute's Richard V. Reeves, in addition to proposing several pubic policy changes to loosen the upper-class grip on economic advancement like curbing exclusionary zoning and eliminating tax subsidies for the wealthy, urged an end to legacy preferences, as well as new steps to fund college attendance more fairly for the benefit of middle- and low-income families. (Reeves 2017, 125-152)

The Jack Kent Cooke Foundation's comprehensive "True Merit" report (cited in previous chapters) made multiple suggestions to advance the interests of low-income applicants — including a "poverty preference" that could provide some balance against the multiple wealth preferences. The report concluded that "[b]eing admitted to a selective institution is actually *harder* for the high-achieving, low-income student than for others." (Giancola and Kahlenberg 2016, 29) (Emphasis in original) The Foundation's CEO also proposed specific suggestions in a 2018 *New York Times* op-ed including a ban on legacy admissions and an end to using demonstrated interest as a factor in admissions decisions. He also advocated hiring more college counselors in public high schools to reduce the ratios of students to counselors, which have reached as high as nearly 500 to 1. (Levy and Tyre 2018)

Julie Lythcott-Haims, author of *How to Raise an Adult*, told the *Palo Alto Weekly* shortly after the admissions bribery indictments that college officials should rethink the broken admission system with three tangible steps: make SAT and ACT tests optional; require applicants to disclose if they were helped writing essays; and refuse to submit data to the *US News* rankings. (Kadvany 2019)

As the first sentences were being handed down, the *Wall Street Journal* listed ten steps to reform admissions that had been suggested to its reporters by high school and private counselors, parents, students and even some admissions officers. These proposals started with getting rid of college rankings and their "easily manipulated" algorithms, and also included ending legacy and athletic preferences, early decision, and requirements for submission of SAT and ACT test results. In addition, the *Journal* article favored limiting the number of colleges to which students may apply. (Korn November 30-December 1, 2019)

Professor Lani Guinier of the Harvard Law School suggested in a 1997 *New York Times* op-ed allocating admissions by a lottery among all qualified applicants, an idea taken up since then by reformers inside and outside academia. Colleges would set their own minimum standards for admission and use algorithms as scoring rubrics for criteria like test scores, class rank and grades, extracurricular activities, and personal essays to create a pool of "qualified" applicants for their lotteries. Perhaps some of those applicants would have their names entered more than once in the pool to reflect "qualities that are considered valuable" by the college. (Guinier 1997) A similar kind of lottery with an individual weighting scheme was considered in *Atlantic* during the Asian American discrimination suit against Harvard in 2018. (Wong 2018)

Others proposed extra-weighting individual applicants in admission lotteries to achieve particular college priorities such as diversity goals. (Conley 2018) But that approach could also open the door to tipping the scales in favor of wealthy and well-connected applicants, just as happens under the present system.

Admissions from a lottery pool (apart from the effects of extra weighting for some categories) would be designed to be entirely randomized. Applicants would order their allotment of college choices in advance, and would be matched to their top-ranked school if their names were drawn by it, and so on. Such a lottery system essentially assumes that all applicants will win a lottery admission to at least one college that fits their talents and their shopping lists. But colleges would want to keep drawing names from their pools only until they filled their own enrollment goals. Best of luck to the applicant with perfect grades and track record who never gets a winning draw!

The randomness of admissions outcomes under a lottery would have several effects besides reducing the wealth-related dominance of the current "holistic" black box admissions model. Social scientists would have a field day measuring the outcomes of these new lottery cohorts during college and post-graduation. Professors at elite colleges would face new challenges in sustaining their school's reputation for turning out the best and the brightest, since they might not be starting out with that sort of student body from the get go. (Conley ibid.) Lotteries could reduce concerns about discrimination against certain types of individuals (depending on the screening criteria and weightings for entry to the pool) — but it could also leave diversity agendas in tatters.

Lotteries could inadvertently lead to undesirable and even inequitable consequences, including severe differentials in gender, racial, ethnic and economic in the student population. Lotteries would also likely undercut some desirable social, artistic and cultural aspects of the full college experience. "A lottery could also rob students of a sense of ownership over their destiny. If getting in to Stanford or Harvard is like winning Powerball, students might come to see their fate as largely tied to uncontrollable forces." (Finger and Gift 2019) College symphonies and club soccer teams might lack a percussion section or a competent goalie for years. Yes, with lotteries the vagaries of luck would replace the influence of the buck. But the luck of the draw is its own form of black box.

Moreover, like the notion of elite colleges foregoing cooperation with the *US News* rankings or calling a halt to early decision or rewarding demonstrated interest, lotteries would achieve their perceived benefits only if the vast majority of colleges adopted them and fully cooperated in their operation and execution. If they did so cooperate by accepting the outcomes, and observing the rules against poaching students they really want, those practices might well by perceived by the "right" Justice Department as restraint of trade in violation of our antitrust laws. (Wong ibid.)

Under current law and public policy, whether lotteries or any other admissions reform proposals could be instituted depends entirely on whether the leading elite colleges and their admissions trade associations would voluntarily make substantial changes in their very successful business models. The examples cited in chapter 6 of inaction and lip-service regarding even their own signed commitments to the Harvard School of Education's strong recommendation on how to make college admissions a more humane and inclusive process illustrate just how unlikely that outcome would be. Former Vassar president Catherine Bond Hill observed that there are just too many economic incentives pushing admissions offices to follow the "car dealer" model rather than the "church" model of social conscience. (Hill 2015)

As long as any changes would be dependent on initiatives, decisions and actions taken within the "self-governing" status of the existing admissions system, the data and analysis in this book tells us that elite colleges would prioritize outcomes that are in their own best interests, not those of applicants generally. Perhaps the best way forward, then, is best exemplified by recent activity in the state legislature of California — which at times has also led the nation in initiating forceful responses to long-needed changes in public policy, such as regarding marriage equality and climate change. Responding to specific aspects of the admissions bribery scandal, legislators in the Golden State have introduced bills that would ban preferential admission for legacies and children of donors at all state colleges, as well as private colleges that receive state tuition grants. Other proposals would set up a statewide registry of private admissions consultants, and require more oversight at public colleges — including three senior administration sign offs — for any "admissions by exception" to normal standards. (Gluckman March 29, 2019) New Mexico's government has also taken steps to make tuition for all state colleges free to state residents, regardless of family income, to encourage promising low-income students to apply and admissions officers to select them. (Romero and Goldstein 2019)

These state-level governmental initiatives indicate an emerging recognition that relying on voluntary admissions reform by elite colleges is essentially a non-starter due to the countervailing demands of their business models. Actions by California, New Mexico and other states on their own, however, have proved to be no match for the national power of elite schools that managed in the past to turn aside similar efforts by Senators Ted Kennedy and Chuck Grassley in their primes. But more recently, Jon Boeckenstedt, associate vice president for enrollment management and marketing at DePaul University, commenting on the 2019 bribery and fraudulent applications indictments, told the *Chronicle of Higher Education* that "'[b]esides the federal government, there is really no governing body to manage to oversee things like this.'" (Hoover March 13, 2019 #1)

We can perhaps leave it to federal law enforcement officers to discover and root out the egregious cases of manipulation of admissions results by fraudulent schemes. The investigation leading to the indictment announced by the US Attorney for Massachusetts, however, was initiated because of an unexpected tip from a parent participating in the scheme who was targeted for unrelated fraudulent conduct. College financing is not within the jurisdiction of the federal Consumer Finance Protection Bureau, despite the sheer size of the dollar amount required to pay for a college education and the $1.5 trillion (and counting) level of the debt incurred to do so — effectively a lifetime mortgage on students' future earnings. Student loan indebtedness, moreover, cannot be discharged in bankruptcy.

We must, therefore, renew a focus on Congress as the *only* institution with the power to reform the corruption within the college admissions system, a role that body has studiously avoided up to now. Public outrage triggered by the indictment provides an opportunity to again push for federal legislative action — this time, even more comprehensive than Kennedy, Grassley and others attempted about decades ago. Michael Dannenberg, a former aide to Senator Ted Kennedy and longtime advocate for policies to lessen the power of wealth in admissions, told the *Wall Street Journal* just after the bribery indictments: "'Now, we're seeing there's this sort of confluence of events that heighten the likelihood of Congress addressing these admission and enrollments issues that undermine diversity.'" (Hackman March 15, 2019)

There Are Multiple Successful Precedents for Federal Legislation and Regulation of Unfair and Coercive Markets and College Practices Detrimental to Student Welfare

Congress holds authority under the Constitution to regulate the type of interstate commerce that American higher education surely constitutes. Congress also holds the leverage to alter colleges' behavior because of these schools' reliance on federal aid to education in all its many forms, including tax deductions granted to donors to these colleges, and their non-profit tax-exempt status.

The pathway for Congress to truly effect reform of college admissions practices has already been established in the many statutes that address serious corruption in financial and trading markets infected with serious imbalances in terms of market power and access to material information as between buyers and sellers. Those reforms all centered on assuring fairness through mandatory substantive disclosures and transparency of process, backed by federal power and leverage. These models seem particularly apt for reforming college admissions, which has become much too dependent on secrecy and obfuscation to achieve mainly self-interested financial goals.

The main examples of these reforms in the financial area are:

- The Securities Acts of the 1930s and later amendments: stock-offering fraud protections; registration of broker dealers and stock offerings; prescribed forms and content of prospectuses and mandated quarterly reports by publicly traded companies; reporting rules regarding trading in company securities by controlling shareholders and senior officers; and a new federal agency (the SEC) to supervise financial markets and police insider trading and other transactions.

- The Williams Act policing and setting disclosure norms for tender offers for public company shares.

- The Sarbanes-Oxley Act requiring officers and accountants to certify prescribed financials and risk assessment measures, including directly mandating board structure and conduct norms beyond what traditional state law requirements.

- The Dodd-Frank Act: requiring mortgage financing disclosures and limits on risky bank trading with depositors' money; annual risk assessment stress tests for systemically important financial institutions that can bring down the economy; stricter capital requirements, rating agency process, and communication reforms.

- The Consumer Financial Protection Bureau: requiring disclosure in credit, mortgages, and other financial dealings; fines and other remedies for unauthorized and undisclosed fees and other forms of tampering with customer accounts.

What all these statutes and entities, many of which have been emulated in countries around the world, have in common is using mandatory disclosure to create a more fair and honest balance in competitive markets between those in control of material information and those who need it to make rational decisions. They all use the federal authority over interstate commerce. Advocates of a "hands-off" regime in terms of government involvement in higher education cite court cases that recognize that colleges should be extended leeway in admissions in order to protect academic freedom. Academic freedom was recognized under the First and Fourteenth Amendments in the case of a professor who was unconstitutionally jailed for refusing to disclose aspects of a lecture to a state legislature.

Others argue that the concept of "expressive association" recognized to some extent by the Supreme Court wraps college admissions in a cloak of immunity from any legislative or governmental action. (Vance 2012) But Richard Kahlenberg, in his essay on "Ten Myths About Legacy Preferences in College Admissions, " pointed out that the courts have specifically held that private schools cannot engage in racial discrimination in enrollment decisions, cannot employ racial quotas, or award bonus points specifically to minority students. (Kahlenberg 2010) In short, there is neither an absolute constitutional right to freedom of admission decisions preferences, nor a constitutional privilege of blanket immunity from government regulation of admissions — whether at state-sponsored colleges or private colleges that receive government funds to support their missions.

Moreover, federal legislative involvement into higher education operations has been in place for decades, and not just with financial aid and research dollars. The 1965 Higher Education Act, reauthorized and signed by presidents eight times since then, is higher education's "foundational law...flush with regulations that are fundamental to institutions' daily operations." (Harris 2017) The simple fact is that higher education as we now know it in the United States would not survive a semester without the Higher Education Act or something very much like it. Federal administrations and legislators from both sides of the aisle routinely initiate efforts to amend or even repeal and replace that Act to address a broad range of public policy issues relating to college education, including assistance for historically black colleges, regulation of college accreditors, simplification of financial aid forms, student debt repayment and collection processes, and student data privacy. (Douglas-Gabriel 2016; Simonton 2018).

The Obama administration employed the leverage of federal law and financial support for student tuition payments to impose real reforms banning *for-profit* colleges' deceptive marketing practices and requiring disclosure of actual graduation rates. The Trump administration has sought to make substantial changes to those requirements and to use the same federal leverage to assure freedom of speech on state and other non-profit college campuses. (Hackman March 20, 2019; Kreighbaum 2019) President Obama also used authority under Title IX of the Higher Education Act's ban on sexual discrimination (previously employed to force equivalent distribution of college athletic scholarship and related sports opportunities between men and women) to impose a a new regime for investigating and adjudicating sexual assault, dating violence and sexual harassment cases on the nation's college campuses. The Trump administration also addressed that subject, in different ways but under the same authority. (Wilson 2017; Harris ibid.; Green 2020)

Academia traditionally resists identifying students as *consumers*, viewing that word as a pejorative, merely transactional diminution of the educational vocation. This essentially self-protective posture, however, denies students basic protections we take for granted in other core elements of our lives and financial choices. It is time this particular college tradition is laid to rest through appropriately drafted federal legislation and regulations mandating the Department of Education to deal with admissions corruption in at least as holistic a manner as the elite colleges contend they approach their admissions decisions.

In this book *elite colleges* are defined broadly as those (numbering around 120) having $500 million or more in endowments and a 35 percent or lower overall acceptance rate, which covers the top three levels of selectivity as commonly measured but eliminates highly specialized art and religious schools that also have low admissions rates but not material clout in setting admissions market practices. A much smaller group of about two-dozen ultra-elite schools that have endowments exceeding $1 billion and regularly admit less than 20 percent of applicants have enormous influence on the overall structure and practices of the admissions process that prevails among the thousands of non-profit colleges in the United States. Certain aspects of new federal legislation and regulation of the admissions game should be more demanding of these ultra-elite, "systemically important" (to borrow a phrase from the Dodd-Frank rules for financial institutions) elite colleges. They effectively set the "terms of trade" as well as the marketing terms and ante for the college admissions system as a whole. If we can close the avenues of corruption at the most elite level, there is a reasonable chance the system as a whole will respond and benefit, as will all college applicants.

Most of the colleges involved in the admissions bribery scandal are belong in the systemically important elite category. Nancy Leopold, executive director of College Tracks (a non-profit advising disadvantaged students) has reminded us, the admissions system was "rigged in favor of privileged students" even before bribery or donating takes rig it more. "It's easy to miss that in the sensationalism of eye-popping amounts of money and celebrities." (Hoover March 13, 2019. (No. 1)) We know that the rigged high affluence admission lanes set up to favor the wealthy and well connected — legacies, donors' children, early decision, certain non-scholarship athletes — are in common use among the most elite schools, often accounting for a majority of their first-year enrollments. Other elite colleges and tuition-dependent schools have little choice but to emulate them with their own black boxes.

Immediately after the bribery indictments, Alan Morrison and Richard Kahlenberg asserted that the admissions "[d]eck is stacked in favor of the rich" — and that "it is time to pull the curtain back on special preferences so that their existence and extent are subject to full debate, both on campus and off." They argued for what their article headlined as "Radical Transparency," including annual data on the economic makeup of entering classes. (Morrison and Kahlenburg 2019) If special preferential admissions were forcefully and fully exposed and, in some cases, even eliminated at the top ranks of the elite institutions with the most exclusionary admissions rates and the highest levels of endowed resources, it would truly be a game-changer in terms of transparency, equity and fairness. To paraphrase the Bible, from those to whom much has been donated, much should be expected.

CHAPTER 8

Reform as Reality: The Transparency, Equity, and Fairness in College Admissions Act of 2021 ("TEFCA")

Mandatory Annual Public Disclosure of Specific Data on Formerly Secret Admissions Preferences and Their Impact on Overall Admissions Statistics

Because black box secrecy continues to provide the essential cover for corruption of the admissions process in favor of wealthy and well-connected applicants, comprehensive reform must start with mandatory and verified annual disclosure of critical statistical details specific to the historical hooks and ladders that elite colleges employ in preferencing those applicants above and apart from the general pool. These forms of reserved seating in elite college entering classes effectively discriminate against prospective students who were not born to wealth and or to parents who graduated from college.

TEFCA's mandated disclosures will finally reveal not only to those students and families directly affected but also to the public generally the full extent that exclusionary admissions lanes not only discriminate directly against first-generation applicants but also often foreclose to all other applicants a substantial percentage of the nominally available admission slots at our most elite colleges. The special lanes can capture even a majority of admissions opportunities when combined with the early decision option that is itself is tethered to applicant wealth.

This mandated disclosure will apply first to the four major categories of preferential admissions consideration for the wealthy and well-connected at elite colleges: (1) legacies, (2) donors' relatives; (3) coach-referred athletes (other than in revenue sports), and (4) children of their own faculty and staff or from colleges on a reciprocal basis.

Some have suggested (in the context of the Harvard Asian-American admissions discrimination case) that if affirmative action based on racial minority status is ever declared unconstitutional, preferences-based admission consideration for first generation and socioeconomically disadvantaged status should take its place, at least at all public colleges. (Gluckman October 22, 2018) Many colleges already have such categories for special consideration in place or plan to add them. Many colleges have already undertaken special recruiting activities focused on poor communities voluntarily, and it is important to capture and compare full data on the impact of those programs on admissions with those schools' preferences for wealthy and well-connected applicants. Accordingly, data for college programs with special application review processes and standards for low-income applicants (5) will also be a required reporting category.

The new transparency defining the contours of special admission lanes will not preclude other limitations on these preferences included in other provisions of TEFCA. Moreover, the coercive early decision option, which can account for nearly majority of ultra-elite college admissions on its own, will be subject to an outright prohibition under another provision of TEFCA.

Because elite colleges have led the way in creating high affluence admissions lanes as core elements of their admissions models, TEFCA will feature distinct categories of colleges in terms of levels of disclosure detail: (I) all private and public non-profit colleges that receive the benefit of any federal funding (including aid to students and research grants) to support their mission); (II) a much smaller group of around 120 *elite colleges*, with endowments of at least $500 million and acceptance rates of 35 percent or less; and (III) about two dozen *systemically important* elite colleges with endowments of at least $1 billion and acceptance rates not greater than 20 percent.

The elite colleges are those where exclusionary black box admission lanes have the greatest impact on the general applicant pool. The most detailed admissions disclosures under TEFCA would apply to the systemically important elite schools because they essentially set the "rules of the road" other admission departments must follow to stay in the game. A similar category was created under federal disclosure rules for financial firms with the most impact on the overall health of the entire financial system.

The mandated data must be disclosed before the official start of each annual admissions cycle, and must include the following data:

For all colleges: the immediately prior three-year rolling average totals for first-year applications, admissions, and enrollment (including all academic terms), and the median and 25th and 75th percentile cut-off values for SAT, ACT or other standard admission tests, and whether they are required or optional, for both admitted candidates and enrolled students.

For elite colleges: in addition, the same data as above for each of the distinct categories of applicants (enumerated (1) through (5) above) given special consideration in their admission processes.

For systemically important elite colleges: in addition, the total number of admitted and enrolled (including grants of deferred enrollment) students in each of categories (1) to (5) whose applications would not have survived the college's initial screening process but for membership in one or more of those categories.

The required disclosures must be timely posted for a year on the college's admissions and applicant recruiting websites, and reported simultaneously to the Department of Education, which would also be required to publicly post such data immediately (subject to investigation of any reasonable suspicion of fraudulent submissions). The TEFCA disclosures will be additional to and not displace any existing disclosure requirements with respect to the College Scoreboard or any other reporting mandates of federal law or Department of Education regulations, or state law. Data disclosures on each college's websites must be no more than two clicks away from the undergraduate admissions home page and signified by a prominently visible icon or link. A link to such data must also appear prominently in any online brochure sent to potential applicants by the college.

For all TEFCA purposes, *donors' relatives* would be defined to include any applicant as to whom the admissions office was informed by any source to be of interest to the advancement or development office or higher university authority (such as the president's office or a board member) in connection with an actual or potential donation to the college by spouse, parent or grandparent (including adoptive) or blood relative of that applicant to the level of aunt, uncle or first cousin.

The term *coach-referred athletes* would include any applicant as to whom the admissions office was informed by any source to be of interest to the athletic department, other than applicants under consideration for athletic scholarships for the school's top three revenue-producing sports. To assure the integrity of the new disclosures, the Department of Education would be empowered under TEFCA to impose further standard definitions of terms.

Ban Coercive Early Decision Admissions and Other Practices That Work to Favor Rich Applicants or Disadvantage Those from Middle- and Lower-Income Families

Another admissions practice that is not one of the four major direct wealth preferences but far outweighs each of those in terms of impact on overall admission access is the early decision option, which, as currently structured, is an inherently coercive, wealth-biased, but very effective yield and revenue management tool for admissions departments. Going forward under TEFCA, no college — systemically important or otherwise — would be permitted to require any student to accept an offer of admission in advance as a prerequisite to that application being considered at any stage. This new rule would bring a universal end to early decision admissions as we know them, but without precluding the far more applicant-friendly and far less wealth-biased *early action* option.

No federal rule imaginable could prevent an applicant who reaches an early and definitive top choice for enrollment from voluntarily promising to accept admission if offered, provided that the financial aid package, if relevant, proved to be acceptable. But under TEFCA, the colleges would no longer be able to create the conditions under which any such offer (solicited or unsolicited) would be enforceable, or limit any applicant to one choice of college only in order to be considered early.

No prohibitive federal legislative action under TEFCA would be required with respect to the current early action application procedures, because in that process the interests of applicants and admissions offices are more fairly balanced than under the early decision model. Some elite colleges admissions officials have expressed their support for the early action option, which usually has about the same submission deadline as early decision but allows the successful applicant until the regular cycle's typical May 1 deadline to choose whether to accept or not. Some admissions officers at elite colleges have expressed their support for the early action option because it gives them more time to court high-quality applicants, knowing that there will be serious competition for them.

Systemically important elite colleges, however, would be required *if they offer the early action option* to make it available to all applicants, and add it to the list of distinctive admissions pathways subject to the new rolling three-year-average data disclosure requirements. These records would reveal over time whether early action applicants were being admitted with differentiated test score ranges, which, in a fair market, all potential applicants would have the right to know. If the data showed such a pattern of material advantage at systemically important schools, the Department of Education would be empowered to extend this disclosure requirement to all elite colleges. In the matter of assessing applicants' *demonstrated interest*, TEFCA would bar any admissions department of an elite college from assigning special or extra weight to the fact that an applicant was able to visit its campus in person.

Additional TEFCA rules would bar any communications between any college's financial aid offices and advancement or development departments with respect to FAFSA or other financial disclosures from applicants' families that the college requires regardless of whether an applicant is applying for aid. This provision would prevent such private information from being used to reveal to fundraising departments the potential to seek donations from a particularly rich family in connection with an application.

Disclosure of Elite Colleges' Initial Application Screening Algorithms and Related Weightings

Each elite college's admissions department would also be required, before the beginning of each admissions cycle year, to disclose a material summary of its algorithmic or other standards for the initial screening of applications so that they will not be passed forward for any further consideration. This disclosure must show both the applicable classes of data considered in such first-stage assessment whether done by humans or machines. The categories covered could include, for example, weighted and un-weighted GPAs, class rank, test score results, extracurricular participation, community service, recommendations, and interviews if referenced in front-end screening decisions. If applicable, the precise relative numerical weight assigned must be disclosed for each category, not merely a general sense of its relative importance.

The admissions office would be free to note that they retain the right to waive these requirements in any case (but TEFCA will also require specific disclosure and sign-off procedures for exceptions possibly linked to outside and wealth-related influences, as described below). Publication of the heretofore secret initial cut benchmarks could discourage applications that have no chance of surviving that cut, but which even the most elite colleges seem to encourage only to pad their selectivity rankings.

Further Controls on Formerly Secret and Undocumented Admission "Tips" for Legacies, Donors' Children and Special Sports Athletes at Elite Colleges

A full and direct prohibition against admitting any applicants from the four historical wealth- and connection-related preference lanes would be rightly unenforceable. Elite colleges will of course continue to be able to admit applicants who happen to be legacies, donor's children, faculty children and aristocratic sports athletes to their entering classes, subject to the new disclosure requirement and also to the following limitations on the process of selection.

Beginning with third academic admissions cycle after the enactment of TEFCA, there could be no more generalized extra weight assigned to an applicant's status in one of those four categories that an elite college otherwise provides in favor of first-generation or lower-income categories of applicants. And if the colleges offer no such special admissions break for those in economically disadvantaged groups, then there will no permissible "tips" in the process for any of the wealth-connected categories. Moreover, as a check on compliance, all elite colleges will still have to disclose all TEFCA-required data relating to admissions and enrollment in terms of each category TEFCA has singled out.

In order to support the objective of *fair play* rather than *pay to play*, moreover, admissions departments of elite colleges would be required to separately track and disclose any admissions involving legacy, donor-related, or coach-referred applicants that do not meet the specific minimum admission screening standards that also must be disclosed under TEFCA, and provide evidence of high-level sign-offs on such extraordinary admissions with advance written explanations and approvals by the admissions dean and the school official to whom the dean (and, in the case of athletes, the athletic director) reports. This provision of TEFCA recognizes that any such admission, where the favored applicant has test scores below the school's average or median for otherwise-accepted applicants, automatically raises the bar for those with no such preferences in order for the admissions office to meet the test score data it wants to present to the public, and especially to the *US News* selectivity rankings. A similar proposal has been under consideration in the California legislature to apply to all "admissions by exception" to that state's public colleges and private schools that get state tuition support funds for their students.

In terms of federal jurisdiction applicable to these unprecedented disclosures and limitations on admissions preferences, bills have previously introduced in Congress to require colleges to disclose their firearms policies and security event records in any admissions brochures they publish. For-profit colleges have been required in the past to limit their tuition receipts from federal grants to not more than 85 percent of their total tuition revenue. None of TEFCA's mandatory disclosures or rules regarding admissions preferences would amount to any federal constraint on final admissions decisions, or impose any governmental admissions criteria or quotas. TEFCA would simply level the playing field for all applicants while bringing what has been kept secret by most elite colleges into the open.

Require Admissions Officials to Certify the Truthfulness of Their Published Marketing Materials

TEFCA would direct the Department of Education to require deans of admission to certify that all the required disclosures, as well as their brochures and other applicant recruiting materials and application websites, are accurate and complete as required and contain no misstatements or omissions of material facts. Penalties for false certification would start with warnings and then proceed to suspension without pay from their duties for a period of time, with repeated violations of a serious nature warranting loss of their position (as sometimes is the case as punishment for NCAA rule violations in intercollege sports recruiting offices).

Prohibit Federal Tax Deductions for Donations Made "in Contemplation of" Specific Individual Admissions Decisions and Other Admission-Related Tax Reforms

There is one special preferential admissions consideration, however, that merits immediate and direct federal intervention on the tax policy side: namely, donor-related admissions. Without parsing the fine distinctions between a true quid pro quo and a carefully choreographed pas de deux (as the *New York Times* called it) TEFCA will establish a rebuttable presumption that any donation, pledge, or committed bequest by a related party (to be defined to include a range of family members and any donor-directed charitable or other trust funds they control) within a two-year window before and after an admissions decision with respect to a related party as being made in contemplation of an affirmative admissions outcome and therefore not eligible for a tax deduction as a charitable contribution.

This presumption would be rebuttable, for example, in the case of the unanticipated death of a related party triggering a bequest made before the window period. Under TEFCA's rule, there would no doubt still be circumstances in which the advancement office would notify admissions of an admissions case in which a significant potential disposition toward giving may be involved. Hence, TEFCA's disclosure requirements tracking donor-related admissions would continue to be in effect for all elite colleges.

New tax rules in TEFCA would also require faculty and staff members of a college with annual compensation over $150,000 from the school to report 25 percent of the value of any tuition and other discounts received in respect to enrollment of their children as income for federal income tax purposes, unless their children qualified for such discounts on a basis other than simply being offspring of a faculty or staff member as certified in writing by the dean of admissions and director of financial aid.

Facilitate Test-Optional Policies

In relation to the fraught subject of test score considerations in the admissions process, all colleges would be encouraged by TEFLA financial incentives to adopt at least a modified form of the test-optional policy, whereby applicants could submit (at their own risk) in lieu of SAT or ACT results a test or other evidence of their readiness to undertake college-level work. All colleges would be required to disclose whether they have adopted any such policies when they publish any standardized test score data regarding their entering classes pursuant to TEFCA requirements or otherwise.

Considering that the *most* the College Board is able to assert unequivocally about the relevance of its SAT to admissions decisions is that it is a better predictor of first-year college performance than GPAs, elite colleges should be taking the lead in experimentation with alternatives to the current standard tests in any event, and TEFCA would make supporting funding available to any colleges that wish to try various forms of test-optional policies as well as alternative testing regimes.

Crack Down on Admissions Cheating, Support Registration of Consulting Services and Proper Guidance Counseling in Public Schools, and Ban Other Questionable Admission Practices

Applicants have been known to cheat not just in their high school classes, but also in taking standardized tests. In a survey of 40,000 high school students, 80 percent said they had copied another's homework, and 59 percent said they had cheated on a test during the prior year. As part of their application process, students would be required under TEFCA to affirm that they have not violated any rules regarding test taking, and that they have not falsely claimed any disability or other condition that has allowed them to take the test under special arrangements. They will also be required to certify that the essays they submit on the Common App or required by any particular college's admissions processes are substantially their own work. Any false declaration in these matters would justify withdrawal of an admissions offer. Under TEFCA, fair dealing between colleges and applicants must be a two-way street.

States would be provided federal funding to support development of registration, basic disclosure requirement and codes of conduct for private admission consulting firms and individuals above a certain revenue level of in-state revenue, and to support reducing the ratio of public high school admissions counselors to students to levels consistent with being able to properly serve and write well informed recommendation letters for their caseloads in their particular schools.

TEFCA will also ban application fees at systemically important colleges — which are frequently waived in any event to encourage more applications as the admissions calendar draws to a close. TEFCA would also prohibit the practice of sending "likely letters" to applicants to entice them to give advance commitments to accept an offer in order to secure the pending bid. Under TEFCA, this or any other form of "early decision light" will go the way of the currently prevailing early decision process.

Require Annual Compliance Audits of Standardized Test Administration, Data Privacy Safeguards, and Effective Opt-Outs for Test-Takers' Regarding Their Personal Data

Meanwhile, the new rules established under TEFCA would also require providers of any standardized test used for college admissions decisions to engage in an annual audit (to be filed with the Department of Education) by a competent professional organization as to security, anti-cheating measures, and test monitoring. They would also have to publicly disclose any material weaknesses revealed in such audits and how they are addressing them.

The providers of the PSAT, SAT and ACT and other standardized admissions tests would also be forbidden to sell to a college or any other entity the personal contact details (including mail and email addresses, text, phone, or other contact details) or other information they obtain with respect to persons who have taken any of their tests, based on the statistical level of their test performance or otherwise, without an advance "opt-in" executed by the test taker at the time the test is taken or at the time the test taker receives the results. This requirement also would be subject to the audit mandates relating to test security and monitoring procedures. In a time when personal privacy is becoming a luxury good, it is important to use an "opt-in" rather than "opt-out" test for what applicants and their families want.

Some applicants may well find it advantageous to agree to such sales of their data in order to receive more information on college options from a wider set of resources than they are familiar with, but that should be a deliberate choice made with clear disclosure. It is also possible that preventing unwanted disclosure of personal information that will trigger an incessant marketing deluge will help reduce the application packing that colleges engage in to manipulate the denominator of their admissions-to-applications ratios and their related selectivity rankings.

Rather than limiting high school student choices in terms of APs, TEFCA would require all elite colleges to disclose whether and which AP grades will be given extra weight when they recalculate transcripts and which AP courses and levels of performance will assure waivers of related common core or prerequisite courses.

The College Board's Common App should also be voluntarily reformed to limit more tightly the number of nonacademic extracurricular activities other than sports that can be submitted. It has been allowing up to ten, which can pressure students to fill in all ten, sometimes with marginal or even fabricated entries.

Annual Reports to High Schools on Admissions Outcomes, and Public Disclosure of Any Material Violation of the TEFCA Admission Practices and Disclosure Rules

The number of applications any college receives from each high school annually, as well as the numbers accepted and attending, would have to be disclosed to the high school before the start of the next admissions year cycle. This will be particularly helpful to over-loaded public high school college admissions counselors in terms of advising their seniors on their admissions chances at particular schools.

The legislation would also require the Department of Education to publish annual reports, accessible online, that summarize significant patterns in admissions outcomes emerging from the new disclosures mandated by TEFCA, and identify any colleges that have violated any of those requirements or other mandated admissions practice changes, and reveal any sanctions imposed with respect to such violations, including potential denial of federal aid eligibility for those colleges that consistently fail to meet their obligations under TEFCA.

Help Colleges Support and Graduate Economically Disadvantaged Students

Companion legislation to TEFCA will provide federal appropriations to restore cuts and increase support for several programs designed to support middle- and low-income and first-generation college applicants, including students who have been in the foster care system and thus suffer a college attendance profile in the single digits. Federal assistance would include strengthened funding for the Federal Work-Study and Supplemental Educational Opportunity Grant programs, as well as doubling funding for Pell grants, making them available year-round including for summer study by students who must work their way through college as quickly as possible. (See Douglas-Gabriel 2016)

Companion legislation to TEFCA would also expand the annual federal 1.4 percent tax on college endowment earnings to apply to all nonprofit private colleges with net investment assets of $250,000 or more per student, and require that receipts from this tax be applied in part to expand Pell grant capacity. TEFCA will also create a dollar-for-dollar exemption from the endowment tax for colleges that increase their financial support for low-income students.

TEFCA will provide special funding for disadvantaged students to take AP and International Baccalaureate classes and tests, as well as subsidies to enable them to take standardized admission tests early and often to take better advantage (which wealthier students already do) of super-scoring by elite admissions offices that evaluate them using only their best scores on each major test segment and overall. (Chinoy 2018)

TEFCA will also be accompanied by financial incentives for all colleges — allocated with reference to their relative financial resources — to place more emphasis on achieving economic diversity within their entering classes and to sustain that diversity with programs to ensure that relative newcomers to their college environments develop a real sense of belonging, and have their basic human needs accounted for, like enough food and access to wellness care, during their time in college.

Respond to the COVID-19 Impact on Colleges with a National Plan to Radically Expand College and Broadband Access

The severe impact of COVID-19 on college resources, budgets, operations, and students has also presented an opportunity to greatly extend admission opportunities with state-of-the-art forms of online learning that colleges have been forced to adopt. Collegiate "telelearning" could well become as commonplace as telecommuting and telemedicine. Including suggestions already put forward by Paul N. Friga of the University of North Carolina and Angel B. Perez, chief executive of the National Association for College Admission Counseling (See Friga April 22, 2020 and Perez 2020), TEFCA would fund a five-year, multi-billion federal "College Access Assurance Plan" including:

(A) A research surge to design and implement a revised "common app" with a new online template where applicants can demonstrate their portfolios of subject matter mastery and the personal development needed for college studies.

(B) A comprehensive examination of higher education business models to identify and facilitate potential administrative efficiencies; operational process improvements; more educationally productive year-round usage of campus facilities; improved transparency of student activity fees and dining hall charges to prevent overcharging in relation to value delivered; academic term structures and delivery options not tied to 19th century agrarian calendars; and novel approaches to tuition charges and payment options — all in order to "bend the college cost curve" downward by 20 percent within five years.

(C) A crash program to help every non-profit college develop best practice online educational options and choices appropriate to its mission, including support for acquiring the requisite hardware, software and connectivity; hiring instructional design talent; development and training of online instructors; and orientation of online students to a level of comfort and satisfaction so that no tuition discounts versus in-person courses would be objectively justified.

(D) A national infrastructure proje deliver affordable state-of-the-art high-speed broadband and connective hardware and software to every American household within five years.

Citizens and their leaders alike will hopefully recognize that assuring access to college through a transparent, equitable, fair, and affordable admissions process that works for qualified students of all economic, racial and ethnic backgrounds — using 21st century technology rather than enshrining 19th century class distinctions — would restore the historic promise of economic and social mobility in America. The financial commitments part and parcel of TEFCA recognize that comprehensive reform of college admissions must be accompanied by an equivalent expansion of federal resources necessary to make that American promise a reality.

Appendix: Turning Admissions Risk Upside Down: An Alternative Path to Transparent and Fair Outcomes for Applicants and Colleges Alike

If the reforms proposed in TEFCA are not adopted, or if it were to fall short in terms assuring comprehensively to replace and reform the current college admissions transparent, fair, and equitable access to higher education to all capable applicants at a reasonable cost — in terms of money, time, and anxiety — even more radical measures must be considered that, while preserving the most useful and potentially beneficial aspects of the current system, would decisively alter the balance of market power in admissions that currently favors the richest applicants and the richest colleges.

1. Adapt and repurpose the Common Application into a national application database where all prospective students would submit their grades, test scores, extracurricular activities, and standard essays, which would be immediately accessible to all colleges.

2. Allow students to submit a list of up to ten colleges where they want to pursue admission, along with (a) completed standard FAFSA forms based on the latest available parental tax data and (b) any additional essay-type material or test scores required by those colleges, which in each case would be made available to the colleges listed.

3. Authorize each college, within a set period of time in early spring, to extend (a) a "bid" (defined below) for any of the students who listed it and provided the materials required, and/or (b) a full bid based solely on the Common Application of any student, or (c) a conditional bid to any student submitting a Common Application whom the college itself wishes to pursue, subject to receiving further material. This means some applicants could get bids from schools they had not focused on themselves.

4. Each bid would include the proposed tuition, room, and board costs net of related financial aid or work-study packages that the college commits to extend to the student. There would then be a thirty-day window for negotiations between the prospective students and colleges relating to those terms.

5. After a first round of such bidding, negotiation, and decisions, there would be a second round available for both colleges and applicants to match up under the same process if not satisfied with the results of the first round.

6. All the new mandatory disclosure rules under TEFCA outlined in chapter 8 would apply to this new admissions process, so we would be able to see if any discriminatory preferences were evident in admissions results. The new system would essentially turn the current admissions process (and seller-buyer market power relationship) upside down: colleges would be strongly incentivized to put their best bids forward to get the students they want most.

7. The current, highly problematic bookends of the admissions calendar — early decision and the dreaded wait list — would become unnecessary and irrelevant. Moreover, the students from the wealthiest families would forgo the relative exclusivity they enjoy in pursuing early decision admissions: all applicants, once admissions bids come out, would have the same opportunity to know right away the aid package on the table and share the same time frame for comparing and negotiating final terms.

This new admissions matching and bidding system, based on the existing Common Application processes, would relieve the undue risks and burdens of the admissions processes now borne by high school students. It would also incentivize colleges, which would under this new system carry more of those risks and, to mitigate their own stresses by more, not less, transparency and real, academically-sound selectivity.

The current elite college rankings-driven selectivity game we know and loathe would effectively be a thing of the past. Applicants would have much better up-front data on their real chances for admission to a particular college. There is even the prospect that the bidding process would at last begin to bend the college cost curve down, as well as the trillion-dollar student debt burden overhanging the economy. That result could be the best college admissions outcome of all.

References

Books:

Armstrong, Elizabeth A., and Laura T. Hamilton. 2016. *Paying for the Party: How College Maintains Inequality.* Cambridge, MA: Harvard University Press

Avery, Christopher, Andrew Fairbanks and Richard Zeckhauser. 2004. *The Early Admissions Game.* Boston, MA: Harvard University Press.

Bruni, Frank. 2015. *Where You Go Is Not Who You'll Be: An Antidote to the College Admissions Mania.* New York, NY: Grand Central Publishing

Deresiewicz, William. 2014. *Excellent Sheep: The Miseducation of the American Elite and the Way to a Meaningful Life.* New York, NY: Free Press

Espeland, Wendy Nelson and Michael Sauder. 2016. *Engines of Anxiety: Academic Rankings, Reputation, and Accountability.* New York, NY: Russell Sage Foundation

Golden, Daniel. 2006. *The Price of Admission: How America's Ruling Class Buys Its Way Into Elite Colleges — and Who Gets Left Outside the Gates.* New York, NY: Crown Publishing

Kahlenberg, Richard D., ed. 2010. *Affirmative Action for the Rich: Legacy Preferences in College Admissions*. New York, NY: The Century Foundation

Kester, Eric. 2012. *That Book About Harvard*. Naperville, I: Sourcebooks

Koch, James V. 2019. *The Impoverishment of the American College Student*. Washington, D.C.: Brookings Institution Press

Lythcott-Haims, Julie. 2015. *How to Raise an Adult*. New York, NY: Henry Holt and Company, LLC.

O'Shaughnessy, Lynn. 2015. *The College Solution*, 2nd ed. Upper Saddle River, NJ: Pearson Education, Inc.

Putnam, Robert D. 2016. *Our Kids: The American Dream in Crisis*. New York: Simon & Shuster

Reeves, Richard V. 2017. *Dream Hoarders: How the Upper Middle Class Is Leaving Everyone Else in the Dust, Why That Is a Problem, and What to Do About It*. Washington, D.C.: Brookings Institution Press

Springer, Sally P., Jon Reider, and Joyce Vining Morgan. 2015. *Admission Matters: What Students and Parents Need to Know About Getting into College*, 3rd ed. San Francisco: Jossey Bass

Steinberg, Jacques. 2003. *The Gatekeepers*. New York, NY: Penguin Books

Tough, Paul. 2019. *The Years That Matter Most: How College Makes or Breaks Us*. Boston, MA: Houghton Mifflin Harcourt

The following publications or other news media are cited multiple times in connection with material in the text:

Atlantic
Axios

Bloomberg Businessweek
CNBC
CNN
Inside Higher Ed
Politico
Chronicle of Higher Education
Economist
Financial Times
The Hill
New York Times
Palo Alto Weekly
Wall Street Journal
Washington Post
Time
Town & Country

Articles, reports and other media cited in the text:

Where authors are cited for multiple articles in the same year, the full date is shown directly after their name as well to facilitate identification with text notations. Where authors are cited for articles in multiple years, the entries are listed in reverse chronological order.

2019 Annual Report: "Education — Supporting School Success." 2019. *Bloomberg Philanthropies*. December 24, 2019

Advertisement. 2019. "Summer Travel Programs: Student Programs." *New York Times*. January 8, 2019.

Allen, Mike. 2019. "1 big thing…#UToo: University shortcuts for the rich." *Axios AM*. March 16, 2019.

Anderson, Jenny. 2019. "America's top colleges are not the engines of social mobility they say they are." *Quartz*. September 13, 2019.

Anderson, Nick. 2020. "College students want answers about fall, but schools may not have them for months." *Washington Post.* April 22, 2020

Anderson, Nick. 2020. "College students are rebelling against full tuition after classes go online." *Washington Post.* April 16, 2020.

Anderson, Nick. 2019. "Federal judge rules Harvard does not discriminate against Asian Americans in admissions." *Washington Post.* October 1, 2019.

Anderson, Nick. 2019. "Study: Universal SAT testing in Virginia would identify more prospective students for major universities." *Washington Post.* June 25, 2019.

Anderson, Nick. 2019. "Attention college shoppers: These schools are slashing their prices." *Washington Post.* January 19, 2019.

Anderson, Nick. 2019. "Early college admissions by the numbers." *Washington Post.* January 7, 2019.

Anderson, Nick. 2018. "U.S. News colleges rankings: UCLA ties Berkeley, West Point leap frogs Annapolis." *Washington Post.* September 12, 2018.

Anderson, Nick. 2018. "A shakeup in elite admissions: U-Chicago drops SAT/ACT testing requirement." June 14, 2018.

Anderson, Nick. 2020. "College students want answers about fall, but schools may not have them for months." *Washington Post.* April 22, 2020

Anderson, Nick. 2020. "College students are rebelling against full tuition after classes go online." *Washington Post.* April 16, 2020.

Anderson, Nick. 2018. "How to protect Harvard admissions secrets? Judge says it's like shielding 'recipe for Coke.'" *Washington Post*. April 10, 2018.

Anderson, Nick. 2016. "Surge in foreign students may be crowding Americans out of elite colleges." *Washington Post*. December 21, 2016.

Anderson, Nick. 2016. "A college-admissions edge for the wealthy: Early decision." *Washington Post*. March 31, 2016.

Anderson, Nick. 2016. "'Read me!': Students race to craft forceful essays as deadlines near." *Washington Post*. October 28, 2017.

Anderson, Nick. 2014. "Colleges often give discounts to the rich. But here's one that gave up on 'merit' aid." *Washington Post*. December 24, 2014.

Anderson, Nick and Susan Svrluga. 2019. "Varsity athletes, admissions and enrollment at top colleges," *Washington Post*. June 12, 2019.

Andriotis, AnnaMaria. 2019. "Student Debt At 65." *Wall Street Journal*. February 23, 2019.

Asimov, Nanette. 2019. "Audit finds weaknesses in UC admissions process, echoing national scandal." *San Francisco Chronicle*. July 17, 2019.

Baldridge, Susan Campbell, Susan Shaman and Robert Zemsky. 2020. "Will Your College Close." *Chronicle of Higher Education*. February 10, 2020.

Barnard, Brennan. 2019. "The Debate Over Early Decision In College Admission: Who Is It Good For?" *Forbes*. June 13, 2019.

Barnard, Brennan. 2016. In Strauss, Valerie. "How college admissions has turned in something akin to 'The Hunger Games'." *Washington Post.* March 28, 2016.

Barnard, Brennan, Richard Weissbourd and Trisha Ross Anderson. 2020. "Will the Pandemic Revolutionize College Admissions?" *Wall Street Journal.* May 30-31, 2020.

Barrett, Devlin and Matt Zapotoski. 2019. "FBI accuses wealthy parents, including celebrities, in college-entrance bribery scheme." *Washington Post.* March 12, 2019.

Bartlett, Tom. 2019. "What the Admissions Scandal Reveals About Secrecy, Privilege and the Nature of Merit." *Chronicle of Higher Education.* March 15, 2019.

Bauman, Dan. 2019. "How Choosing Prestige Is Starting to Strain Some Elite Institutions." *Chronicle of Higher Education.* November 14, 2019.

Bauman, Dan and Tyler Davis. 2018. "How the NCAA's March Madness Windfall makes Its Way to Colleges." *Chronicle of Higher Education.* March 12, 2018.

Belkin, Douglas. 2019. *"SAT to Give Students 'Adversity Score' to Capture Social and Economic Backgrounds." Wall Street Journal.* May 16, 2019.

Belkin, Douglas. 2019. "New Front in College Admissions: Nudging Students to Decide Early." *Wall Street Journal.* January 2, 2019.

Belkin, Douglas. 2019. "SAT to Give Students 'Adversity Score' to Capture Social and Economic Backgrounds" *Wall Street Journal.*

May 16, 2019

Berman, Jillian. 2017. "New York Fed president: Legacy admissions to college is hurting economic mobility." *MarketWatch*. October 7, 2017.

Berrett, Dan. 2019. "Hampshire College to Admit Pared-Down Freshman Class Next Year." *Chronicle of Higher Education*. February 2, 2019.

Biemiller, Lawrence. 2018. "Can a Signature Program Save Your College?" *Chronicle of Higher Education*. March 11, 2018.

Biemiller, Lawrence. 2017. "Struggling Mills College Look to a 'Signature Significance' to Boost Its Fortunes." *Chronicle of Higher Education*. May 18, 2017.

Binkley, Collin. 2018. "Most big public colleges don't track suicides, AP finds." *Associated Press*. January 2, 2018.

Binkley, Collin and Hannah Fingerhut. "Poll: Americans split on college admissions fairness." *Associated Press*. April 24, 2019.

Blackford, Linda. 2019. "Students end hunger strike after UK president agrees to cover mural, take other steps." *Lexington Herald Leader*. August 3, 2019.

Blumenstyk, Goldie. 2019. "This Map Paints a Given Picture of America's Economic Divide. Colleges Shouldn't Run from Them." *Chronicle of Higher Education*. July 17, 2019.

Blumenstyk, Goldie. 2019. "Why Don't Colleges Do More to Help Students in Need? Money, Attitude and More." *Chronicle of Higher Education*. July 12, 2019.

Boeckenstedt, Jon. 2020. "Will Coronavirus End the SAT?" *Chronicle of Higher Education*. April 30, 2020.

Boland, Ed. 2016. "Former Yale admissions officer reveals secrets of who gets in." *New York Post*. February 7, 2016.

Botstein, Leon. 2019. "Meritocracy Isn't Broken. Assessment Is." In "Does meritocracy stall social mobility, entrench an undeserving elite and undermine trust in higher education?" *The Chronicle of Higher Education*. September 13, 2019.

Brenoff, Ann. 2016. "The 9 Things That Are Wrong With The College Application Process." *Huffington Post*. January 21, 2016.
Brittain, John and Eric L. Bloom. "Admitting the Truth: The Effect of Affirmative Action, Legacy Preferences, and The Meritocratic Ideal on Students of Color in College Admissions." In Kahlenberg, ed., *Affirmative Action for the Rich*, 123-42.

Brooks, David. 2018. "A New Cold War is Waged." *New York Times*. October 30, 2018.

Brown, Forrest. 2014. "The Legend of the Z-list." *Harvard Crimson*. August 3, 2014.

Brown, Sandy. 2017. "The Surprising Value That Need-Based Aid Brings." *Chronicle of Higher Education*. January 1, 2017.

Brown, Sarah. 2019. "Here's Why Alaska's Governor Thinks His University System Needs Steep Cuts — And Why Experts Say He's Wrong." *Chronicle of Higher Education*. July 25, 2019.

Bruni, Frank. 2019. "When Did College Turn So Cruel?" *New York Times*. September 3, 2019.

Bruni, Frank. 2017. "Lifting Kids to College." *New York Times*. April 26, 2017.

Bruni, Frank. 2016. "The Plague of 'Early Decision.'" *The Bulletin*. December 21, 2016.

Bruni, Frank. 2016. "College Admissions Shocker." *New York Times*. March 30, 2016.

Burwell, Sylvia Mathews. 2018. "The Mental Health Crisis on Campuses." *Foreign Affairs*. November/December 2018.

Carlson, Scott. 2020. "At the Precipice: 6 in 10 Colleges Say They Missed Fall Enrollment Goals." *Chronicle of Higher Education*. February 24, 2020.

Carlson, Scott. 2016. "When College Was a Public Good." *Chronicle of Higher Education*. November 27, 2016.

Camera, Lauren. 2019. "The Higher Education Apocalypse." *US News*. March 23, 2019.

Chaffin, Joshua. 2019. "How wealthy Americans get their kids into school." *Financial Times*. March 12, 2019.

Chan, J. Clara. 2017. "On Social Media, They Represent the College 24/7." *Chronicle of Higher Education*. September 17, 2017.

Chan, J. Clara. 2017. "Yelp for Colleges? An Economist Rates Its Usefulness." *Chronicle of Higher Education*. June 12, 2017.

Cherney, Elyssa. 2020. "College students are unlikely to get tuition refunds after coronavirus campus shutdown. But it won't be for lack of trying." *Chicago Tribune*. April 9, 2020.

Chetty, Raj, Nathaniel Hendren, Patrick Kline, and Emmanuel Saez. 2014. "Where Is the Land of Opportunity? The Geography of Intergenerational Mobility in the United States." *Quarterly Journal of Economics*. 129 (4), 1553-1623.

Chetty, Raj, John M. Friedman, Emmanuel Saez, Nicholas Turner, and Danny Yagan. 2017. "Mobility Report Cards: The Role of Colleges in International Mobility." *Equality of Opportunity Project*. Working Paper Number 23618, revised Version December 2017.

Chin, Allison. 2019. "Patients are desperate to resemble their doctored selfies. Plastic surgeons alarmed by 'Snapchat dysmorphia.'" *Washington Post*. August 6, 2019.

Chinoy, Sahil. 2018. "A Surprisingly Simple Way to Help Level The Playing Field of College Admissions." *New York Times*. August 27, 2018.

Chua, Amy et al. 2020. "To the Class of 2020: Commencement Advice for a Moment of Crisis." *Wall Street Journal*. May 2-3. 2020, Section C1-4.

Clotfelter, Charles T. 2017. "How Rich Universities Get Richer…and leave everyone else behind." *Chronicle of Higher Education*. October 27, 2017.

Coffman, Chad, Tara P. O'Neil, and Brian Starr. "An Empirical Analysis of the Impact of Legacy of Preferences on Alumni Giving at Top Universities" in Kahlenberg, ed. 2010 ibid., 101-21.

College Raptor. 2019. "Largest Endowments for 2019." https://www.collegeraptor.com/college-rankings/details/Endowment

Crowe, Cailin. 2018. "Moody's Gives Higher Ed a Negative

Outlook, Again." *Chronicle of Higher Education.* December 4, 2018.

Conley, Bill. 2019. "The Great Enrollment Crash." *The Chronicle Review.* September 6, 2019.

Conley, Dalton. 2018. "Enough fretting over college admissions. It's time for a lottery." *Washington Post.* August 13, 2018.

CTE Policy Watch. 2019. "Changes to College Scorecard Announced." May 22, 2019.

Dannenburg, Michael. 2018. "Memorandum: Elite College Admissions" *Education Reform Now.* June 26, 2018.

Davorken, Ann Kearns and Karon Grigonas. 2019. "Changing Landscapes of College Admissions." *Higher Education Analytics Center.* June 10, 2019.

Desai, Saahil. 2018. "College Sports Are Affirmative Action for Rich White Students." *Atlantic.* October 23, 2018.

Diep, Francie, 2020. "Why One Former Campus Leader Thinks College Rankings Should Stop During the Pandemic." *Chronicle of Higher Education.* May 21, 2020.

Dimon, Jamie. 2019. Chairman and CEO Letter to Shareholders." *JPMorgan Chase & Co. Annual Report.* August 2018.

Douglas-Gabriel, Danielle. 2017. "This trend could destabilize some small private college if it continues." *Washington Post.* May 15, 2017.

Douglas-Gabriel, Danielle. 2016. "House rejects proposal to review year-round Pell Grants." *Washington Post.* July 7, 2016.

Douglas-Gabriel, Danielle. 2016. "Illinois budget battle leads Moody's to downgrade several state universities." *Washington Post.* February 25, 2016.

Douthat, Ross. 2019. "The College Admissions Trilemma." *New York Times.* September 21, 2019.

Douthat, Ross. 2017. "How to Fix the Republican Tax Plan." *New York Times.* November 15, 2017.

Douthat, Ross. 2014. "College, the Great Unequalizer." *New York Times.* May 3, 2014.

Dremann, Sue. 2015. "Gunn graduate's message: 'We are fighters'." *Palo Alto Weekly.* June 3, 2015.

Dreier, Peter and Richard D. Kahlenberg. 2014. "Making Top Colleges Less Aristocratic and More Meritocratic. *New York Times.* September 12, 2014.

Dried, Nadia. 2016. "How College Recruiters Are Using Snapchat, the App That Half of High Schoolers Use." *Chronicle of Higher Education.* October 12, 2016.

Druckerman, Pamela. 2019. "Helicopter Parenting Works." *New York Times.* February 6, 2019.

Ducharme, Jamie. 2019. "A gender gap no one wants to close." *Time.* June 3-10, 2019.

Dudley, William C. 2017. "The Monetary Policy Outlook and the Importance of Higher Education for Economic Mobility." *Federal Reserve Bank of New York.* October 6, 2017.

Dunn, Carrie. 2019. "'A deep and boiling anger': NBC/WSJ poll finds a pessimistic America despite economic satisfaction." *NBC News: Meet the Press.* August 25, 2019.

Economist. 2019. "Measuring the 1%." November 30, 2019.

Economist. 2019. "Bribe styles of the rich and famous." March 16, 2019.

Editorial, *Palo Alto Weekly.* 2019. "The audacity of privilege." *Palo alto Weekly.* March 22, 2019.

Editorial, *Wall Street Journal.* 2017. "What Is Harvard Hiding?" *Wall Street Journal.* August 7, 2017.

Editorial Board, *New York Times.* 2019. "Turns Out There's a Proper Way to Buy Your Kid a College Slot." *New York Times.* March 12, 2019.

Editorial Board, *New York Times.* 2017. "The Corruption at the Heart of March Madness." *New York Times.* September 28, 2017.

Editorial Board, *New York Times.* 2017. "Haunted by Student Debt Past Age 50." *New York Times.* February 13, 2017.

Editorial Board, *New York Times.* 2017. "Haunted by Student Debt Past age 50." *New York Times.* February 13, 2017.

Education Dive Staff https://www.educationdive.com/news/how-many-colleges-and-universities-have-closed-since-2016/539379. November 1, 2019.

Ellis, Lindsay. 2019. "'Everything Must Go!' A Rash of College Closures Keeps This Liquidation Firm Busy." *Chronicle of Higher Education.* June 17, 2019.

Email to author. 2018. "Tips for a successful college tour."

gooddecisions@collegefactual.com. July 10, 2018.

England, Jason. 2019. "Higher Education and the Illusion of Meritocracy." *Chronicle of Higher Education.* March 13, 2019.

England, Jason. 2017. "Admissions Confidential." *Chronicle of Higher Education.* December 3, 2017.

Ethan, Leyton, Kaylio, Ugwall and Waverly. 2019. *The Campanile,* Palo Alto High School. Editorial May 2019; Letter April 2019.

Eustachewich, Lia and Ruth Brown. 2018. "Emails show Harvard favored applicants with ties to big donors." *New York Post.* October 18, 2018.

Ezeugo, Ernest and Clare McCann. 2017. Chetty vs. Pell: What's the Best Way to Measure a College's Commitment to Low-Income Students?" Blog Post. *New America.* October 3, 2017.

Fallows, James. 2001. "The Early Decision Racket." *Atlantic.* September 2001.

Fernandez, Deidre. 2017. "Want to get into your first-choice college? Better buy a plane ticket." *Boston Globe.* August 21, 2017.

Feuerherd, Ben. 2019 "SAT drops supplemental 'adversity score' amid criticism." *New York Post.* August 28, 2019.

Finger, Leslie and Thomas Gift. 2019. "Some People Want Lottery-Based Admissions. That's a Terrible Idea." *Chronicle of Higher Education.* April 1, 2019.

Fischer, Karen. 2017. "Many Colleges See a Drop in International Students, Chronicle Survey Finds." *Chronicle of Higher Education.* September 6, 2017.

Fischer, Karen, et al. 2016. "Are Colleges Engines of Inequality." *Chronicle of Higher Education.* January 17, 2016.

Fischer, Karen and Jack Stripling. 2014. "An Era of Neglect." *Chronicle of Higher Education.* March 2, 2014.

Flanagan, William S. and Michael E. Xie. 2017. "Median Family Income for Harvard Undergrads Triple National Average." *Harvard Crimson.* January 25, 2017.

Franklin, Delano R. and Samuel W. Zwickel. 2018. "In Admissions, Harvard Favors Those Who Fund It, Internal Emails Show." *Harvard Crimson.* October 18, 2018.

Friga, Paul N. 2020. "How Congress Can Save Colleges." *Chronicle of Higher Education."* of April 22, 2020.

Friga, Paul N. 2020. Under Covid-19, University Budgets Like We've Never Seen Before." *Chronicle of Higher Education.* April 20, 2020.

Friga, Paul N. 2020. "The Hard Choices Presidents Will Have to Make." *Chronicle of Higher Education.* April 3, 2020.

Frye, Alice A. 2018. "Lady Bird's Cheating Problem." *Chronicle of Higher Education."* February 1, 2018.

Furstenburg, Francois. 2020. "University Leaders are Failing. The pandemic reveals ineptitude at the top." *Chronicle of Higher Education.* May 19, 3020

Gardner, Lee. 2020. "Inside the Scramble for Students." *Chronicle of Higher Education.* May 18, 2020

Gardner, Lee. 2020. "How College Leaders Are Planning for the Fall." *Chronicle of Higher Education*. April 17, 2020.

Gardner, Lee. 2018. "How to Identify and Invest in High-Achieving, Low-Income Students." *Chronicle of Higher Education*. February 11, 2018.

Gardner, Lee. 2017. "Brb — Gotta Go Text Teens About College." *Chronicle of Higher Education*. November 16, 2017.

Gee, Kelsey. 2018. "Temple Is Probed Over Online MBA Marketing." *Wall Street Journal*. July 26, 2019.

Georgetown University: Center on Education and the Workforce. 2016. "America's Divided Recovery: College Haves and Have Nots." January 2016

Gerstein, Josh. 2018. "What Is Harvard Trying to Hide?" *Politico*. October 21, 2018.

Getlen, Larry. 2018. "Why the middle class can't afford life in America anymore." *New York Post*. June 22, 2018. (Citing Quart, infra 2018).

Giancola, Jennifer and Richard D. Kahlenberg. 2016. "True Merit: Ensuring Our Brightest Students Have Access to our Best Colleges and Universities." *Jack Kent Cooke Foundation*. January 2016.

Gladwell, Malcolm. 2011. "The Order of Things." *New Yorker*. February 14 and 21, 2011.

Gluckman, Nell. 220. "Elite-College Admissions Has an Image Problem. Would Ending legacy Admissions Help?" *Chronicle of Higher Education*. January 30, 2020.

Gluckman, Nell. 2019. "How The Wealthy and Well-Connected Have Learned to Game The Admissions Process." *Chronicle of Higher Education.* August 2, 2019.

Gluckman, Nell. 2019. "A Fresh Abuse Rattles College Admissions: Parents Give Up Custody of Their Children So They Can Get Student Aid." *Chronicle of Higher Education* July 30, 2019.

Gluckman, Nell. 2019. "California Lawmakers Propose Reforms in Admissions Process. Other States Could Follow." *Chronicle of Higher Education.* March 29, 2019.

Gluckman, Nell. 2018. "Harvard's Admissions Process Was Just Dissected in Federal Court. How Did It Hold Up?" *Chronicle of Higher Education.* November 2, 2018.

Gluckman, Nell. 2018. "What's New in Harvard's Admissions Procedures: Explicit Instructions on Race." *Chronicle of Higher Education.* October 26, 2018.

Gluckman, Nell. 2018. "The Lawsuit Against Harvard Turns into a Courtroom Battle of Economists." *Chronicle of Higher Education.* October 25, 2018.

Gluckman, Nell. 2018. "Harvard Is Challenged on Whether Socioeconomic Status Should Replace Race as Admissions Factor." *Chronicle of Higher Education.* October 22, 2018.

Glynn, Jennifer. 2017. "Opening Doors." *Jack Kent Cooke Foundation.* 2017.

Golden, Daniel. 2019. "'The Epitome of Sleaze': How Rick Singer pulled off his Fraud — and why colleges were complicit." *The Chronicle Review.* October 17, 2019.

Golden, Daniel. 2018. "How the Fight Against Affirmative Action at Harvard Could Threaten Rich Whites." *ProPublica.* July 11, 2018.

Golden, Daniel. 2016. "Jared Kushner Isn't Alone: Universities Still Give Rich and Connected Applicants a Leg Up." *ProPublica.* November 22, 2016.

Golden, Daniel. 2010. "An Analytical Survey of Legacy Preference." In Kahlenberg, ed. 2010 ibid., 71-99.

Goldrick-Rab, Sara. 2018. "It's Hard to Study if You're Hungry." *New York Times.* January 14, 2018.

Goldstein, Dana. 2019. "Reporting on a Very Bad Year for the College Admissions Industry." *New York Times.* August 2, 2019.

Goldstein, Dana. 2017. "When Affirmative Action Isn't Enough." *New York Times.* September 17, 2017.

Gray, Eliza. 2015. "Bubble Trouble For Standardized Testing." *Time.* October 1, 2015.

Green, Erica L. 2020. "New Campus Sexual Misconduct Rules Will Tackle Dating Violence." *New York Times.* February 10, 2020.

Greenspan, Rachel E. 2019. "The College Board Is Rolling Out a New SAT 'Adversity Score.' Here's How it Could Impact College Admissions." *Time.* May 16, 2019.

Guinier, Lani. 1997. "The Real Bias in Higher Education." *New York Times.* June 24, 1997.

Gross, Sybilla. 2020. "Universities Forced to Face Addiction to Foreign Students' Money." *Bloomberg.* April 4, 2006.

Guyut, Katherine and Isabel V. Sawhill. 2020. "Telecommuting will likely continue long after the pandemic." *Brookings*. April 6, 2020.

Hackman, Michelle. 2019. "Trump to Issue Order Tying Federal Grant to Free Speech on Campus." *Wall Street Journal*. March 20, 2019.

Hackman, Michelle. 2019. "College-Admission Scandal Draws Scrutiny in Washington." *Wall Street Journal*. March 15, 2019.

Han, Crystal, Ozan Jaquette and Karina Salazar. 2019. "Recruiting the Out-of-State University: Off-campus recruiting by public research universities." *Joyce Foundation*. March 2019.

Harper, Stephen J. 2016. "What Rankings Have Wrought." Review of Engines of Anxiety; Academic Rankings, Reputation and Accountability," by Wendy Nelson Espeland and Michael Sauder. *Chronicle of Higher Education*. July 31, 2016.

Harris, Adam. 2017. 'What Would the Repeal of Higher Ed's Foundational Law Mean for Colleges?" *Chronicle of Higher Education*. June 23, 2017.

Hart, Kim and Allison Snyder. 2020. "How the coronavirus pandemic will transform teaching." *Axios*. May 9, 2020.

Hartocollis, Anemona and Kate Taylor. 2019. "Elite Colleges Announce Record Low Admissions Rates in Wake of College Cheating Scandal." *New York Times*. March 29, 2019.

Hartocollis, Anemona. 2018. "Is an Extroverted Applicant Better Suited for Harvard Than an Introvert?" *New York Times*. October 25, 2018.

Hartocollis, Anemona. 2018. "Harvard Rated Asian-American

Applicants Lower on Personality Traits, Suit Says." June 15, 2018.

Hartocollis, Anemona, Amy Harman, and Mitch Smith. 2018. "'Lopping,' 'Tips' and the 'Z-list': Bias Lawsuit Explores Harvard's Admissions Secrets." *New York Times.* July 28, 2018.

Heffernan, Lisa and Jennifer Wallace. 2016. "To get into college, Harvard report advocates for kindness instead of overachieving." *Washington Post.* January 20, 2016.

Henninger, Daniel. 2019. "The College Admissions Mess." *Wall Street Journal.* May 23, 2019.

Hensley-Clancy, Molly. 2017. "Asians With 'Very Familiar Profiles': How Princeton's Admissions Officers Talk About Race." *BuzzFeed News.* May 19, 2017.

Hess, Abigail J. 2018. "New study finds that 36 percent of college students don't have enough to eat." *CNBC.* April 6, 2018.

Hesse, Tom 2017. "In Admissions Hunt, Some Colleges Consult the King of Clicks: BuzzFeed." *Chronicle of Higher Education.* February 14, 2017.

Hill, Catherine Bond. 2019. "Should All College Admissions Be Need-Blind?' Yes." *Wall Street Journal.* March 18, 2019.

Hill, Catherine Bond. 2015. 'Income Inequality and Higher Education." *The Presidency: American Council on Education — Leadership Advocacy, Summer 2015 edition.* June 10, 2015.

Holmes, Lindsay and Anna Almendrala. 2016. "There's Been A Startling Rise In Suicide Rates In The U.S." *Huffington Post.* April 22, 2016.

Hoover, Eric. 2020. "AP Tests During Covid-19. Heartbreak, Technical Glitches, and Anonymous Intrigue." *Chronicle of Higher Education*. May 15, 2020.

Hoover, Eric. 2020. "Colleges Are Urged to Reassess Admissions Policies Because of 'Extraordinary Hardships' Covid-19 Poses." *Chronicle of Higher Education*. April 29, 2020.

Hoover, Eric. 2020. "Distance Learning." *Chronicle of Higher Education*. April 24, 2020.

Hoover, Eric. 2020. "'Act Now!' Say Hello to the New Enrollment Playbook." *Chronicle of Higher Education*. February 11, 2020.

Hoover, Eric. 2019. "Let's Clarify a Few Things About the New 'Adversity Score'. (First, Stop Calling it That.)" *Chronicle of Higher Education*, May 23, 2019.

Hoover, Eric 2019. "Why Are SAT Takers Getting an 'Adversity Score'? Here's Some Context." *Chronicle of Higher Education*. May 16, 2019.

Hoover, Eric. 2019. "Admission Officers Didn't Cause the Scandal. But They Helped Shape the Culture That Spawned It." *Chronicle of Higher Education*. March 13, 2019. (No. 1)

Hoover, Eric. 2019. "Bribery Scandal Reveals 'Weak Spots' in the Admissions System." *Chronicle of Higher Education*. March 13, 2019.

Hoover, Eric. 2018. "Breaking Open the 'Black Box' of Elite Admissions." *Chronicle of Higher Education.* December 12, 2018.

Hoover, Eric. 2018. "Both Sides at Harvard Trial Agree on One Thing: 'The Wolf of Racial Bias' Is at the Door." *Chronicle of Higher*

Education. November 4, 2018.

Hoover, Eric. 2018. "As Harvard Trial Winds Down, Admissions Director Takes the Stand — Again." *Chronicle of Higher Education*. November 1, 2018.

Hoover, Eric. 2018. "Harvard's Star Witness Testified All Day. Here Are 4 Moments That Mattered." *Chronicle of Higher Education*. October 31, 2018.

Hoover, Eric. 2018. "Dueling Economists: Rival Analyses of Harvard's Admission Process Emerge at Trial." *Chronicle of Higher Education*. October 30, 2018.

Hoover, Eric. 2018. "Harvard Asks Court to Keep Information on Individual Applicants and 'Granular' Admissions Details Under Seal." *Chronicle of Higher Education*. June 24, 2018.

Hoover, Eric. 2018. "Some Colleges Share Lists of Early Decision Admits. Now the Justice Department Is Investigating." *Chronicle of Higher Education*. April 8, 2018.

Hoover, Eric. 2018. "Reading an Application in Under 10 Minutes? Way Too Fast, One Admissions Dean Says." *Chronicle of Higher Education*. February 1, 2018.

Hoover, Eric. 2017. "Demographic Changes as Destiny in College Admissions? It's Complicated." *Chronicle of Higher Education*. December 14, 2017, citing Nathan D. Grawe, author of *Demographics and the Demand* for *Higher Education*. 2018. Baltimore, MD: Johns Hopkins University Press.

Hoover, Eric. 2017. 'Wait, Will Anyone Investigate Legacy Admissions?" *Chronicle of Higher Education*. August 3, 2017.

Hoover, Eric. 2016. "Foundation Urges Admissions Offices to Create a 'Poverty Preference'." *Chronicle of Higher Education*. January 11, 2016.

Hoover, Eric. 2015. "College Admissions, Frozen in Time." *Chronicle of Higher Education*. May 26, 2015.

Hoover, Eric and Sara Lipka. 2016. "Enrollment Goals Remain Elusive for Small Colleges." *Chronicle of Higher Education*. December 11, 2016.

Hoover, Eric and Beckie Supiano. 2015. "College Admissions Isn't Fair…Whatever That Means." *Chronicle of Higher Education*. October 2, 2015.

Hoxby, Caroline M. and Christopher Avery. 2012. "The Missing 'One-Off': The Hidden Supply of High-Achieving, Low-Income Students." *National Bureau of Economic Research*. December 2012.

Hubler, Shawn. 2020. "University of California Will End Use of SAT and ACT in Admissions." *New York Times*. May 21, 2020.

Hurtado, Patricia, Janelle Lawrence and Sydney Maki. 2018. "Harvard Study Found Asian-American Admissions Bias, Suit Claims." *Bloomberg*. June 15, 2018.

Ingraham, Christopher. 2020. "U.N. warns that runaway inequality is destabilizing the world's democracies." *Washington Post*. February 11, 2020.

Insurance Journal. 2016. "95% of Post-Recession Jobs Went to College Educated: Study." June 30, 2016, citing *Georgetown University: Center for Education and the Workforce*, ibid.)

Jaquette, Ozan and Karina Salazar. 2018. "Colleges Recruit at Richer, Whiter High Schools." *New York Times*. April 13, 2018.

Jaschik, Scott. 2019. "Private Nonprofit College Closures, 2016-Present: The List Colleges Don't Want to Join." *Inside Higher Ed*. June 13, 2019.

Jaschik, Scott. 2019. "Where Colleges Recruit…And Where They Don't." *Inside Higher Ed*. April 16, 2019.

Jaschik, Scott. 2019. "Where Do Colleges Recruit? Wealthy and White High Schools." *Inside Higher Ed*. April 1, 2019.

Jaschik, Scott. 2017. "The 2017 Survey of Admissions Directors: Pressure All Around." *Inside Higher Ed*. September 13, 2017.

Jaschik, Scott and Doug Lederman, eds. 2017. "2017 Survey of College and University Admissions Directors: A Study by Higher Ed and Gallup." *Inside Higher Ed*.

Jia, Emil. 2018. "The Legacy of Legacy." *Harvard Political Review*. April 30, 2018.

Johnson, Steven. 2019. "'Better, not Bigger': As Private Colleges Hunger for Students, One University Slims Down." *Chronicle of Higher Education*. July 17, 2019.

Johnson, Steven. 2019. "Private Colleges Set New Record in Tuition Discounts." *Washington Post*. May 10, 2019.

June, Audrey Williams. 2018. "Harvard's Racial Diversity Is on Trial. But What Do We Know About Its Economic Diversity?" *Chronicle of Higher Education*. October 24, 2018.

Kadvany, Elena. 202. "'I didn't get to say goodbye': Graduating seniors grapple with unexpected ending to their high school careers." *Palo Alto Weekly.* May 8, 2020.

Kadvany, Elena. 2019. "Pressure over college admissions 'out of control'." March 15, 2019.

Kahlenberg, Richard D. 2018. "A New Call to End Legacy Admissions." *Atlantic.* February 14, 2018.

Kahlenberg, Richard D. 2018. "10 Myths About Legacy Preferences in College Admissions." *Chronicle of Higher Education.* September 22, 2010.

Kamenetz, Anya. 2016. "5 Ways Elite-College Admissions Shut Out Poor Kids." *nprED.* January 15, 2016.

Kapp, Diana. 2015. "Why Are Palo Alto's kids killing themselves?" *San Francisco Magazine.* May 18, 2015.

Katzman, John and Steve Cohen. 2017. "Let's Agree: Racial Affirmative Action Failed." *Wall Street Journal.* October 27, 2017.

Kelderman, Eric. 2020. "Can 'White Resentment' Help Explain Higher-Education Cuts?" *Chronicle of Higher Education.* January 24, 2020.

Kelderman, Eric. 2019. "Enrollment Shortfalls Spread to More Campuses." *Chronicle of Higher Education.* May 20, 2019.

Kelderman, Eric. 2018. "Why College Mergers Need to be More Than Just Cutting Administrators." *Chronicle of Higher Education.* April 27, 2018.

Kelliher, Fiona. 2018. "The Meaning of Middle Class." *Palo Alto Weekly.* February 9, 2018.

Kirwan, William E. (Brit) and Arne Duncan. 2016. Speed Up the Glacial Pace of NCAA Reform." *Chronicle of Higher Education.* October 31, 2016.

Kochkodin, Brandon. 2019. "Notre Dame and Baylor Admit More Legacies Than Harvard and Yale." *Bloomberg.* March 21, 2019.

Korn, Melissa, Douglas Belkin, and Juliet Chung. 2020. "Coronavirus Pushes Colleges to the Breaking Point, Forcing 'Hard Choices' About Education." *Wall Street Journal.* April 30, 2020

Korn, Melissa. 2019. "How to fix College Admissions." *Wall Street Journal.* November 29, 2019.

Korn, Melissa. 2019. "Oberlin, University of Chicago and Other Elite Colleges Extend Application Deadlines." *Wall Street Journal.* January 29, 2019.

Korn, Melissa. 2018. "Harvard Admissions Dean Largely Ignored Report on Factors Affecting Asian-American Applicants." *Wall Street Journal.* October 17, 2018.

Korn, Melissa. 2018. "Williams, Wesleyan, Middlebury Among Targets of Federal Early-Admissions Probe." *Wall Street Journal.* April 11, 2018.

Korn, Melissa, 2018. "How Much Does Being a Legacy Help Your College Admissions Odds." *Wall Street Journal.* July 9, 2018.

Korn, Melissa. 2018. "The Decision That Hurts Your Chances of Getting Into Harvard." *Wall Street Journal.* March 28, 2018.

Korn, Melissa. 2017. "Cash-*Strapped* Private Colleges Cut Programs, Sell Assets." *Wall Street Journal.* September1, 2017.

Korn, Melissa, 2017. "Private Colleges See Record Discounting Pressure From Cost-Conscious Families." *Wall Street Journal.* May 15, 2017.

Kreighbaum, Andrew. 2019. "Trump Signs Broad Executive Order." *Inside Higher Ed.* March 22, 2019.

Kreighbaum, Andrew. 2018. "College Scorecard Drops National Comparison Data." *Inside Higher Ed.* October 1, 2018.

Kutner, Max. 2014. "How to Game the College Rankings." *Boston Globe.* August 26, 2014*: Boston Magazine.* September 2014.

Kuncel, Nathaniel and Paul Sackett. 2018. "The Gatekeeper Tests." *Wall Street Journal.* March 10-11, 2018.

Kvaal, James. 2017. "Colleges Can Help Students Move Up. Let's Make It Easier." *Chronicle of Higher Education.* February 19, 2017.

Larson, Carlton F. W. 2010. "Legacy Preferences and the Constitutional Prohibition on Titles of Nobility." In Kahlenberg, ed. 2010 ibid., 145-172.

Larson, Lucas Smolcic, Julia Rock, Harry August, and Jesse Barber. 2019. "VIP dinners offer peek at culture of privilege at Brown University." *Providence Journal.* February 24, 2019.

Laterman, Kaya. 2019. "Tuition or Dinner? Nearly Half of College Students Surveyed in New Report Are Going Hungry." *New York Times.* May 2, 2019.

Leonhardt, David. 2017. "America's Great Working-Class Colleges." *New York Times.* January 18, 2017.

Levy, Harold O. 2017. "Colleges Should Abandon Early Admission." *Inside Higher Ed.* January 12, 2017.

Levy, Harold O. and Peg Tyre. 2018. "How to Level the College Playing Field." *New York Times.* April 7, 2018.

Lewin, Tamar. 2011. "Harvard and Princeton Restore Early Admission." *New York Times.* February 24, 2011.

MacMillan, Douglas and Nick Anderson. 2019. "Student tracking, secret scores: How college admissions officers rank prospects before they apply." *Washington Post.* October 14, 2019.

Maldonado, Camilo. 2019. "Price of College Increasing Almost 8 Times Faster Than Wages." *Forbes.* July 24, 2018.

Manchester, Julia. 2019. "11 percent say they'd pay a bribe to get their kids into a top college: poll." *The Hill.* March 22, 2019.

Mangan, Katherine. 2019. "Public Universities Work Hard to Make Up for Budget Cuts. But In-State Students May be Paying the Price." *Chronicle of Higher Education.* March 26 2019.

Mangan, Katherine. 2019. "'Like a Slap in the Face'. Advocates Say Bribery Scheme Will Harm Students With Learning Disabilities." *Chronicle of Higher Education.* March 13, 2019.

Mangan, Katherine. 2018. "Northern Michigan U. Compensates 4 Who Were Threatened With Punishment for Speaking of Suicides." *Chronicle of Higher Education.* November 12, 2018.

Manzi, Jim. 2008. "Is Harvard Just a Tax-free Hedge Fund?"

National Review. May 12, 2008.

Marcus, Jon. "Transforming Higher Ed?" *New York Times.* April 24, 2020.

Marcus, Jon. 2017. "The newest advantage of being rich in America? Higher grades." *The Hechinger Report.* August 16, 2017.

Marcus, Jon. 2014. "New study quantifies impact of ratings." *The Hechinger Report.* January 16, 2014.

Marcus, Jon. 2013. "In a new age of college transparency, who's checking the facts?" *The Hechinger Report.* March 20, 2013.

Margolin, Emma. 2016. "Adolescent Suicide Spike leaving Families in Agony." *NBC News.* December 5, 2016.

Markovits, Daniel. 2019. "American Universities Must Choose: Do They Want to Be Equal or Elite?" *Time.* September 12, 2019.

MarksJarvis, Gail. 2016. "Workers with college degrees now outnumber those with high school degrees, study finds." *Chicago Tribune.* July !, 2016, citing Georgetown University: Center on Education and the Workforce., ibid.

May, Patrick. 2018. "'Me, rich?' Here's what Palo Altans think about themselves." *Bay Area News Group.* February 24, 2018.

Mazur, Eric and Bob Kerrey. 2020. "Higher Ed's Coronavirus Opportunity." *Wall Street Journal.* May 11, 2020.

McClay, Wilfred. M. 2017. "Higher Ed's Dysfunctional Devotion to Meritocracy." *The Chronicle Review.* December 3 2017.

McGinty, Jo Craven. 2016. "For Enrollment managers, a New

College Try." *Wall Street Journal.* May 28-29, 2016.

McMurtrie, Beth. 2019. "How Well Do Elite Colleges Contribute to the Public Good?" *Chronicle of Higher Education.* April 11, 2019.

Medina, Jennifer. 2019. "What's Life Like as a Student at U.S.C.? Depends on the Size of the Bank Account." *New York Times.* April 3, 2019.

Median, Jennifer, Katie Benner, and Kate Taylor. 2o19. "Actresses, Business Leaders and Other Wealthy Parents Charged in U.S. College Entry Fraud." *New York Times.* March 12, 2019.

Menand, Louis. 2003. "The Thin Envelope" *New Yorker.* March 20, 2003.

Meyer, Caroline. 2019. "Breaking down the early decision choice." *The Cavalier Daily.* June 21, 2019.

Mitchell, Josh. 2019. "The Long Road to the Student Debt Crisis." *Wall Street Journal.* June 7-8, 2019.

Moody, Josh. 2019. "20 Public Schools With Low Acceptance Rates." *US News.* September 19, 2019.

Moore, Justine. 2013. "Connection to University can affect admission decision." *Stanford Daily.* March 12, 2013.

Morrison, Alan B. and Richard Kahlenburg. 2019. "Admissions Policies Lack Credibility. The Cure: Radical Transparency" *Chronicle of Higher Education.* March 21, 2019.

Morrison, Patt. 2019. "Column: College admissions scandal shows how desperate the privileged are to keep it that way." *Los Angeles Times.* March 20, 2019.

Morse, Robert, Eric Brooks, and Matt Mason. 2019. "2020 Best Colleges Rankings Coming Sept. 9, 2019." *US News*. August 19, 2019.

Morse, Robert, Matt Mason, and Eric Brooks. 2019. "Updates to 5 Schools' 2019 Best Colleges Rankings Data." *US News*. July 25, 2019.

Morton, Jennifer. 2019. 'The False Promise of Elite Education." *Chronicle of Higher Education*. March 29, 2019.

NACUBO (National Association of College and University Business Officers). 2018. "State of College Admissions? Executive Summary."

Nadworny, Elissa. 2017. "High-Achieving, Low Income Students: Where Elite Colleges Are Falling Short." *NPR*. August 2017, citing and quoting Jennifer Glynn, 2017, "Opening Doors," *Jack Kent Cooke Foundation*.

National Center for Education Statistics. 2019. "Immediate College Enrollment Rates." February 2019.

Nietzel, Michael T. 2019. "U.S. News Releases Its Annual College Ranking. Here's What's Wrong With Them." *Forbes*. September 9, 2019.

Nguyen, Terry. 2019. "Want to Learn How the World Sees Your College? Look on YouTube." *Chronicle of Higher Education*. January 22, 2019.

Olsen-Phillips, Peter. 2016. "Free Entrance Exams Opens a Path to College." *Chronicle of Higher Education*. August 14, 2016.

Orentlicher, David. 2016. "Economic Inequality and College Admissions Policies." *Cornell Journal of Law and Public Policy, Volume 26, pp. 104-105.*

Patel, Vimal. 2019. "How Rising College Costs and Student Debt Contribute to a Social-Mobility 'Crisis'." *Chronicle of Higher Education.* July 8, 2019.

Perry, Andre M. 2019. "The college admissions scandal proves that we need affirmative action." *The Avenue: Brookings.* March 14, 2019.

Pennington, Bill. 2019. "The Real Cost of Diversifying College Rosters." *New York Times.* November 7, 2019.

Pennington, Bill. 2019. "Admissions Scandal Stokes Hard Questions on Recruited Athletes." *New York Times.* March 19, 2019.

Perez, Angel B. 2020. "Simplify Everything," in "The Coronavirus Enrollment Crash." *Chronicle of Higher Education.* May 7. 2020.

Perez-Pena, Richard and Daniel E. Slotnik. 2012. "Gaming the College Rankings." *New York Times.* January 31, 2012.

PrepScholar. circa 2016. "Williams College Requirements for Admission."

Pettit, Emma. 2018. 'A Fifth of Private Colleges Report First-Year Discount Rate of 60 Percent, Moody's Says." *Chronicle of Higher Education.* November 14, 2018.

Press Release. 2019. "Secretary DeVos Delivers on Promise to Expand College Scorecard, Provide Meaningful Information to Students on Educational Options and Outcomes." *U.S. Department of Education.* May 21, 2019.

Press Release. 2016. "Colleges and Universities Agree to Expand Access and Opportunity for Talented Lower-Income Students with American Talent Initiative Supported by Bloomberg Philanthropies." *Bloomberg Philanthropies.* December 13, 2016.

Quart, Alissa. *2018.* 'Squeezed: Why Our Families Cant Afford America." *Ecco.* 2018.

Quintana, Chris. 2018. "In Unusual Letter, Democratic Senators Ask 'U.S. News' to Change Emphasis of College Rankings." *Chronicle of Higher Education.* December 3, 2018.

Ratnesar, Romesh. 2019. "The way out of college admissions hell …is video games." *Bloomberg Businessweek.* March 25, 2019.

Rawls, T. H. 2017. "College Legacy Admissions: Affirmative Action for Whites." *New York Times.* August 6, 2017.

Reeves, Richard V. and Eleanor Krause. 2018. "Raj Chetty in 14 charts: Big findings on opportunity and mobility we should all know." *Brookings.* January 11, 2018.

Reeves, Richard V. 2017. "Colleges and the end of Upward Mobility." *Chronicle of Higher Education.* December 3, 2017.

Reeves, Richard V. 2017. "Stop Pretending You're Not Rich.' *New York Times.* June 10, 2017.

Remnick, David. 2018. "Andrea Ocasio-Cortez's Historic Win and the Future of the Democratic Party." *New Yorker.* July 16, 2018.

Rim, Christopher. 2020. "Princeton Is The First Ivy League School To Cancel 'Early Action' Applications Due to Covid-19." *Forbes.* June 19, 2020.

Robinson, Marilynne. 2020. "What Kind of Country Do We Want." *New York Review of Books*. June 11, 2020

Romero, Simon and Dana Goldstein. 2019. "New Mexico Announces Plan for Free College for State Residents." *New York Times*. September 18, 2019.

Root, Jay and Shannon Najmabadi. 2019. "After new admissions scandal, former Regent Wallace Hall says University of Texas' rules are a 'joke'." *Texas Tribune*. March 15, 2019.

Rosen, Tali. 2020. "There Is No Vaccine for Teenage Despair." *New York Times*. May 7, 2020.

Rosenburg, Brian. 2019. "This Is Higher Education's Gilded Age." *Chronicle of Higher Education*. February 2, 2019.

Ryan, Aidan F. 2018. "In First Day of Testimony, Khurana Says It's Okay Harvard Skews Wealthy." *Harvard Crimson*. October 23, 2018.

Sachs, Peter. 2010. "The Political Economy of Legacy Admissions," in Kahlenberg, ed. 2010 ibid., 211-36.

Sanchez, Erica L. 2017. "How Libraries Discriminate Against Undocumented Children." *Time.com./4962107/libraries-discriminte-undocumented-children*. October 17, 2027.

Saul, Stephanie. 2016. "Public Colleges Chase Out-of-State Students, and Tuition." *New York Times*. July 7, 2016.

Saul, Stephanie. 2016. "A Push to Make Harvard Free Also Questions the Role of Race in Admissions." *New York Times*. January 14, 2016.

Scherrer, Robert. 2015. "College Applications, Parental Exasperations." *Wall Street Journal.* October 7, 2015.

Scheve, Kenneth F. and Matthew J. Slaughter. 2018. "How to Save Globalization." *Foreign Affairs.* November/December 2018.

Schmidt, Peter. 2010. "A History of Legacy Preferences and Privilege," in Kahlenberg, ed. 2010 ibid., 33-69.

Schwartz, Yishai. 2017. "Admissions Anxiety." *Town & Country.* August 2017. See also "The T&C Guide to College: A $1.7 Million Map to Getting In." *Town & Country.* August 2017, and Schwartz, Yishai 2017. "For Parents Willing to Pay Thousands, College Counselors Promise to Make Ivy League Dreams a Reality." *Town & Country.* June 28, 2017.

Scott, Sam, 2016. "The Gravity of Inequality." *Stanford Alumni Magazine.* November/December 2016.

Selingo, Jeffrey. 2020. "Behind the Curtain of Elite College Admissions." *Wall Street Journal.* August 29-30, 2020.

Selingo, Jeffrey J. 2020 "Colleges Need to Rethink Their Market — and Maybe Their Mission." *Chronicle of Higher Education.* February 16, 2020.

Selingo, Jeffrey J. 2017. "Americans love higher education, just not their universities." *Washington Post.* July 18, 2017.

Selingo, Jeffrey J. 2017. "Can the Middle Class Afford College?' *Washington Post.* May 8, 2017.

Selingo, Jeffrey J. 2017. "How higher education made President Trump." *Washington Post.* February 16, 2017.

Selingo, Jeffrey J. 2017. "Small colleges fight to survive, amid warning of shaky finances." *Washington Post.* February 13, 2017.

Selingo, Jeffrey J. 2004. "U.S. Public's Confidence in Higher Education Remains High." *Chronicle of Higher Education.* May 7, 2004.

Seltzer, Rick. 2020. "How Much Are Most Colleges Paying in Endowment Tax?" *Inside Higher Ed.* February 18, 2020.

Shadowen, Steve and Sozi P. Tulante. 2010. "A Legal Challenge to Preferences as a Violation of the Equal Protection Clause of the Constitution and the Civil Rights Act of 1866," in Kahlenburg, ed. 2010 ibid., 173-97.

Sherman, Erik. 2016. "College Educated Get all Post-Recession Jobs — Even Low-Pay Ones." *Forbes.* July 2, 2016.

Simon, Cecilia Capuzzi. 2015. "The Test-Optional Surge." *New York Times.* October 28, 2015.

Simonton, Teghan. 2018. "How Republican and Democratic Wish Lists on Higher Education Stack Up." *Chronicle of Higher Education.* July 24, 2018.

Singer, Natasha. 2018. 'For Sale: Survey Data on Millions of High School Students." *Chronicle of Higher Education.* July 29, 2018.

Singh, R. Guru. 2019. "I Pledge $5,000 to My Alma Mater if it Will End Legacy Preferences." *Inside HigherEd.* February 11,.2019

Smialek, Jeanna. 2019. "Inequality Is Holding Economies Back. Education Could Be One Solution." *Bloomberg Businessweek.* March 20, 2019.

Smithey, Cole. 2017. "Lady Bird—Revisited." *Smart New Media*. December 7, 2017.

Stauffer, Rainesford. 2019. "I learned in College that Admission Has Always Been for Sale." *New York Times*. March 13, 2019.

Stewart, Matthew. 2018. 'The 9.9 Percent Is the New American Aristocracy." *Atlantic*. June 2018.

Strauss, Valerie. 2019. "For decades, students at an elite school published a map with seniors' college plans. This year, they decided it fed a 'toxic' school culture." *Washington Post*. June 11, 2019.

Strauss, Valerie. 2019. "The college admissions scandal proves that we need affirmative action." *Washington Post*. March 14, 2019.

Strauss, Valerie. 2019. "The College Board is changing sign-up rules for AP tests. Critics say it's an undue burden on students." *Washington Post*. February 7, 2019.

Strauss, Valerie. 2018. "No, private schools aren't better at educating kids than public schools. Why this new study matters." *Washington Post*. July 26, 2018.

Strauss, Valerie. 2017. "Yes, the Republican tax bill would help rich parents send their kids to private school." *Washington Post*. November 8, 2017.

Strauss, Valerie. 2017. "Can coaching truly boost SAT scores? For years, the College Board said no. Now it says yes." *Washington Post*. May 9, 2017.

Stripling, Jack. 2019. "The Origins of an Admission-Bribery Mastermind Are Buried in a Confidential Report." *Chronicle of*

Higher Education. May 29, 2019.

Stripling, Jack. 2019. "'It's an Aristocracy': What the Admissions Bribery Scandal Has Exposed about Class on Campus." *Chronicle of Higher Education.* April 17, 2019.

Stripling, Jack and Eric Hoover. 2015. "In Admissions, the Powerful Weigh In." *Chronicle of Higher Education.* November 29, 2015.

Student Poll. 2016. "College-Bound Students Use a Wide Variety of College Ranking Sources." *Art & Science Group LLC. Volume 12, Issue 3.* December 2016.

Supiano, Beckie. 2020. "'On a Desert Island With Your Students': Professors Discuss the Weirdness of Teaching Remotely in a Pandemic." *Chronicle of Higher Education.* April 7, 2020.

Supiano, Beckie. 2019. "Low-Income Students Told Brown U. That Textbook Prices Limited their Choice. Here's What the University is Doing." *Chronicle of Higher Education.* April 11, 2019.

Supiano, Beckie. 2019. "They're Already Rich. Why Were These Parents So Fixated on Elite Colleges?" *Chronicle of Higher Education.* March 13, 2019.

Svrluga, Susan. 2019. "University of Oklahoma forfeits its ranking on the U.S. News list after acknowledging inflated data." *Washington Post.* May 24, 2019.

Svrluga, Susan. 2016. "The controversy at Mount St. Mary's goes national after professors are fired." *Washington Post,* February 9, 2016.

Tanzi, Alexandre and Michael Sasso. 2019. "Richest 1% of

Americans Close to Surpassing Wealth of Middle Class." *Bloomberg.com/news/article/2019-11-09/one-percenters-close-to-surpassing-wealth-of-u-s-middle-class*. November 9, 2019

The Hill. 2019. "11 percent say they'd pay a bribe to get kids into a top college: poll." March 22, 2019.

The Upshot. 2017. "Some Colleges Have More Students From the Top 1 Percent Than the Bottom 60. Find Yours." *New York Times Interactive*. January 18, 2017.

Thomas, Kei-Sygh. 2018. "When 1 in 10 Kids on Campus Doesn't Have Enough to Eat: Inside the Campaign to Help Feed Hungry College Students." *the74million.org*. January 9, 2018

Thomason, Andy. 2019. "In Bribery Scheme, Coaches Sold the 'Admission Slots' to Nonathletes. Wait, Coaches Influence Admissions?" *Chronicle of Higher Education*. March 13, 2019.

Thompson, Carolyn. 2019. "College Board Says It Is Replacing SAT 'Adversity Score'." *Associated Press*. August 20, 2019.

Todd, Sarah. 2019. "A new statistic reveals the startling privilege of white kids admitted to Harvard." *Quartz*. September 24, 2019.

Tough, Paul. 2019. "What Admissions Offices Really Want. *New York Times Magazine*. September 10, 2019.

Top Hat. 2020. "Adrift in a Pandemic: Survey of 3,089 Students Finds Uncertainty About Returning to College." May 1, 2020.

U.S. Department of Education. 2019. "Immediate College Enrollment Rate." *National Center for Education Statistics*.

Vance, Lawrence M. 2012. "Does the First Amendment Protect

the Freedom of Association?" *The Future of Freedom Foundation*. May 9, 2012.

Vasquez, Michael and Dan Bauman. 2019. "How America's College-Closure Crisis Leaves Families Devastated." *Chronicle of Higher Education*. April 4, 2019.

Vassar College. 2018. "Is that a fact?" *Vassar College Brochure*. 2018.

Vedder, Richard K. 2012. "Princeton Reaps Tax Breaks as State Colleges Beg." *Bloomberg Opinion*. March 18, 2012.

Warikoo, Natasha and Nadirah Farah Foley. 2018. "How Elite Schools Stay So White." *New York Times*. July 24, 2018.

Weintraub, Karen, Joelle Renstrom and Nick Anderson. 2019. "Felicity Huffman gets 14 days in jail in college admission scandal." *Washington Post*. September 13, 2019.

Weissbourd, Richard, Lloyd Thacker et al. 2016. "Turning the Tide." *Harvard Graduate School of Education*. January 20, 2016.

Wells, Carrie. 2016. "Fired Mount St. Mary's faculty reinstated after public furor." *Baltimore Sun*. February 12, 2016.

Wermund, Benjamin. 2017. "How U.S. News college rankings promote economic inequality on campus." *Politico*. September 10, 2017.

Wilson, Robin. 2017. "How a 20-page Letter Changed the Way Higher Education Handles Sexual Assault." *Chronicle of Higher Education*. February 8, 2017.

Wong, Alia 2018. ""Lotteries May Be the Fairest Way to Fix Elite-

College Admissions." *Atlantic*. August 1, 2018.

Zahneis, Megan. 2018. "Temple U. Says Several Programs Submitted False Data to 'U.S. News'." *Chronicle of Higher Education*. July 25, 2018.

Zauzmer, Julie M. 2010. "Z-listed Students Experience Year Off." *Harvard Crimson*. March 30, 2010.

Zhou, Li. 2015. "Obama's New College Scorecard Flips the Focus of Rankings " *Atlantic*. September 15, 2015.

Zwick, Rebecca. 2017. "Why Applying to College Is So Confusing." *New York Times*. December 5, 2017.

ABOUT THE AUTHOR

During his four-decade professional career, Terry Connelly practiced corporate law with Cravath, Swaine & Moore in New York City and London; served as chief of staff of global investment banking at Salomon Brothers and head of global investment banking at Cowen & Company; was director of strategic services at Ernst & Young Australia and an adjunct lecturer at Queensland University of Technology; and is dean emeritus of the Ageno School of Business at Golden Gate University in San Francisco.

Terry is a past fellow of the Aspen Institute, and has served as chair of the Corporate Finance Committee of the Securities Industry Association; board president of the Carter Burden Center in New York City; vice-chair of the board of Trevor Day School in Manhattan; vice chair of the board of the Public Religion Research Institute in Washington, D.C.; chair of the Program Council of the Toor-Cummings Center for International Studies and the Liberal

Arts at Connecticut College; chair of the board of the Cardiac Therapy Foundation in Palo Alto, CA.; and member of the finance board of the Catholic Community at Stanford University. He has previously co-authored two books dealing with higher education: *The Responsibility of Dissent* with John F. Hunt (1969), and *Riptide: The New Normal in Higher Education*, with Dan Angel (2011).

Born and raised in Lincoln, Nebraska, Terry holds a BA in Politics from The Catholic University of America, where he was elected to *Phi Beta Kappa*. He earned a JD from New York University School of Law, where he was a Root-Tilden Scholar and articles editor of the *Law Review*. He lives with his wife and family in Palo Alto, CA.

www.ingramcontent.com/pod-product-compliance
Lightning Source LLC
Chambersburg PA
CBHW021348210526
45463CB00001B/20